First World War
and Army of Occupation
War Diary
France, Belgium and Germany

30 DIVISION
Divisional Troops
Royal Army Medical Corps
97 Field Ambulance
2 November 1915 - 2 July 1919

WO95/2324/2

The Naval & Military Press Ltd
www.nmarchive.com
Published in association with The National Archives

Published by

The Naval & Military Press Ltd

Unit 10 Ridgewood Industrial Park,

Uckfield, East Sussex,

TN22 5QE England

Tel: +44 (0) 1825 749494

www.naval-military-press.com

www.nmarchive.com

This diary has been reprinted in facsimile from the original. Any imperfections are inevitably reproduced and the quality may fall short of modern type and cartographic standards.

© **Crown Copyright**
Images reproduced by permission of The National Archives, London, England, 2015.

Contents

Document type	Place/Title	Date From	Date To
Heading	WO95/2324 97 Field Ambulance Nov 15-Aug 19		
Heading	30th Division Medical 97th Field Ambulance Nov 1915 July 1919		
Heading	30th Division 97th 7 a Vol I Nov 15		
War Diary	Larkhill	02/11/1915	07/11/1915
War Diary	In Chamal	08/11/1915	08/11/1915
War Diary	Havre	09/11/1915	09/11/1915
War Diary	Bethencourt	11/11/1915	16/11/1915
War Diary	Villers Bocage	17/11/1915	17/11/1915
War Diary	Mirvaux	18/11/1915	27/11/1915
War Diary	Canaples	28/11/1915	28/11/1915
War Diary	Fienvillers	29/11/1915	30/11/1915
Heading	30th Div 97th 7a. Vol 2 171/7909 December 1915		
Heading	War Diary of 97th (C.P.) F. A. R.A.M.C. from December 1/15 to December 31/15 Volume II		
War Diary	Fienvillers	01/12/1915	31/12/1915
Heading	Plews of Latrines Functions 18.12.15		
Diagram etc	Latrines Fienvillers		
Heading	Please of Latrines Functions 18.12.15		
Diagram etc	Cooking Oven Fienvillers		
Diagram etc	Fienvillers		
Diagram etc	Scheme of Work at Fienvillers		
Heading	30th Div F/180/2 Jan 1916		
Heading	War Diary of 97th (C.P.) Field Ambulance R.A.M.C. from January 1/16 to January 31/16 Volume III		
War Diary	Fienvillers	01/01/1916	10/01/1916
War Diary	Naours	11/01/1916	11/01/1916
War Diary	La Houssoye	12/01/1916	12/01/1916
War Diary	Chipilly	13/01/1916	31/01/1916
Diagram etc	Cooking Oven Fienvillers		
Diagram etc	Drying Room Fienvillers		
Miscellaneous	Wash House Fienvillers		
Miscellaneous	Chipilly Incinerator Half Inch Scale		
Heading	97th Field Ambulance Feb March 1916		
Heading	97th FA. Vol 4		
Heading	97 Field Amb Vol 5		
War Diary	Chipilly	01/02/1916	17/03/1916
War Diary	Allonville	18/03/1916	01/04/1916
Heading	30th Div No 97 F. Amb. April 1916		
War Diary	Allonville	01/04/1916	29/04/1916
War Diary	Sailly Laurette	30/04/1916	30/04/1916
Heading	30th Div No 97 F. Amb. May 1916		
War Diary	Sailly Laurette	01/06/1916	01/06/1916
War Diary	Sailly-Laurette	02/06/1916	06/06/1916
War Diary	Sailly Laurette	06/05/1916	07/05/1916
War Diary	Sailly Laurette	08/05/1916	31/05/1916
Heading	97th Field Ambulance 140/1949 Jun 1916		
War Diary	Sailly Laurette	01/06/1916	15/06/1916
War Diary	Bray	16/06/1916	19/06/1916
War Diary	Abu Gessing Stn Billon Bug Outs	20/06/1916	25/06/1916

War Diary	Ads.	25/06/1916	30/06/1916
Miscellaneous	To ADMS 30 Division	27/03/1917	27/03/1917
Miscellaneous	To ADMS 30 Division	06/05/1917	06/05/1917
Miscellaneous	The D.M.S. Third Army	29/03/1917	29/03/1917
Miscellaneous	DG 250/4. D.M.S. Third Army.	20/03/1917	20/03/1917
Heading	30 Division No 97 Field Ambulance July 1916		
War Diary	A.D.S.	01/07/1916	08/07/1916
War Diary	Dive Copse	09/07/1916	09/07/1916
War Diary	Billon Fm	09/07/1916	15/07/1916
War Diary	Corbie	16/07/1916	24/07/1916
War Diary	Corbie III Corps Regt St.	25/07/1916	29/07/1916
War Diary	Corbie	30/07/1916	31/07/1916
Miscellaneous	30th Division A	08/08/1916	08/08/1916
Heading	War Diary of 97th (C.P.) Field Ambulance R.A.M.C. for the month of August 1916 Volume 10		
War Diary	Corbie	01/08/1916	02/08/1916
War Diary	Huppy	03/08/1916	04/08/1916
War Diary	Calonne Sur La Lys	05/08/1916	09/08/1916
War Diary	Annezin	10/08/1916	31/08/1916
Heading	War Diary of 97th (C.P.) Field Ambulance for the month of September 1916 Volume XI		
War Diary	Annezin	01/09/1916	16/09/1916
War Diary	Busnes	17/09/1916	18/09/1916
War Diary	Sezaincourt	19/09/1916	20/09/1916
War Diary	Ollincourt	21/09/1916	30/09/1916
Heading	War Diary of 97 Field Ambulance for the month of October 1916 Volume XII		
War Diary	Ollincourt	01/10/1916	03/10/1916
War Diary	Dernancourt	04/10/1916	04/10/1916
War Diary	Becordel	05/10/1916	10/10/1916
War Diary	Medical Dump X. 29 D 3.2	11/10/1916	20/10/1916
War Diary	Becordel	21/06/1916	23/06/1916
War Diary	Buire	24/10/1916	31/10/1916
Operation(al) Order(s)	Operation Order By Lieut Col. B.S. Appendix A	28/10/1916	28/10/1916
Operation(al) Order(s)	Operation Orders By Lieut Col B.B. Burke D.S.O. Commanding 97th (C.P.) Field Ambulance, R.A.M.C.	29/10/1916	29/10/1916
Heading	War Diary of 97 Field Ambulance for the month of November 1916 Volume XIII		
War Diary	La Herliere	01/11/1916	30/11/1916
Heading	War Diary of 97 Field Ambulance for the month of December 1916 Volume XIV		
War Diary	La Herline	01/12/1916	11/12/1916
War Diary	Laherliere	12/12/1916	31/12/1916
Heading	War Diary of 97 Field Ambulance for the month of January 1917 Volume XV		
War Diary	Laherliere	01/01/1917	06/01/1917
War Diary	Mondicourt	07/01/1917	31/01/1917
Heading	War Diary of 97 Field Ambulance for the month of February 1917 Volume XVI		
War Diary	Mondumt	01/01/1917	28/01/1917
Heading	War Diary of 97 Field Ambulance for the month of March 1917 Volume XVII		
War Diary	Mondi court	01/03/1917	31/03/1917
Heading	War Diary of 97th Field Ambulance for the month of April 1917 Volume XVIII		
War Diary	Mandicourt	01/04/1917	02/04/1917

War Diary	Bowmicourt	03/04/1917	19/04/1917
War Diary	Nenvill-Vitasse	20/04/1917	30/04/1917
Miscellaneous	Summary of Medical War Diaries For 97th F.A. 30th Divn. 7th Corps, 3rd Army 18th Corps from 12/4/17.	12/04/1917	12/04/1917
Miscellaneous	97th F.A. 30th Divn. 7th Corps 3rd Army. O.C. Lt. Col. L.D. Shaw. 18th Corps from 12/4/17	12/04/1917	12/04/1917
Miscellaneous	97th F.A. 30th Divn. 18th Corps 3rd Army. O.C. Lt. Col. L.D. Shaw.	18/04/1917	18/04/1917
Miscellaneous	97th F.A. 30th Divn. 7th Corps. 3rd Amry. O.C. Lt. Col. L.D. Shaw	18/04/1917	18/04/1917
Miscellaneous	97th F.A. 30th Divn. 7th Corps. 3rd Army. O.C. Lt. Col. L.D. Shaw. 19th Corps from 29/4/17.	29/04/1917	29/04/1917
Miscellaneous	97th F.A. 30th Divn. 19th Corps 3rd. Army. O.C. Lt. Col. L.D. Shaw.	29/04/1917	29/04/1917
Miscellaneous	97th F.A. 30th Divn. 7th Corps 3rd Army. O.C. Lt. Col. L.D. Shaw. 18th Corps from 12/4/17	12/04/1917	12/04/1917
Miscellaneous	97th F.A. 30th Divn. 18th Corps 3rd Army. O.C. Lt. Col. L.D. Shaw. 7th Corps from 18/4/17.	18/04/1917	18/04/1917
Miscellaneous	97th F.A. 30th Divn. 7th Corps 3rd Army. O.C. Lt. Col. L.D. Shaw.	18/04/1917	18/04/1917
Miscellaneous	97th F.A. 30th Divn. 7th Corps. 3rd Army. O.C. Lt. Col. L.D. Shaw. 19th Corps from 29/4/17.	29/04/1917	29/04/1917
Miscellaneous	97th F.A. 30th Divn. 19th Corps. 3rd Army. O.C. Lt. Col. L.D. Shaw.	29/04/1917	29/04/1917
Heading	War Diary of 97th Field Ambulance for the month of may 1917 Volume XIX		
War Diary	Frame Court	01/05/1917	03/05/1917
War Diary	Bachimont	04/05/1917	19/05/1917
War Diary	Ecoivres	20/05/1917	20/05/1917
War Diary	Conteville	21/05/1917	21/05/1917
War Diary	Lespesses	21/05/1917	23/05/1917
War Diary	Thiennes	24/05/1917	24/05/1917
War Diary	Rouge Croix Sheet 27 In 40000 W.9.D 7.7.	25/05/1917	25/05/1917
War Diary	Beauvoorde Farm Sheet 27 1-40000 K. 34.c. 8.9.	26/05/1917	28/05/1917
War Diary	Brandhoek Sheet 28 1 in 40000 G. 6. D. 4.0.	29/05/1917	31/05/1917
Miscellaneous	Summary Of Medical War Diaries For 97th F.A. 30th Divn. 7th Corps, 3rd Army 18th Corps from 12/4/17.	12/04/1917	12/04/1917
Miscellaneous	97th F.A. 30th Divn. 19th Corps. 3rd Army. O.C. Lt. Col. L.D. Shaw. 11th Corps, 2nd Army from 20/5/17.	20/05/1917	20/05/1917
Heading	War Diary of 97th Field Ambulance for the month of June 1917 Volume XX		
War Diary	Brandhoek Sheet 28 1 in 40000 9.6. D 4.0.	01/06/1917	12/06/1917
War Diary	Brandhoek Sheet 28 in 40000 G 12 b 5.9.	13/06/1917	21/06/1917
War Diary	Wippenhoek Sheet 27 1 in 40000 28 D 0.7	22/06/1917	30/06/1917
Heading	War Diary of 97th Field Ambulance for the month of July 1917 Volume XXI		
War Diary	Wippenhoek L 24328	01/07/1917	06/07/1917
War Diary	Hazehons Sheet 5. A. 1/10000	07/07/1917	15/07/1917
War Diary	Ruminghem	16/07/1917	18/07/1917
War Diary	Ouderzeele	19/07/1917	19/07/1917
War Diary	Wippenhoek	20/07/1917	31/07/1917
Heading	War Diary of 97th Field Ambulance for the month of August 1917 Volume XXII		
War Diary	Wippenhoek	01/08/1917	07/08/1917
War Diary	Outtersteene Sheet 36 M F 8 B 9.3	08/08/1917	09/08/1917
War Diary	St Jans Cappell Sheet 27 X 12.9.9.9	11/08/1917	22/08/1917

War Diary	St Jans Cappell	23/08/1917	23/08/1917
War Diary	Dranoutre Sheet 28 M 36 C 22	24/08/1917	31/08/1917
Heading	War Diary of 97th Field Ambulance for the month of September 1917 Volume XXII		
War Diary	Dranoutre	01/09/1917	30/09/1917
Heading	War Diary of 97th Field Ambulance for the month of October 1917 Volume XXIV		
War Diary	Dranoutre Sheet 28 M 36.6.22	01/10/1917	16/10/1917
War Diary	Dranoutre	16/10/1917	31/10/1917
Heading	War Diary of 97th Field Ambulance for the month of November 1917 Volume XXV		
War Diary	Dranoutre M 36 C 43	01/11/1917	14/11/1917
War Diary	Tyrone Farm M 36992	15/11/1917	25/11/1917
War Diary	Woodcote House 120 C 43 Sheet 28	26/11/1917	30/11/1917
Heading	War Diary of 97th Field Ambulance for the month of December 1917 Volume XXVI		
War Diary	Woodcote House I. 20. C. 4.3 (Sheet 28)	01/12/1917	02/12/1917
War Diary	Woodcote House	03/12/1917	31/12/1917
Heading	War Diary of 97th Field Ambulance for the month of January 1918 Volume XVII		
War Diary	Woodcote House I. 20. C.4.3. (Sheet 28)	01/01/1918	02/01/1918
War Diary	Woodcote House	03/01/1918	05/01/1918
War Diary	La. Clytte N 7. C 3.5 Sheet 28	06/01/1918	06/01/1918
War Diary	Wardrecques E. 4. Central (Hazebrouck) Sheet 5A	07/01/1918	08/01/1918
War Diary	Wardrecques	09/01/1918	12/01/1918
War Diary	Le Paraclet T. 25. b. 8.7 Sheet 62 D	13/01/1918	13/01/1918
War Diary	Bayonvillers W.2.a.9.8 Sheet 62 D	14/01/1918	14/01/1918
War Diary	Rosieres F. 8. a. 3.8 Sheet 66 E	15/01/1918	16/01/1918
War Diary	Rosieres	17/01/1918	17/01/1918
War Diary	Guerbigny Q. 27. b. 9.9. Sheet 66 E	18/01/1918	18/01/1918
War Diary	Omencourt N. 24. a. 2.2. Sheet 66d	19/01/1918	20/01/1918
War Diary	Omencourt	21/01/1918	26/01/1918
War Diary	Chauny A 26.a. 2.6 Sheet 70 D	27/01/1918	28/01/1918
War Diary	Chauny	29/01/1918	31/01/1918
Heading	No. 97. F.A. Feb 1918		
War Diary	Chauny A 26.a. 2.6 Sheet 70 D	01/02/1918	02/02/1918
War Diary	Chauny	03/02/1918	08/02/1918
War Diary	Rimbercourt D. 10. a. 3.3. Sheet 70 E	09/02/1918	09/02/1918
War Diary	Omencourt N. 24. a. 2.2. Sheet 66D	10/02/1918	10/02/1918
War Diary	Omencourt	11/02/1918	21/02/1918
War Diary	Dury K 30.c.9.7 Sheet 66D	22/02/1918	22/02/1918
War Diary	Dury	23/02/1918	28/02/1918
Heading	War Diary of 97th Field Ambulance for the month of March 1918 Volume XXIX		
War Diary	Dury K 30.c.9.7. Sheet 66D	01/03/1918	02/03/1918
War Diary	Dury	03/03/1918	21/03/1918
War Diary	Esmery Hallon	22/03/1918	22/03/1918
War Diary	Roiglise	23/03/1918	24/03/1918
War Diary	Hangest	25/03/1918	26/03/1918
War Diary	Moreuil	27/03/1918	27/03/1918
War Diary	Rouvrel	28/03/1918	28/03/1918
War Diary	Goyencourt	29/03/1918	29/03/1918
War Diary	Saleux	30/03/1918	31/03/1918
Heading	97th Field Ambulance Apr 1918		
War Diary	Offeux Sheet Abbeville 14 1/100.000	01/04/1918	02/04/1918
War Diary	Offeux	03/04/1918	05/04/1918

War Diary	Elverdinghe B. 15.a.57 Sheet 28	06/04/1918	06/04/1918
War Diary	Canada Farm A.18.a.27 Sheet 28	07/04/1918	08/04/1918
War Diary	Canada Farm	09/04/1918	23/04/1918
War Diary	Point Du Jour G.30.a 8.8. Sheet 27	24/04/1918	24/04/1918
War Diary	Point Du Jour	25/04/1918	30/04/1918
Heading	No. 97 F.A. May 1918		
War Diary	Point Du Jour G. 30. a. 8.8. Sheet 27	01/05/1918	04/05/1918
War Diary	Point Du Jour	05/05/1918	16/05/1918
War Diary	Mesnil Val 6.E.0.50 Sheet 14 Abbeville	17/05/1918	19/05/1918
War Diary	Mesnil Val	20/05/1918	31/05/1918
Heading	97th F.A. June 1918		
War Diary	Mesnil Val 6.E. O. 50 Sheet 14 Abbeville	01/06/1918	02/06/1918
War Diary	Biencourt 1. I. 30. 71. Sheet 16 Dieppe	03/06/1918	03/06/1918
War Diary	Biencourt	04/06/1918	26/06/1918
War Diary	Forest L'Abbaye J. 4. 90.50 Sheet 14 Abbeville	27/06/1918	27/06/1918
War Diary	Helvelinghem G. 30. G. 8.6. Sheet 27a	28/06/1918	30/06/1918
Heading	97th F.A. July 1918		
War Diary	Helvelinghem G. 30. b. 8.6 Sheet 27 A	01/07/1918	03/07/1918
War Diary	Helvelinghem	04/07/1918	08/07/1918
War Diary	St Momelin Sheet 5A Hazebrouck	09/07/1918	09/07/1918
War Diary	Maison Blanche O. 26. C. 3.0 Sheet 27	10/07/1918	12/07/1918
War Diary	Maison Blanche	13/07/1918	20/07/1918
War Diary	Steenvoorde P 6.9. L. 6 Sheet 27	21/07/1918	21/07/1918
War Diary	Steenvoorde	02/07/1918	31/07/1918
Heading	97th F.A. Aug 1918		
War Diary	Steenvoorde P 6 a 46 Sheet 27	01/08/1918	03/08/1918
War Diary	Steenvoorde	04/08/1918	09/08/1918
War Diary	Godewaersvelde Q. 6 a. central sheet 27	10/08/1918	12/08/1918
War Diary	Godewaersvelde	13/08/1918	30/08/1918
War Diary	LeBrebant Sheet 28 G31 d52	31/08/1918	31/08/1918
Diagram etc	Sketch To Illustrate The Method Of Evacuating		
Heading	97th F. Amb. Sept 1918		
War Diary	Le Brebant Sheet 23 G. 31. d 5.2	01/09/1918	01/09/1918
War Diary	Locre M 29 a 75 Sheet 28	02/09/1918	02/09/1918
War Diary	Locre	03/09/1918	05/09/1918
War Diary	Hagedoorne Sheet 28 S. 3.a 3.9	06/09/1918	08/09/1918
War Diary	Hagedoorne	09/09/1918	12/09/1918
War Diary	Westoutre M9. C. 4.8 Sheet 28	13/09/1918	14/09/1918
War Diary	Westoutre	15/09/1918	28/09/1918
War Diary	Locre Sheet 28 M 29.a 75	29/09/1918	30/09/1918
Heading	97th F.A. Oct. 1918		
War Diary	Neuve Eglise T. 10. Central Sheet 28	01/10/1918	02/10/1918
War Diary	Aircraft Farm N 32 9.2.3 Sheet 28	03/10/1918	03/10/1918
War Diary	Aircraft Farm	04/10/1918	09/10/1918
War Diary	Head Wytschaete N. 30 a 1.7 Sheet 28	10/10/1918	12/10/1918
War Diary	N 30. A. 1.7 Sheet 28	13/10/1918	16/10/1918
War Diary	Hollebeke P. 7. C. Central	17/10/1918	17/10/1918
War Diary	Roncq X. 7. d. 9.7. Sheet 28	18/10/1918	18/10/1918
War Diary	Roncq	19/10/1918	20/10/1918
War Diary	Sterrenhoek S. 4. b. 5.6. Sheet 29	21/10/1918	21/10/1918
War Diary	Coyghem U. 19 C. 4.7 Sheet 29	22/10/1918	24/10/1918
War Diary	Coyghem	25/10/1918	27/10/1918
War Diary	Rolleghem T. 2. a. 2.6 Sheet 29	28/10/1918	30/10/1918
War Diary	Rolleghem	31/10/1918	31/10/1918
Heading	No 97 F. A. Nov. 1918		
War Diary	Rolleghem T. 2. a. 2.6 Sheet 29	01/11/1918	03/11/1918

War Diary	Rolleghem	04/11/1918	04/11/1918
War Diary	Hoogmolen O 23. d. 59 Sheet 29	05/11/1918	06/11/1918
War Diary	Hoogmolen	07/11/1918	08/11/1918
War Diary	Autryve V. 8. a. 5.4. Sheet 29	09/11/1918	09/11/1918
War Diary	Watripont E. 5. b. 9.3 Sheet 37	10/11/1918	10/11/1918
War Diary	Flobecq T. 27. a. 8.5 Sheet 30q	11/11/1918	12/11/1918
War Diary	Flobecq	13/11/1918	13/11/1918
War Diary	Renaix X 16. d. central Sheet 29	14/11/1918	15/11/1918
War Diary	Heestert P. 29 b. 45 Sheet 29	16/11/1918	16/11/1918
War Diary	Aelbeke M. 29. c. 8.4 Sheet 29	17/11/1918	18/11/1918
War Diary	Aelbeke	19/11/1918	27/11/1918
War Diary	La Vigne E.I.a. 4.4. Sheet 36	28/11/1918	28/11/1918
War Diary	La Hutte Farm D. 26. a. 5.5 Sheet 36	29/11/1918	29/11/1918
War Diary	Laventie M. 4. b. 1.9. Sheet 36	30/11/1918	30/11/1918
Heading	No. 97 F. A. Dec. 1918		
War Diary	St Venant P. 10. C. 1.9 Sheet 36 A	01/12/1918	01/12/1918
War Diary	Ebblinghem T. 18. C. 9.8. Sheet 27	02/12/1918	03/12/1918
War Diary	Ebblinghem	04/12/1918	31/12/1918
Heading	30th Div Box 2100 No 97 F.A. Jan 1919		
War Diary	Ebblinghem	01/01/1919	06/01/1919
War Diary	Arneke	07/01/1919	07/01/1919
War Diary	Socx	08/01/1919	08/01/1919
War Diary	Dunkirk	09/01/1919	31/01/1919
Heading	97th F.A. Feb. 1919		
War Diary	Dunkirk	01/02/1919	28/02/1919
Heading	97th F.A. Mar-Apr 1919		
War Diary	Dunkirk	01/03/1919	31/03/1919
War Diary	St Pol-Sur-Mer	01/04/1919	30/04/1919
Heading	97th F.A. May 1919		
War Diary	Dunkerque St Pol.	01/05/1919	03/06/1919
Heading	97th. F.A. June 1919		
War Diary	Dunkerque St Pol.	03/06/1919	25/06/1919
Heading	97th F.A. July 1919		
War Diary	Dunkerque St Pol S/Mer	02/07/1919	02/07/1919

WO 95/2324
97 Field Ambulance
Nov '15 – Aug '19

30TH DIVISION
MEDICAL

97TH FIELD AMBULANCE
NOV 1915 - DEC ~~1918~~ July 1919

$$\frac{7634}{121}$$

30 lbs Kieserin

97 £ 7 a.
T 1704
tot I

Nov. 1915

Nov. 15

WAR DIARY
or
INTELLIGENCE SUMMARY

(Erase heading not required.)

Army Form C. 2118

Instructions regarding War Diaries and Intelligence Summaries are contained in F. S. Regs., Part II. and the Staff Manual respectively. Title Pages will be prepared in manuscript.

Place	Date	Hour	Summary of Events and Information	Remarks and references to Appendices
LARKHILL	2-11-15	10 pm	Arrived LARKHILL 24 Camp CANADA Lines & mobilised – full strength of Regular Perm. personnel 10 Officers 182 men – Camp a new one & very clean & comfortable – Two other ambulances of the 30th Division in Camp viz 96th (P) Field Ambulance 9 m. L.A. (I.E) G.S.O.	
LARKHILL	3-11-15	10 pm	Busy drawing equipment from Ordnance. G.S.O.	
LARKHILL	4-11-15	10 pm	ditto A.S.C. 38 men attached – 54 horses & horse vehicles taken over today. G.S.O.	
LARKHILL	5-11-15	10.30 am	Received stores drawn – received orders to entrain daily recording moving from the TCO Cadet – G.S.O.	
"	6-11-15	10 pm	Icently all equipment drawn except Motor Transport & 10 pr and Ordnance Stores – Only one type of both & second type for entrained AMESBURY Monday morning G.S.O.	
"	7-11-15	10 pm	Orders this morning to entrain at AMESBURY 1.45 am. G.S.O.	
In Channel	8-11-15	10 pm	On board MONA'S Queen bound for transport – left AMESBURY 2 am. this morning arrived SOUTHAMPTON 3.20 am – Lieut C.A.R. GATLEY reports sick furnished admitted to NETLEY – on board are Reg. to Br. MANCHESTER Reg. for Sig. walling Coy R.E. & 6 land officers & 101 men – Rest of Staff personnel	

1875 Wt. W593/826 1,000,000 4/15 J.B.C. & A. A.D.S.S./Forms/C. 2118.

WAR DIARY
or
INTELLIGENCE SUMMARY

Army Form C. 2118

Place	Date	Hour	Summary of Events and Information	Remarks and references to Appendices
HAVRE	9-11-15	10 p.m.	ASC with Horse Transport & 2 Officers have embarked at 4 pm on AUSTRALIND & left for HAVRE. we embarked on MONA'S 2 men 5 pm & left SOUTHAMPTON 8.30 pm. Lost sight on voyage heavy sea-storm - party on MONASQUEEN arrived HAVRE 2:15 am. Disembarked 7.30 am - from Stannate on board on day went - proceeded to Rest Camp no 5 - party on AUSTRALIND arrived HAVRE 8 am. I arrived no 5 - 3.30 here. food obtained on board by their party in attendance no pay rect - one casualty in this party a Pvt bicycle Corps servicharfed 4.20 Fleury. Enter heavy Hailstorm - G.A.R.	S.L.R.
BETHENCOURT	11-11-15	10 p.m.	HAVRE nov 10 to left Rest Camp 4.40 am - in heavy Hailstorm. GARE DES MARCHANDISE 6.15 Entrain Leave HAVRE 8.20 A.M. - here in Cattle trucks - Gaps in floor which are however covered with Duckboards	

1875 Wt. W503/826 1,000,000 4/15 J.B.C. & A. A.D.S.S./Forms/C. 2118.

Army Form C. 2118

WAR DIARY
or
INTELLIGENCE SUMMARY
(Erase heading not required.)

Instructions regarding War Diaries and Intelligence Summaries are contained in F. S. Regs., Part II. and the Staff Manual respectively. Title Pages will be prepared in manuscript.

Place	Date	Hour	Summary of Events and Information	Remarks and references to Appendices
			Men slept most of the journey. 1 June. 9–10·15 halt 2 hrs at MONTDIDIER BUCHY coffee & cognac(brandy) for men by French Officials – arrived from PONT REMY, detrain – 9 p.m. move off VIA POIX, POZUEREL LONG, L'ETOILE – Hours halt for meal for men – FLIXECOURT to BETHENCOURT via Redwator for Bullock – arrived here 5 a.m. distance only 12 miles but been tired out after these nights without sleep – men & Officers in billets & comfortable – 2 June. A.D.M.S. 20th Division visits us & fixes site for Hospital – Deficiencies wh. D. C. of M.S. Motor Transport – Successes – Boots for men, 1/2 old ones – 9 tables & seats of mourning Stove – G.C. Ott – Infiltrates DE RICE joins today also lieu Anglaust too unwell –	
BETHENCOURT 12·11·15 10 p.m.				

Army Form C. 2118

WAR DIARY
or
INTELLIGENCE SUMMARY
(Erase heading not required.)

Instructions regarding War Diaries and Intelligence Summaries are contained in F. S. Regs., Part II. and the Staff Manual respectively. Title Pages will be prepared in manuscript.

Place	Date	Hour	Summary of Events and Information	Remarks and references to Appendices
BETHENCOURT	13-11-15	10 p.m.	Hospital of 12 beds opened in main street 30 yds N of Church — appointed Lieut MACFARLANE Sanitary Officer — C. of E.R. LIEUT FOOTE appointed Billeting Officer — Court of Enquiry held by me — Inspector of H.Q.IV.S. held visit Lieut DEWAR recovered — LIEUTS MALLOCH & THOMPSON returned to respective units this eve of bicycle — I unding no fault attached to loco 67204 & the POOL — we are shell deficient in our incoherenced Newport. C.O.M. Lieut T. ANDERSON sent from Field Ambulance for Temporary Duty with XV Field Park at BELLOY — SUR-SOM ME — C.R.E.	
BETHENCOURT	14-11-15	10 p.m.	SUNDAY — Have 4 chaplains & their between attachés. Do us for Review — trial draw	

1875. Wt. W593/826 1,000,000 4/15 J.B.C. & A. A.D.S.S./Forms/C. 2118.

WAR DIARY
or
INTELLIGENCE SUMMARY

Army Form C. 2118

(Erase heading not required.)

Instructions regarding War Diaries and Intelligence Summaries are contained in F.S. Regs., Part II. and the Staff Manual respectively. Title Pages will be prepared in manuscript.

Place	Date	Hour	Summary of Events and Information	Remarks and references to Appendices
			DADMS this morning. Be Informed in writing by ADMS. mechanical transport — Receive 6 new lorries — Motor ambulances — (5 Sunbeam 2 Ford) One hd. Mot. Cycle & one cyclist — Washing shed 2 cycles — Motor cyclist to over ord. strength to be here from August 1915 — Mot. cyclist to be at AMC Headqrs. for dispatch of Mr Luntenan & detachers — Dis Headquarters — Topography — Clay overlying chalk — all except very light kitchen cases — G.S.H. Casualties	
Bethencourt	10/15	10 pm	Infant record record 1300 funnel paid out to Pay all Sunbeam need new covers & new heavy hard worn during night — Indent No. FLISECOURT to Hendon at Ailly — L. HADTCOCHER	

WAR DIARY
or
INTELLIGENCE SUMMARY

Army Form C. 2118

Saw A.D.M.S. about Lectures – Also 3 or 4 Chaplains appeared – These Chaplains & their four fortunes [horses] to other Heavy Brigade – A.D.M.S. agrees to see that they keep supplied & by cyclist orders told them I could apply & free for Chaplains Wherever & keep them exercised I regard a service of the regaining item – Score McSweeney's been seen a sister Ambulance but only by G.O.C. Div. Gave me a brother on to Brigade Hearth: Sent down Sgt – Major to the Ambulance and supplies to keep us lines seen Charges he saw in the Div. accounted to be sick Cleared from 9th Bde by motor Ambulance to our Dressing Station at BETHENCOURT
Parallel instructions for 97th F.A. carried out in accordance to brop. [?] laid down by A.D.M.S

WAR DIARY
or
INTELLIGENCE SUMMARY

Army Form C. 2118

Place	Date	Hour	Summary of Events and Information	Remarks and references to Appendices
Bethune	16/1/15	10 pm	Horse Township Rider Struck off Strength — Trier — sight draught cad old age — Bay riding Catafalark.

17th June D. J. Innes Bevan
Casualties R.A.M.C. not 19th —   Wdr 18 — 10 Pleeding W.A.R Gallery
Admissions to F.A. from 17th June of 19th — 3/4 M.A.H.R. — 2 } Burials
                                                    Upper Ditch — 3 } Total 10 pr week
                                                    St Pass   — 1
                                         Henry Ford Enott Easy with — twelve Beds
Re: Ground this not Enquired — Ambulances behind dept —
Wd — to Bgde Headqrs (913) to cut more tomorrow —
Lieut For to Process of night to load all sick
only the closed — Reports Drug Thus Proof 93 men as empty
Muriel tomorrow — Reports the deaths etc —
Brigade Headqrs — Wither ice estang of Kainethof
Steven — POW Lieut Dewar & Major I Dunbeaver
+ faces etc huft 22nd & 24th M.O. + P.R.
+ follow behind Steven — Lieut Malock Dane
                                  P/M Dunbeaver in Pow Col J. Kegg
                                  horse ambulances of each up | |

1875 Wt. W593/826 1,000,000 4/15 J.B.C. & A. A.D.S.S./Forms/C.2118.

Army Form C. 2118

WAR DIARY
or
INTELLIGENCE SUMMARY

(Erase heading not required.)

Place	Date	Hour	Summary of Events and Information	Remarks and references to Appendices
	17/7/15		infty D 20 + 21 T MOHR. R. Skeeeu johns column — Marching to the second bivy	
			97th to ANSO. Afternoon from BETHENCOURT	To clear FLESSELLES 12 htrs. X ands ST OUEN 9.45
			VIGNACOURT & FLESSELLES Reconnoiter — VILLERS-BOCAGE	
			We unfortunately have to leave the Brigade as in concentration after closer to the front — to have now to clear sick from as they left — Our Evening Stations in advance (Brigade) Recedeeey evacuate my sick back again from the Brigade to O.C.S. at ST OVEN — D.a.M.	
VILLERS BOCAGE	17/7/15	10am	left BETHENCOURT 8.10 AM loads covered 3 hours with South / Bakery etc — Cleared ST OVEN of British St OVEN hotels up 8.0 AM — feel intense St OVEN hotels up	

WAR DIARY or INTELLIGENCE SUMMARY

Army Form C. 2118

Engineers transport — or first Bus — 3 out our transport — roads terribly slippery in places. Lieut Porter following out first A.D.[?]s. Large lures harnessed & horseback. Got our transport as held up on Trenchell 1/2 mile Cambrai side of Corbie — March on preserved by orders to Lieut Porter to join Army at VILLERS-BOCAGE. Personnel Cleared FLESSELLES 12.20. Horn arrived VILLE & BOCAGE 1.30 pm. Lieut Porter & Transport arrive 2.85 — was somewhat [?]. Lieut Devoy E B Luckens reports — [?] of — 22 no MOHRS R13.

22 no MOHRS R13, the whole way (8 patches up the road) —
I think I had tried to see a few —
19 Sore feet —
24 to MOHRS R. 16. The whole way, 2 patches on the road —
all sore feet —

WAR DIARY or INTELLIGENCE SUMMARY

Army Form C. 2118

Lieut Malloch reports true that his 3 H Ambulances the Sunbeam 9 on Pow car Cursed — 20th M.C.H.R.R. carried 7 the whole way & picked up 17 in various I suez & has Stretchers & Stretcher the rest feet

21/11 M.C.H.R.D. carried 30 the whole way. the Stretchers & one Stretcher couple.

Billets at Villers Bocage for heep of Horses indifferent — horses stabled in street place of Shoeing the MAIRIE.
HEADQRS Bn of FLESSELLES
HEADQRS Bn Brigade at VAUX-EN-AMIENOIS.

WAR DIARY
or
INTELLIGENCE SUMMARY
(Erase heading not required.)

Army Form C. 2118

Place	Date	Hour	Summary of Events and Information	Remarks and references to Appendices
			Received Reinf of NCOs & men and 1 officer on this trying day - lots of NCOs and men received a had more than 6 weeks service - been absolutely nothing - Transport baggage - Chaplains lorry - up the whole of the C.S. overhead waggon - what with Mens Valises - Tent ropes & Alternative Baggage — Room return to be reach 164 gallon Glenley continuing - Tonight's March take place tomorrow — Ecole Bellevigneau from MOLLIENS-au-BOIS. MIRVAUX. by 10.30 AM 97th F.D. AMB. VILLERS-BOCAGE (until ebene V.B) G.C.P.F.	
MIRVAUX. 10PM 15/7/15			LEFT VILLER BOCAGE 10.15 A.M. Bittely coDel Jong Veerkamp Recruiting out transport trophy of yesterday—Promkay available & by hand knew cow Church Deffre heavy no Good	

WAR DIARY
or
INTELLIGENCE SUMMARY
(Erase heading not required.)

Army Form C. 2118

Instructions regarding War Diaries and Intelligence Summaries are contained in F. S. Regs., Part II. and the Staff Manual respectively. Title Pages will be prepared in manuscript.

Place	Date	Hour	Summary of Events and Information	Remarks and references to Appendices
			Gave orders for reveley, Major A.S.C. transport & ambulance, furnished trolley & gotten french labour. 8 helpers for parties — put in 3 coolies. This was done — and of day run of 3 shifts of pairs. 15 francs accepted by Major — wrote coleman worked off 10.15 — road greasy & rolly — on arrived MIRVAUX transport & all at 12 noon. Casualties in war or received — ADM from ACC in village to keep filled — no place available to open dressing station. Saw Mayor with interpreter. Found it in the church damp but clean — will reopen in useful — Evening go to see ADMS (2nd ed.) at Hendgers & Hendges Brigade at Chateau MOLLIENS-au-BOIS — garage & lorry S. & R. V.I. Brigade at 9 AM each morning we are in this area — This evening a Chaplain (R.C. of C.) complained he wont sleep in his billet as RAMC fellow in there. P.C.M.	

WAR DIARY
or
INTELLIGENCE SUMMARY

Army Form C. 2118

Place	Date	Hour	Summary of Events and Information	Remarks and references to Appendices
MIRVAUX	19/7/15	10pm	Visited all billets been in Square of Mirvaux late in Spite of Cold are crowded — rides Mieraucourt — billets find that the billets of the complaining chaplaining Mother (then angry) the Piers — Saw ADMS — Thaw Set in — Saw FCD.D. — On Clay overlay chalk — We are still in advance of Rail Railway — relics —	

STOVEN
R.C. Station
W.

● BN MOHR R.

● BN M & HR R.
● BN TRAIN

Bus & Hops

● BN MOHR. R.

MIRVAUX E

roughly 14 miles

We have

● BN M OHR. R.

● BN MOHR.R. We have now to collect left from Battalion behind to MIRVAUX & figures available through Métonne Route to ST. OUEN

F. SEH.

Place	Date	Hour	Summary of Events and Information	Remarks and references to Appendices
MIRVAUX.	20/11/15	10 pm	Orders from Div Headqrs. Before we all go to Eurenepont Cich to HIGHLAND C.C. Station at VILLERS-BOCAGE only 4½ miles to our East instead of 14 miles — A.S.C. Div from Corned MIRVAUX — one field hospital & large new hut de with the only Deep well in the village near it — So we took Church leaving it yesterday cleaned then we went in & then our new dressing Station in it — it is just enough due W. Church — Tomorrow A.C.C.S. is opened Motor Ambulances to Evacuate our sick thro this city it shows the only we are short in advance for 91st Brigade —	

WAR DIARY
or
INTELLIGENCE SUMMARY
(Erase heading not required.)

Army Form C. 2118

Place	Date	Hour	Summary of Events and Information	Remarks and references to Appendices
MIYAUK	2/11/15	10hr	COZO & saw no fatigue — G.O.C. Division visits us before we change Dressing Station — gives us orders to two Chaplains & asked for Ambulance on Sundays if can be spared — arrange to do so — Seems the Chaplains Department is badly organised — shows he recognises on several occasions deficiency ethic or several scale as a deep enhances department. R.A.M.C. — Men very cheerful but disorientated as we in our very burns inhibitates her forgotten & no known had enno — as been in other units of this Division had — I believe 96th F.A. lovers suffers the severe as our own.	
		17.00	travel hrs long & men & wind out in full marching order left in place —	

Army Form C. 2118

WAR DIARY
or
INTELLIGENCE SUMMARY
(Erase heading not required.)

Instructions regarding War Diaries and Intelligence Summaries are contained in F. S. Regs., Part II. and the Staff Manual respectively. Title Pages will be prepared in manuscript.

Place	Date	Hour	Summary of Events and Information	Remarks and references to Appendices
			New Dressing Station becoming well — busy morning — Medical conference re preparation of POULAINVILLE — interviewing A.D.M.S. 3rd Div re present — Cars today — Heavy firing N.R. front G.O.R.	
MOLYVANE	24/7/16	10pm	Here A.D.M.S. 30th Div re transport of nurses & ecclesiastic outfits — receiving husky — D.M.S. 3rd Army wishes us — saw no hospitals — was to meet all him we had just evacuated the Church but it was too damp for ADS for patients — He said he did not like the Church having used it — Why had he not taken Chateau of MOLLIENS-au-BOIS	

Wt. W593/826 1,000,000 4/15 J.B.C.&A. A.D.S.S./Forms/C. 2118.

Army Form C. 2118

WAR DIARY or INTELLIGENCE SUMMARY

Place	Date	Hour	Summary of Events and Information	Remarks and references to Appendices

9/11/15 — hrs HQ 91st Brigade Headquarters —
Great correspondents from HQ & also from the Brigade
Very recent letters — the letters from home show
they have received home-draws with me — since 9-11-15
I have received 14 letters from only three have
been received & all these had been *(marked by)*
(when I was out before some of my letters were (?)
by Censor & after being censored in mil? all my letters
were received *(also many news of very long)*
are very anxious about their second winter.

Casualties RAMC Nov 16th — to 22nd
to 87270 the Officer AE — to C.C.S. (HIGHLAND)
by ambulance —

A Divisions to FA forme 91st Brigade — Nov 16 — Nov 22nd
20th MOHRR 6 · 21st NOHRR 3
22nd MOHRR 6 · 24th MOHRR 9 Total 31
97 to FA 2
3 A.C.C.

WAR DIARY
or
INTELLIGENCE SUMMARY

Army Form C. 2118

Place	Date	Hour	Summary of Events and Information	Remarks and references to Appendices
MIRVAUX	23/10/18	10 pm	Reinforcements H.T. Cnl Henry brought HQrs. gee-up. GSM.	
			Re. Billeting over keenest trouble for every day. Information re. new billeting areas. Hospital accommodation is very bad. Billeting in the best in the Village. If billeting for F.A. were arranged by Field head Qts. it would be easier. Getting Lenihan A/Quartermaster for our F.A. as Gnery Bryant headge changes for us. — Saw ADMS as to where red carbolic & Echusol F.S. regulations and concerning the total G.O.D. entering on 20 horses to receive 40 weekly. Echusol received was a month & Echusen monthly.	
			J. Wat Drady at end of month.	

Army Form C. 2118

WAR DIARY
or
INTELLIGENCE SUMMARY
(Erase heading not required.)

Instructions regarding War Diaries and Intelligence Summaries are contained in F.S. Regs., Part II. and the Staff Manual respectively. Title Pages will be prepared in manuscript.

Place	Date	Hour	Summary of Events and Information	Remarks and references to Appendices
MEZVAUX	24/V/15	10 am	Busy with Officers testing men coming & returning waggons & intends? Prisoners — There is fast — warm sevia — J.A.M. Warmer. Gentle rainfall — Heavy Gunning Due East morning with DADMS 30th Div & find places # A minelayer the new Belleting to which to induced softly — HENVILLERS — OUTRE BOIS — BOIS BERGES someonall — In afternoon W/P Inderbeek at BERNAVILLE — HOTEL DE VILLE of which hgs heard Shrops did not force the point — Class of PROUVILLE — HEUZECOURT included town & Such R place in a Maison vide at Le MEILLARD — Wooden floors & friendliness. It was a back with possibilities — Two Douglas Motor cycles arrived today we hear	

1875 Wt. W593/826 1,000,000 4/15 J.B.C. & A. A.D.S.S./Forms/C. 2118.

WAR DIARY
or
INTELLIGENCE SUMMARY

Army Form C. 2118

Place	Date	Hour	Summary of Events and Information	Remarks and references to Appendices
			how over fell considerable of in stop 9 there is 7 indoor ambulances 9 stretcher bearers.	
			G.W.M.	
MIRVAUX	26/11/15		7. FLESSELLES - Accompanied the ADMS by motor to MEILLARD to inspect Site chosen yesterday for hospital. ADMS thinks it very suitable - took to BERNAVILLE see Hotel De Ville impossible as ground floor occupied by school - next DDMS 3rd Army go to FIENVILLERS inspect barn chosen by DDMS suitable for 10 been hind so good in wounds light 9 comfort for wounded as site chosen at Le MEILLARD - Return to Le MEILLARD with DDMS 9 ADMS - ADMS reconnoiters DDMS that Le MEILLARD is better than FIENVILLERS so DDMS accords me to go see self 9 make the horse as comfortable as possible — G.1.S Bgde HMS Trevdrow (we are to have feast)	

WAR DIARY
or
INTELLIGENCE SUMMARY
(Erase heading not required.)

Army Form C. 2118

24th M/H.R. hopes Nov 26th to POMMIER & see HALLOY MARIEUX. Nov 27 to BERLES & POMMIER. See scheme & reviews for instruction —

20th & 21st M/H.R. Nov 26 to POUVILLERS Nov 27 to COVIN — scheme & reviews for instruction —

22nd M/H.R. go straight to ENGLEBELMER MESNIL — they will go by Motor buses —

Relieved by Bgde HeadQrs, 1 Inf/Bgde staying for one night, ambulances & stretcher bearers 24 to go to Recrubigny 2.O. & one for 25 at Tug-beze. The night of 26th between Z.A. bringing any service cases & between D. Regiments — Returning Egys on 27 to Return at night with any delivin cases to Z.A. & to evacuate them with Fd the sick of Regiments from 28 onward will be

Army Form C. 2118

WAR DIARY
or
INTELLIGENCE SUMMARY
(Erase heading not required.)

Instructions regarding War Diaries and Intelligence Summaries are contained in F. S. Regs., Part II. and the Staff Manual respectively. Title Pages will be prepared in manuscript.

Place	Date	Hour	Summary of Events and Information	Remarks and references to Appendices
MIRVAUX	25/8/15		Looked after by F.A. of Brigade to which they were attached for instruction, purposes — Arranged for ride to the Carriere def — S.d.R.	
	26/8/15	10am	All ranks (N.C.O's and men) worked extremely well — excellent nick hot pork & dear boo beefsteaks — Confused buffoon with tea & cold lunch quite good — G.O.C. adequate tune & beef showers — 91st Inf Brigade horses of today — His Excellency returned in the evening — Anxt accompanying no. 24 to M.O.H.R. ridden into cover) 8 — Carried for Exhaustion. Sent artillery no. 21st M.O.H.R. sicks up cattle 2 — Sore feet Sent artillery no. 20th M.O.H.R. broke up horse 1 — Sore feet	

Army Form C. 2118

WAR DIARY
or
INTELLIGENCE SUMMARY
(Erase heading not required.)

Instructions regarding War Diaries and Intelligence Summaries are contained in F. S. Regs., Part II. and the Staff Manual respectively. Title Pages will be prepared in manuscript.

Place	Date	Hour	Summary of Events and Information	Remarks and references to Appendices
MIRVAUX	27/3/18	1pm	Received orders from A.D.M.S. to move to CANAPLES on 28th inst. See A.D.M.S. about it & to arrange to see O.C. 97th Fd. Amb at MONTVILLERS tomorrow — we are to attack for wounded tomorrow at 9.30 by 9.F.A. E.L.M.	
		10.15 AM	Received marching orders from 95th Inf. Brigade. Whole ⟨unit⟩ will march to relieve lines of the 47th Fd Amb. from Louleuleurs hun theopi unit now at Hessellis unit at Belloyjou, rearrangement 97th F.A. MIRVAUX unchanged. Prisoners at VILLERS BOCAGE. — HAVERNAS to CANAPLES CANAPLES	
			It was to move independently on 29th to Le MEILLARD. Later received orders MD108. 97th F.A. move from CANAPLES to FIENVILLERS on the 29th instead of to Le MEILLARD. Three motor ambulances to be sent bring up Reserve Lorries for above up	

1875 Wt. W593/826 1,000,000 4/15 J.B.C. & A. A.D.S.S./Forms/C. 2118.

WAR DIARY
or
INTELLIGENCE SUMMARY
(Erase heading not required.)

Army Form C. 2118

Place	Date	Hour	Summary of Events and Information	Remarks and references to Appendices
			En Route	
			20th M.A.H.R. carried 85 sick all adcases to T.A.	
			21st " " " Cases 3 - one sick but conscious.	
			24th " " " Cases 24 - never took anywhere over 20 feet.	
				J.C.M.
CANAPLES	25/11/15	10 pm	Another reconnaissance was made at 7.4. 8 AM - via MOLLIEN-AU-BOIS - & VILLERS-BOCAGE - arr. at FLESSELLES 10.30 AM - C.O. Office - drove to CANAPLES arriving 12.45 noon - to prepared billeting arrangements have been made for 18 - Staff Officers of the Signals of M.E. is here/ orders of 19th M.A.H.R. for Villebeoy as Emergency B. Light ambulances but 14 M.cars [unclear] to stop [unclear] moved to sleep in small room - Hospital Annex. for us by 19 in M.A.H.R. Col. Clear & acty Bacof- arrange with Col. later to let my patients sleep on floor of MAIRIE which is also	

Army Form C. 2118

WAR DIARY
or
INTELLIGENCE SUMMARY
(Erase heading not required.)

Instructions regarding War Diaries and Intelligence Summaries are contained in F. S. Regs., Part II. and the Staff Manual respectively. Title Pages will be prepared in manuscript.

Place	Date	Hour	Summary of Events and Information	Remarks and references to Appendices
FIENVILLERS.	24/11/18		Orders received of 19th M.A.R.R. Ambulances (two) to take all fit personnel on Secret Co? 19th M.A.A.R. and Secondary 15th M.A.R.R. See A.D.M.S. re two moving transport — A.D.M.S. states records to talk to 15th M in FIENVILLERS re/ADMS states to seize land and Room as soon to arrive at FIENVILLERS 12 noon tomorrow. J.A.R.	
	25/11/18	10am	Ambulance in rates 10.28 am — Received Orders following this morning from G.H.Q. — Proceed via FIEFFES–MONTRELET Arrived FIENVILLERS 1.20pm — Billets arranged by ADMS for men & officers good — Hospital arranged for see later Orders by DDMS 20 Army On 25–11–18. —	

WAR DIARY or INTELLIGENCE SUMMARY

Army Form C. 2118

No Casualties to-day —
Casualties Admitted Nov 23rd — Nov 29th Incl —
Admissions to F.A. Nov 23rd — Nov 29th
R.A.S.C.

20th MOHR	41
21st MOHR	12	4 O.R. Rel.
22nd " " "	13
24th " " "	9

Recruiting Scheme received East 9 weeks
Incl. Incl.s 30ff feef Could be added So —
Visit from D.A.D.M.S. 35th Div — orders issued to
Send 3 Officers — 8 N.C.O. + hospitals to 3 S. MIDLAND
J.A. 48th Div & Div of VAUCHELLES for training for 6 days —
Men take two days Rations & the Strength of new
Eastern Strength Return Dec 1st
VIDE M0122 of 29-11-18 — G.S.E.H.

Army Form C. 2118

WAR DIARY
or
INTELLIGENCE SUMMARY
(Erase heading not required.)

Place	Date	Hour	Summary of Events and Information	Remarks and references to Appendices
FIENVILLERS	30/11/15		New arr. sand off Lieut MALLOCH- For 1st 9 Devons - 8 NCOs Sergts Halliwell - Archibald & LEE Corps Rutherford. Red Xx. Corps. Blain & Jolley & two between re-embarked ex. ADMS orders of MO/22 of 29-11-15- J.R.Gr.	

97th Fa.
tot: 2

121/7909

30 K Kr
F/1211

December 1915

Confidential
War Diary
of
97th (C.P.) F.A., R.A.M.C.
from December 1/15 to December 31/15
Volume II

Place	Date	Hour	Summary of Events and Information	Remarks and references to Appendices
FIENVILLERS	1/2/15	10 AM	Barn as Hospital all very suitable create personal arrangements with owner of barn for use of a large Laboratory of poste here — Inside arrangements for 25 stretchers & more cosy than the barn — the Chateau Rg/Officers Clergy leeds in wards keeps a 1st Aid Hospital but unfortunately we enquired all at ad Division Headquarters are moving — LE MEILLARD & may require Chateau — LIEUT ANDERSON reports for duty — Heavy rain all day — G.J.M	
FIENVILLERS	2/2/15	10 AM	Duties of Corps of Cyclists from M.M.P. They had been sleeping in barn recently occupied by Judicial notes — loses here & Country seeker Reinforced 11/2 G.J.M	

WAR DIARY or INTELLIGENCE SUMMARY

Army Form C. 2118

Place	Date	Hour	Summary of Events and Information	Remarks and references to Appendices
FIENVILLERS	3/10/15	10 pm	Heavy rain all day - G.O.R. Admitted 15 cases of Diarrhoea to Div. Rest Station which is at BERTEAUCOURT. These Div. Rest Stations are a magnificent scheme my officers unable to evacuate to C.C.S. only ended up likely to get well in 10 days - all other cases to Div Rest Station - this means a great saving to the fighting strength of our units - as only 5% of my admissions will go to C.C.Stations - Rain all day - Lieut. G.F.P. Heatherden arrives for duty from 30th Div R.E. Lieut. J.M. Anderson struck off strength sent to 30 Div R.E.	
FIENVILLERS	4/10/15	10 pm	Wired from DMS 3rd Army re beds and three ACE Lids for my F. Ambulance as well as these and 12 Rolls 2 b-bis	

WAR DIARY
or
INTELLIGENCE SUMMARY

(Erase heading not required.)

Army Form C. 2118

Place	Date	Hour	Summary of Events and Information	Remarks and references to Appendices
			He asks why we don't use Chateau - I reply Div Headqrs want it - Discharged to duty all eyecases - one only leaving. To Div Rest Station. Rain all day. G.O.H.	
FIENVILLERS	5/7/15	10 p.m.	Div Headquarters do not Require Chateau but 91st Bgde do want it as their Headquarters they received instructions on firing line tomorrow to 30th Division - Officers leave Chateau & take up our Billets in village - Rain in morning fine in afternoon - Warren - G.O.M.	

WAR DIARY
INTELLIGENCE SUMMARY

Army Form C. 2118

Place	Date	Hour	Summary of Events and Information	Remarks and references to Appendices
FIENVILLERS	6/12/15	10 p.m.	91st Brigade returns to Div. billeting area today – Headqrs in Chateau here – 21st M.G.H.R.R. billeted in village – 24th M.G.H.R. in AUTHEUX – 20th M.G.H.R. in BOIS BERGUES – 22nd M.G.H.R. in CANDAS – Rain all day – A.D. recensions to our F.A. for week ending Dec 8th 90th Brigade:- 16th M.G.H.R. — 2 17th " " — 1 18th " " — 1 19th " " — — Total — 9 5 Cavl. Divs not included, 15 cases of measles all taken in our boots refer to Divr R. stahn	

WAR DIARY
or
INTELLIGENCE SUMMARY

Army Form C. 2118

91st Brigade

20th M.A.R.P.	3
21st " "	1
22 " "	3
24 " "	11
Total	**18**

A.S.C. attached 97 " F.A.	3
" 20 4 Coy	1
" 261 M.T. D.S.C	6 —
M.M.P.	9 — Eye cases — referred below
3rd Div. Signals	2
" Cyclists	1
A.S.C. Motor Dowers	2
Headqrs Staff	1
R.E. 202 Coy	2
Total	**26 —**

Weekly total advances for week of J-y

WAR DIARY
or
INTELLIGENCE SUMMARY

Army Form C. 2118

Place	Date	Hour	Summary of Events and Information	Remarks and references to Appendices
			Send Staff Sergt Aultony meeting Sellers & 10 men for instructions to No 19 O.C.S. at DOWLLENS. Remain for 14 days – G.C.M.	
FIENVILLERS.	7/12/15	10/am	Saw R.E. Officer O.C. A.E. Stores – arranged for fatigue parties for carrying firewood for watering road in courtyard of Hospital – also R.E. Officer Buildg Leeds, plumbing for flooring trace & two R.E. men to supervise our fatigue party. 3 Officers 8 men & 2 batmen return from S.MIDLAND Field Ambulance. Fair i.e. snowing. Rain in afternoon. C.C.M.	

WAR DIARY
or
INTELLIGENCE SUMMARY

Army Form C. 2118

Place	Date	Hour	Summary of Events and Information	Remarks and references to Appendices
FIENVILLERS	8/12/15	10 p.m.	Reinforcement. Lieut A.B. Bolivers from Southampton reports for duty in place of Lieut C.A.R. Gattey - eventually ceft at SOUTHAMPTON and 8 Feb — Lieuts - Postes - Macfarlane & Thompson & men & 2 between posted to 3-S. M IDLAND F. Ambc for 7 days instruction. Fine all day. [signed]	
FIENVILLERS	9/12/15	10 PM	DIV R.O. re Scheme for taking forms for cook house stoves. Raining all morning & drying retorn — take farm in our billetting area — we are allowed 9/6d a day — arrange to pay 3 francs a day for farm buildings as they are in a very delapedated condition. [signed]	

Place	Date	Hour	Summary of Events and Information	Remarks and references to Appendices
LIENVILLERS	9/7/15	10pm	Captain A.A. Fyffe R.A.M.C. S.R. from 37th Division reports for duty, taken on strength accordingly. Renie — all day — G.H. Orders from A.D.M.S. 30th Division — To send M.O. to 37th Div. To replace Captain A.A. Fyffe sent to us recently. Lieut G. Scurr Rauf ordered by me to report ADMS 30th Div & being offrs strength accordingly — G.H.	
FIENVILLERS	11/7/15	10am	Busy field training — C. to 70 Irel fend. D.H.	

Army Form C. 2118

WAR DIARY
or
INTELLIGENCE SUMMARY
(Erase heading not required.)

Instructions regarding War Diaries and Intelligence Summaries are contained in F.S. Regs., Part II. and the Staff Manual respectively. Title Pages will be prepared in manuscript.

Place	Date	Hour	Summary of Events and Information	Remarks and references to Appendices
FIENVILLERS	12/12/15	10pm	A D M S 35th Div visit F.A. Engaged various improvements which will be completed with NCO Sleet. G.S.M.	
FIENVILLERS	13/12/15	6pm	Admissions to Hospital by units for week ending 13-12-15:— 90th Brigade 16. M.G. H.R. R. 6 17 " " " 3 18 " " " 1 19 " " " 4 91st Brigade 20th M.H.H. R. 6 21 " " " 18 22 " " " 2 24 th " " " 33	

1875 Wt. W593/826 1,000,000 4/15 J.B.C. & A. A.D.S.S./Forms/C. 2118.

WAR DIARY
or
INTELLIGENCE SUMMARY

(Erase heading not required.)

Army Form C. 2118

Place	Date	Hour	Summary of Events and Information	Remarks and references to Appendices
FIENVILLERS	14/11/15	2.30 pm	30 Bde attached ASC attached 6 A.T. & O.F. Amb. 1 30 Bde Squadron 4 MMP 1 (Eye own estimate) Total 81 Five but not yet a C.O. — LOA 30 Officers & NCOs sent for instruction to S.S. MIDLAND F.A. returns today. Rain all day. JWW	

Army Form C. 2118

WAR DIARY
or
INTELLIGENCE SUMMARY
(Erase heading not required.)

Instructions regarding War Diaries and Intelligence Summaries are contained in F. S. Regs., Part II. and the Staff Manual respectively. Title Pages will be prepared in manuscript.

Place	Date	Hour	Summary of Events and Information	Remarks and references to Appendices
FIENVILLERS	15/12/15	10am	Visit from ADMS expressed himself satisfied — Send Staff Orderman Ryan & Dr Ross to 3 C.S. MIDLAND FA for instruction — Afternoon 9.9. Our Conferences visit to 3 S.M.F.A. Chapel from 2 to 1. No loss or engagement for Baths and Showers witnessed. They have been there 9 months — Frost in morning inclined to rain in evening. S.M
FIENVILLERS	16/12/15	10pm	Send Lieut Herbette G.F.P. to 3 C.S. MIDLAND FA for instruction — Rain all day — SCR.
FIENVILLERS	17/12/15	10am	Rain all day. SCA.

WAR DIARY or INTELLIGENCE SUMMARY

Army Form C. 2118

Place	Date	Hour	Summary of Events and Information	Remarks and references to Appendices
FIENVILLERS	18/10/15	10am	91st Brigade Consists of Brigade 30th Division to join 7th Division OTd – infty S.C.H.	
FIENVILLERS	19/10/15	10am	21st Brigade arrive today from 7th Division. Consist of 2 YORKS. 2. BEDFORDS. 2. R. SCOTS. 2. WILTS. Two dy. Clear – S.C.H	
FIENVILLERS	20/10/15	10am	attached is a plan of Cooking meur head in the day by this recent – In little wind are now go forards when Enteric meals Cooked – also is a plan off a wound of latrines – ascribed also in same hecenfo. The floors occluded in a well ascribed also in same hecenfo. (tree Cockroach) – Six labour cesspools all the time burned open $q=\eta$	

WAR DIARY
or
INTELLIGENCE SUMMARY

Army Form C. 2118

Place	Date	Hour	Summary of Events and Information	Remarks and references to Appendices
FIENVILLERS	29/12/15	10 am	True Dy. Class—	
			Returned by week ending today.	
			89th Brigade.	
			16th K. Liv. R. — 2	
			19th K. Liv R — 5	
				Total 7
			90th Brigade 16th M.C.H.R.R. — 10	
			17th " " — 6	
			18th " " — 1	
				Total 17
ETEN			91st Brigade	
			20th M.C.H.R.R. — 6	
			21st " " — 13	
			22nd " " — 7	
			24th " " — 47 (all sore feet)	
				Total 70

J.S.M.

WAR DIARY
or
INTELLIGENCE SUMMARY
(Erase heading not required.)

Army Form C. 2118

Place	Date	Hour	Summary of Events and Information	Remarks and references to Appendices
FIENVILLERS	27/12/15	10 am	ASC MT 30th Div H.Q's — 1 " Canal Section no 70 — 1 261 MT Div sup Col — 1 MT 30 Div F.A.H.Q. — 1 30 Div Div H.Q — 1 No 1 Coy ASC — 1 Bgd Div Cyclists — 1 No 3 A.E Signal Sector — 1 Total 8 Rain all day. Lieuts Arkerman & Heathcote returned to Foliestone No 3 E. MIDLAND F.A. 9am Rain all day.	g Coys H.Q 10.55 9am 9am
FIENVILLERS	27/12/15	10 am		

WAR DIARY
or
INTELLIGENCE SUMMARY
(Erase heading not required.)

Army Form C. 2118

Place	Date	Hour	Summary of Events and Information	Remarks and references to Appendices
FIENVILLERS	23/10/15	10 am	Our French interpreter leaves for 19th M.A.R.L. Present arrangement ADMS has one interpreter for his use & for use of the 3 field ambulances. Rain on & off all day. GSOH	
FIENVILLERS	24/10/15	10 am	Visited no 23 F.A. at PROUVIGNY — spleen platoons. Same as yesterday — Our cookery arrangements etc. Near Acheux. FINE day. GSOH	
FIENVILLERS	25/10/15	10 am	X'mas day — divine service 1.15 — RCL had Roast Turkey — sausages — jellies & puds — French visits — 7 — 9 pm officers had all ranks in turn — tables & forms kindly by O.R.S. GSOH	

WAR DIARY or INTELLIGENCE SUMMARY

Army Form C. 2118

Place	Date	Hour	Summary of Events and Information	Remarks and references to Appendices
FIENVILLERS	26/3/15	Noon	21st Brigade - attachments - 2nd Bedford R. leave - 2nd R. Scots leave - Replaced by 18th & 22nd L.W.R & 19th M.O.H.R. - Brigade now is: 2nd WILTS. R, 2nd YORKSHIRE R, 18th K. L. IV - R, 19th M.O.H.R	
			Sent Staff Sergt King, 9. 10 men to 19 D.C.S. for instruction. Showery cold day. Quiet. G.C.M.	
FIENVILLERS	27/3/15	10 pm	Staff Sergt Arranged to collecting 19th M.O.H.R today. Men returned to focus A.M. Picture for week ending return 27th in 90th Brigade. 16 M.C.H.R. 7, 17 " " 4, 18 " " 3, 19 " " 3, Total 17	

Army Form C. 2118

WAR DIARY
or
INTELLIGENCE SUMMARY
(Erase heading not required.)

Instructions regarding War Diaries and Intelligence Summaries are contained in F. S. Regs., Part II. and the Staff Manual respectively. Title Pages will be prepared in manuscript.

Place	Date	Hour	Summary of Events and Information	Remarks and references to Appendices
			21st Brigade 2nd WILTS 14 2nd YORKS 16 2nd R. SUTTS 8 2nd BEDS. 1 — 36 30th DIV. H.Q. to 1st FA — 2 Same 35th Div H.Q. — 1 " Sau Cochin — 1 A.S.E. attached 97 to FA — 1 " No 1 Coy — 1 " M.T. Supp. est — 1 " 208 MT DSC — 2 " 109 Coy — 1 R.E. No 3 Sig. Sec — 1 " No 202 Fld Coy — 3 " Sig Supply team — 1 " 201 Fld Coy — 1 " B Aic Sig Coy — 1 A.C.C. 30 Div — 1 — 18 Showery all day thick Grand Total 7 3 GSO	

Showery all day thick

Army Form C. 2118

WAR DIARY
or
INTELLIGENCE SUMMARY
(Erase heading not required.)

Instructions regarding War Diaries and Intelligence Summaries are contained in F. S. Regs., Part II. and the Staff Manual respectively. Title Pages will be prepared in manuscript.

Place	Date	Hour	Summary of Events and Information	Remarks and references to Appendices
FIENVILLERS	29/12/15	10am	Visit from D.M.S. 3rd Army. Yesterday expressed himself satisfied — afternoon conference of A.D.M.S. 30th Div. & Sanitation & various other matters — Attached is plan of our precis incinerator for our "Winter Palace" tents, covered stores, dining room, drying room & attendants hut & stove — an important improvement in our Cookhouse stove — i.e. a circular boiler made out of an old plan of improvement in our Cookhouse stove — i.e. a circular boiler made out of an old drum. GLM	
FIENVILLERS	29/12/15	10am	Fine dry COD in morning — RAIN in evening. GLM	
FIENVILLERS	30/12/15	10am	Visit from A.D.M.S. expressed himself Satisfied. Fine dry COD GLM	
FIENVILLERS	31/12/15	10pm	Rather Frost tonight but most mild today GLM	

Plans
of
Latrines

Annexure

18/11/15

LATRINES FIENVILLIERS

DEC 15th 1915

PLAN
SCALE HALF INCH

SERGEANTS LATRINES

- 9'-0"
- 7'-0"
- 3'-6"
- 1'-3", 2'-3", 3'-0", 3'-0", 1'-3"
- 4'-1"
- WC
- PIT 3'-0"x3'-0"x5'-0" DEEP FILLED WITH RUBBLE
- URINAL TROUGH
- 2'-6" OPENING
- 2" WASTE PIPE LEADING INTO PIT

LATRINES FOR PRIVATES

- 16'-0"
- 5'-0"
- 8'-0"
- W.C. — 2'-0" × 1'-6" × 2'-0" × 1'-6" × 2'-0" × 1'-6" × 2'-0"
- W.C. W.C.
- URINAL TROUGH — 9'-0"
- PIT 4'-0"x7'-0"x6'-0" DEEP FILLED WITH RUBBLE
- 3" WASTE PIPE LEADING INTO RUBBLE
- 3'-6" OPENING
- SAPLINGS 6'-0" HIGH
- CANVAS SCREEN
- CANVAS SCREEN — 5'-0"
- CANVAS SCREEN — 20'-0"
- 2'-6"

SECTION THRO URINAL TROUGH
- 1" TIMBER LINED WITH TIN
- 4½"×3" TIMBER
- 2'-3"

SECTION THRO W.C.
- BISCUIT TIN
- 1'-8"
- 2'-1"

Plans of Catherine Inverarity 18/1/51

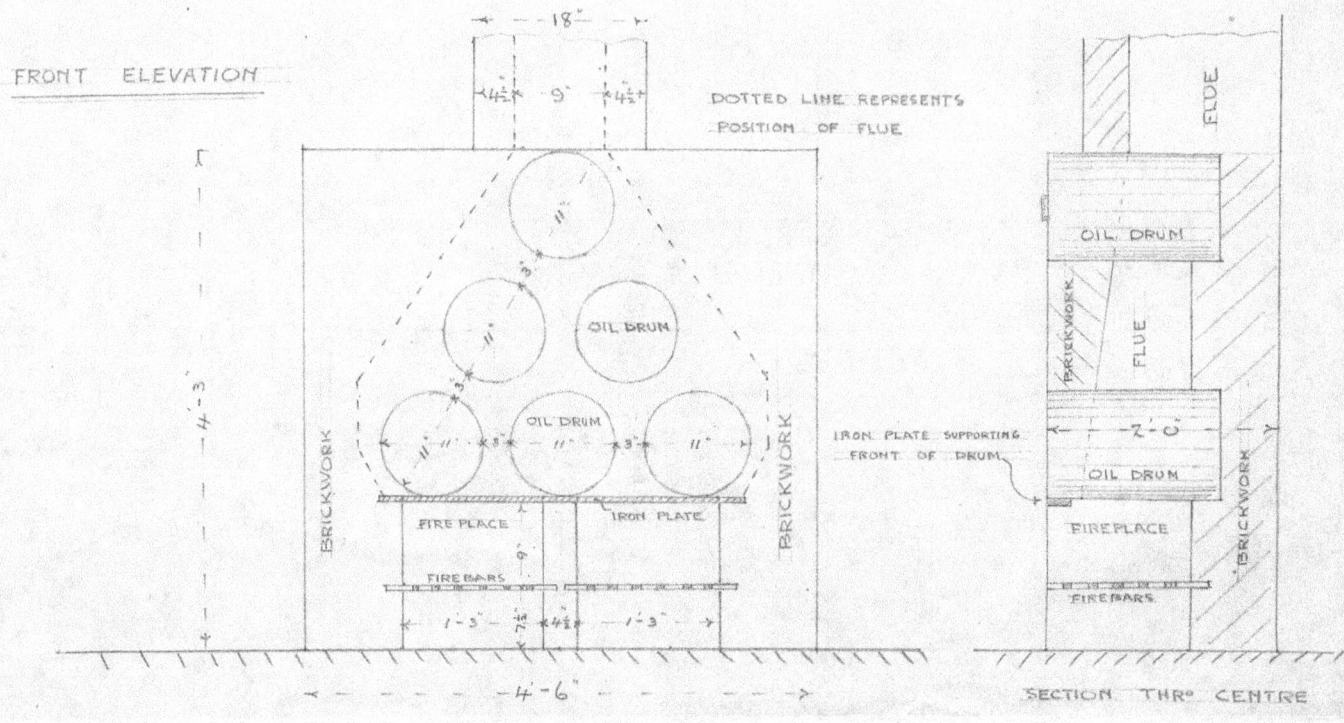
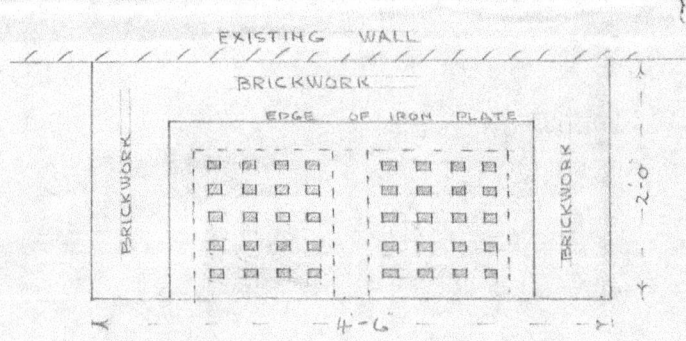

FIENVILLERS

INCINERATOR FOR BURNING FAECES

HALF INCH SCALE

PLAN

- CLAY PARGING
- BRICKWORK
- OIL DRUM
- OIL DRUM
- IRON BARS SUPPORTING OIL DRUMS
- TRENCH FOR FIRE

SECTION AB

- CORRUGATED IRON COVER
- FIRE PLACE

97th Field Ambulance

SCHEME OF WORK
AT
FIENVILLERS

SCALE 1" = 20'-0" APPROX.

BRAZIER SUSPENDED FROM ROOF
ASH TRAY LINED WITH TIN
FLOOR BOARDED WITH 1" BOARDS

STREET

POND

BARN

WORK SHOP

DRYING ROOM

BARN

ROOMS
FORMS

DINING
TABLES

PAVED FOOTPATH

YARD
LEVELLED and DRAINED

BARN

PAVED FOOTPATH

RATION STORES

COOK HOUSE
OVEN

ALDERSHOT OVENS

FIELD TRENCH
FOR DAILIES

STREET

ROAD LEADING TO RESERVOIR

BATH & ABLUTION HOUSE

BRAZIER
WASH TROUGH
FOOT BOARDS
FOOT BOARDS
BATH
15'-0"
15'-0"
WASH TUBS

MAIN ROAD

97th F.a.
tot: 3

3rd Div
F/120/2

Jan 19th

Confidential

War Diary of

97th (C.P.) Field Ambulance R.A.M.C.

from January 1/16 to January 31/16

Volume VII

WAR DIARY
or
INTELLIGENCE SUMMARY
(Erase heading not required.)

Army Form C. 2118

Place	Date	Hour	Summary of Events and Information	Remarks and references to Appendices
FIENVILLERS.	1/1/16	11 am	Rain all day - buggy - Lieut J. Parker goes on leave in Bedford. To visit father dying. G.O.C.	
FIENVILLERS.	2/1/16	10 am	Fd avi all day - G.O.C.	

FIENVILLERS.	3/1/16	10 am	18th LIVERPOOLS & 19th M.H.R.R. march today - 7 days march to AMIENS. Records are -
			In of men admitted to F.A. from Corps -
			9th BRIGADE 2/1st BRIGADE 97th C.P.F.A. 1
			16th MoH.R.R 17 2nd WILTS 12 35th D.v.Cyc 3
			17th " 4 2nd YORKS 12 16 R/12 8
			18th " 5 18th K.L.R 8 1st STAMFS 7
			2nd R.S.Fus 4 19 M.oH.R.R 11 RE 201 Fd Coy 3
			        30 49 RFA 2nd WELSH 1
			                                  RE 202 Fd Coy 4
			                                  A.S.C. Hq 30oy 1
			                                  A.S.A. M.T.35 Div 1
			                                  A.S.C. M.T. 35 Div 1
			                                  FAmo
			                                  A.S.C. Hurdles
			                                  97 C.P.F.A. 1
			                                         29
			
			Dr. O'Neill O.C. Scott
			Rain all day.	

WAR DIARY or INTELLIGENCE SUMMARY

Army Form C. 2118

Place	Date	Hour	Summary of Events and Information	Remarks and references to Appendices
FIENVILLERS	4/1/16	10 pm	Won all day — Lieut Bateman on leave ceded his embussed 3/1st Dee and Yor Ambce — visited ADMS according to geek.	
FIENVILLERS	5/1/16	10 pm	Cured visits ADMS 2nd Div — Snr LIEUT G.F.P. Heathcote to 150 Bgde RFA — Later (his move Cancelled by ADMS) & LIEUT D. Matlock Sent to 150th Bgde RFA — Capt. I.E. Hamilton Returned but for duty from 151st & 152nd Bgdes of 5th Reugh accordingly — Chaplain's place of our Med Dres with brigade — Lieut. W. Ford Selected for temp duty with 2nd York. Lieut D. Morrow attached for duty with 150th G.F.A Brigade RFA	
FIENVILLERS	6/1/16	10 pm	R.A.M.C. Operation order No I by Colonel I.S. Dawson A.D.M.S. Para I 97th Field Ambulance You dishri 9th Field Ambulance heard as No 10 Wmurn (Commander Major Hogges RAMC) on January 11 in relieving CHIPILLY & SAILLY-LE-SEC respectively on January 13th — 97th Field Ambulance will take over the Divisional Rest Station from No 13 Field Ambulance	

Army Form C. 2118

WAR DIARY
or
INTELLIGENCE SUMMARY
(Erase heading not required.)

Instructions regarding War Diaries and Intelligence Summaries are contained in F. S. Regs., Part II. and the Staff Manual respectively. Title Pages will be prepared in manuscript.

Place	Date	Hour	Summary of Events and Information	Remarks and references to Appendices
			The following accompanying Column will report arrival @ Puchevillers Div (D) To 10th Corps in DonT Roycher La Houssoye area – @ T.A. Div on arrival in Vaux Chipilly area (inclf to infant inclusive) MARITABLE Jan 11th Jan 12th Jan 13th 97th Field Ambulance NAOURS CHIPILLY 96th Field Ambulance " LA HOUSSOYE SAILLY LE SEC (1 Section) RAINCAL Day - (afterwards Hamilton Sparks Cashuaf from 15th Bay De R.F.A. Colonel Skeragh?) G.S.O.	
FIENVILLERS 7/1/16		10 a.m.	Rain all Day. Lieut Brennan hand in his leave extended. No W.O.tee to-day. GLA	
FIENVILLERS 8/1/16		10 p.m.	Re Leave Vacation orders list by Col Dawson A.M.S. A.D.M.S. 25th Div – Received Vacation orders? MARCH TABLE for the Section @ Trouchwith us Jan 11 in 12 in 9 13 in – Sent to O.C. C. Section Vero OC 96th O.W. Field Ambulance from CEE Corp GSOfs.	

Army Form C. 2118

WAR DIARY
or
INTELLIGENCE SUMMARY
(Erase heading not required.)

Instructions regarding War Diaries and Intelligence Summaries are contained in F. S. Regs., Part II. and the Staff Manual respectively. Title Pages will be prepared in manuscript.

Place	Date	Hour	Summary of Events and Information	Remarks and references to Appendices
FIENVILLERS	9/1/16	10 p.m.	Officers & Men over Billets & fixtures training to 10th F.A.E. The 36th DIVISION trained 10 h. & to transfer all our potentials to them. Rain all day. J.S.F.	
FIENVILLERS	10/1/16	10 p.m.	Handed over kites, billeting pictures – & potentials of field Ambulance to 10th Field Ambulance which leaves us 36th horses tomorrow 8.30. To arrive new destination Tuesday march – Attached see plans of air drying rooms & washhouse – Rain all day. J.S.F.	
NAOURS	11/1/16	11 a.m.	Marched VIA MONTRELET – FIEFFES. CANAPLES – HAVERNAS – WARGNIES – to billets in NAOURS – started 8.30 AM arrived 12.15. Good Road – distance 11 miles – Fine all day – Evening Signal Rain – No sign of Cavy.S.C.& R or march or feeding a march. Admission to F.A. by march horses 3-1-16 & now 10-1-16. 90th Brigade 16th MCH.R.2 17r. 30 4 18r. 20 1 ——— 6	

WAR DIARY or INTELLIGENCE SUMMARY

Army Form C. 2118

(Erase heading not required.)

Instructions regarding War Diaries and Intelligence Summaries are contained in F.S. Regs., Part II. and the Staff Manual respectively. Title Pages will be prepared in manuscript.

Place	Date	Hour	Summary of Events and Information	Remarks and references to Appendices
LA HOUSSOYE	12/7/16	10 PM	21st Brigade 2nd WILTS 9 97th RFA 3 +S.O.MGCoy 1 2nd YORKS 16 16th R.Rifles 4 RE 11th Coy 2 2nd R.Scots Fus 1 1st S. Lancs 4 19th L.Pool R 7 16th N.L.Pool 1 RE 21st Bgde HqCoy 1 8th N.Lanc Brig Coy 1 — — — RE 30th Div Pioneers 1 11th R.Inns Fus 2 29 2nd Essex 1 Gen Do 4 31st Div (Ulster) DAC 2 1C.C.H.T.Attached 1 97th RFA S.A.A. 34 GRAND TOTAL 69 — Marched — 8.45 AM via TALMAS — SEPTENVILLE — PIERREGOT — MOLLIEN-AU-BOIS — ST GRATIEN — FRECHENCOURT — Battalions joining marched forward to LA HOUSSOYE — the Transport going to LA HOUSSOYE via PONT NOYELLES — fell in left on marshall. Man Sice Ice — Distance 12 miles — Find all day Slightly in the evening	
CHIPILLY	13/7/16	11 PM	Head over afternoon of No 10 Column to Cpt Law A.A.F.Y.F.F. as I have to proceed with him to the less 11 AM) to def me G. Court marshal — Column left LA HOUSSOYE 9 AM marched via LA NEUVILLE — CORBIE —	

WAR DIARY or INTELLIGENCE SUMMARY

Army Form C. 2118

Place	Date	Hour	Summary of Events and Information	Remarks and references to Appendices
CHIPILLY	18/7/16	10pm	VAUX-SUR-SOMME – SAILLY-SEC – SAILLY LORETTE – ᆠ CHIPILLY – arriving 4 pm – Distance 10 miles – men feel no stiff on forth hill – Lieut J. Porter arrives off leave – Col Deverton the 20th is now in action – J.R.H. Last night Lieut A. Gloverior gets to the duties of Town Major in & Bethem [Bray Rest Billets] – Go to F.A.(T.F.) is Brining ambulance etc & no leaders – Arrived Dressing station at BRAY – under orders ADMS. Detail Capt Hamilton – Lieut Kenfork – ts been inspecting 2 men for duty with no 3 Ambulance Elvilla. Also Captain FYFE & 30 men inspecting 2 Red ᆠ Divisional Baths at BRAY. For All Day – G.P.K.	
CHIPILLY	19/7/16	10pm	Under orders ADMS Detail 2 [promoted?] Sergeants X no 5 C.O.S. Corke for permanent duty – Shrekoff? orderly at ADM bureau – Visit from ADMS – also DDMS – Rain all day f.d.f	

1875 Wt. W501/826 1,000,000 4/15 J.B.C. & A. A.D.S.S./Forms/C. 2118.

WAR DIARY
or
INTELLIGENCE SUMMARY
(Erase heading not required.)

Army Form C. 2118

Instructions regarding War Diaries and Intelligence Summaries are contained in F. S. Regs., Part II. and the Staff Manual respectively. Title Pages will be prepared in manuscript.

Place	Date	Hour	Summary of Events and Information	Remarks and references to Appendices
CHIPILLY	16/1/16	10pm	Rain all day. Busy as usual. Town busy or inclined. Apparently responsible for everything but everyone in town – absolutely no field billets – laying down papers – investigating sleeping staffs – also responsible for billeting of no 3rd Divn. Raw wet day.	
CHIPILLY	17/1/16	10pm	Arranging billets for WRDuff DACG Divion 150 officers 530 men + 20 attached 700 horses 9 mules. Fine cold day.	
CHIPILLY	18/1/16	10pm	A busy any full day – visit from ADIVIS.	
CHIPILLY	19/1/16	10pm	DivRO I am appointed Town Major in addition Brig McDerbes No 3 Ambulance Florella by command of ADMS 2Dvn det is furnishing command for echurry etc – No 3 A.F.W. Asking W. Pierstewd Keefstehrtr	

WAR DIARY or INTELLIGENCE SUMMARY

Army Form C. 2118

Place	Date	Hour	Summary of Events and Information	Remarks and references to Appendices
C.H.16,LLY	20/9/16	10am	Endeavoring to obtain D.C.H.16,LLY finishes today - arranged with works for our B Services car on loan as my may wish to escort & refresh of train for wounded - (plan ?) we are expert at trades.	
			Five in vicinity seems in difference.	
C.H.16,LLY	21/9/16	10am	Added orders ADMS 20th Div. F send 12 men wounded underg. C.O.b. 21st Brigade & to 60th Brigade instructed how D.Hopkins to Rendl for the day - knowles & wo Fred for 14 days F to Bakerie & Saulsomps 10 officers & 14 days. Beesy G. all day.	
C.H.16,LLY	22/9/16	10pm	Visit from ADMS. Festive all day.	
C.H.16,LLY	23/9/16	10pm	Busy McCalaurin. Fine all day.	

Army Form C. 2118

WAR DIARY
or
INTELLIGENCE SUMMARY
(Erase heading not required.)

Instructions regarding War Diaries and Intelligence Summaries are contained in F. S. Regs., Part II. and the Staff Manual respectively. Title Pages will be prepared in manuscript.

Place	Date	Hour	Summary of Events and Information	Remarks and references to Appendices.
CHIPILLY	25/7/16	10pm	Busy all day. Ealenchend Dugyle all day.	
PH. PILLY	23/7/16	10pm	FINE —	
CHIPILLY	27/7/16	10pm	Fine —	
CHIPILLY	28/7/16	10pm	Fine —	
CHIPILLY	29/7/16	10pm	Fine —	
CHIPILLY	29/7/16	10pm	Fine — Brothers arranged with Divisions — Inspection Hospitals and trips in their turn — webs of fuel to echo ADMS.	

WAR DIARY
or
INTELLIGENCE SUMMARY

(Erase heading not required.)

Army Form C. 2118

Instructions regarding War Diaries and Intelligence Summaries are contained in F. S. Regs., Part II. and the Staff Manual respectively. Title Pages will be prepared in manuscript.

Place	Date	Hour	Summary of Events and Information	Remarks and references to Appendices
CHIVILLY	23/5/16	10pm	Bell firing -	
CH. pouilly	24/5/16	10pm	Fine - Drill in afternoon - Ought from Lyons Rlieve attached this went for temp duty -	

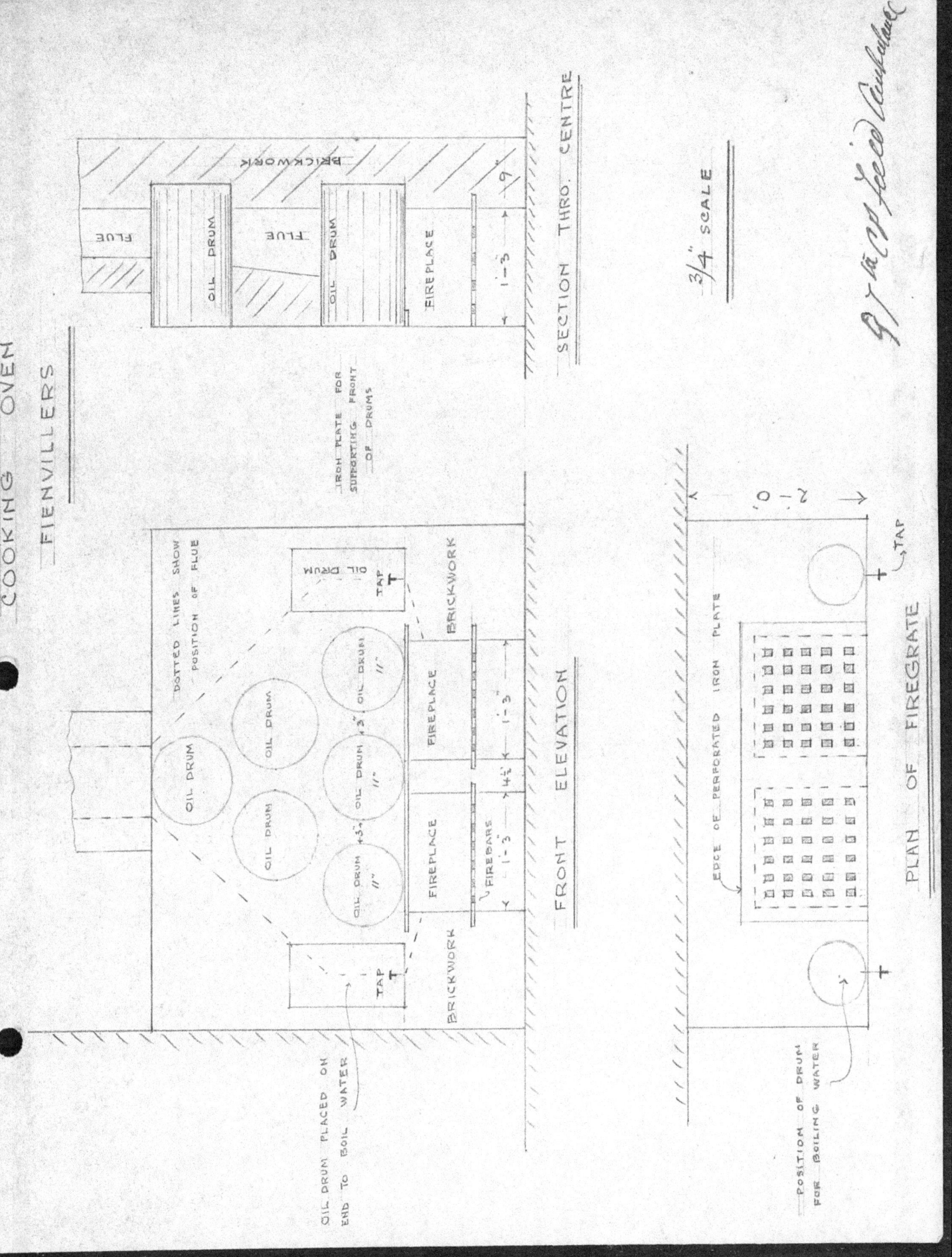

DRYING ROOM
FIENVILLERS

SCALE 3/8" = 1'-0"

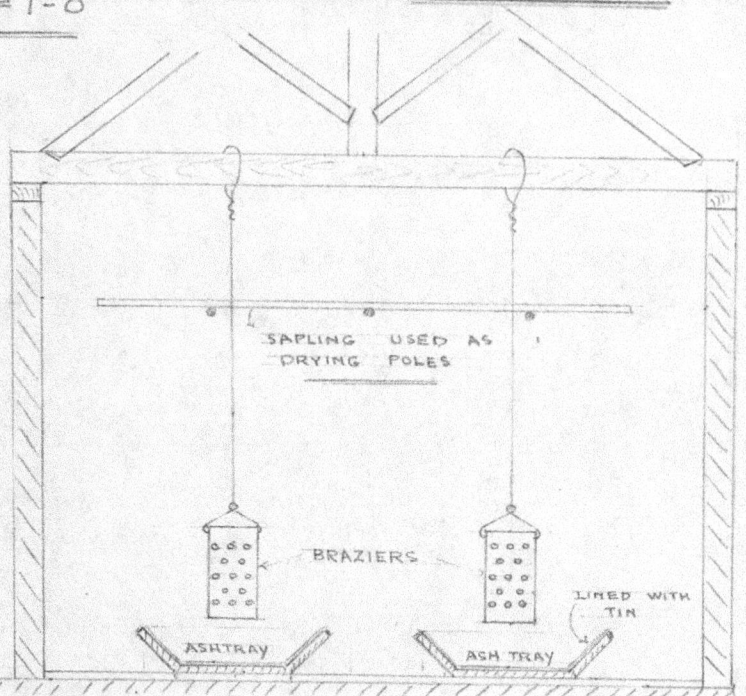

SECTION

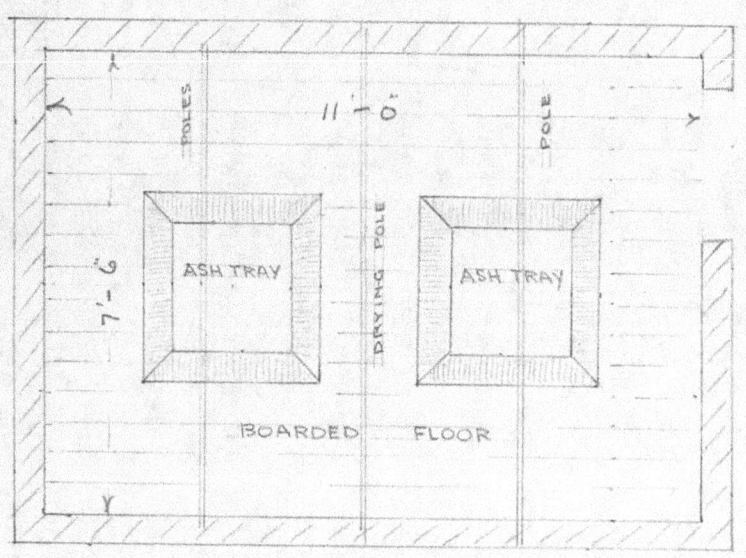

PLAN

WASH HOUSE
FIENVILLERS

SCALE 3/8" = 1'-0"

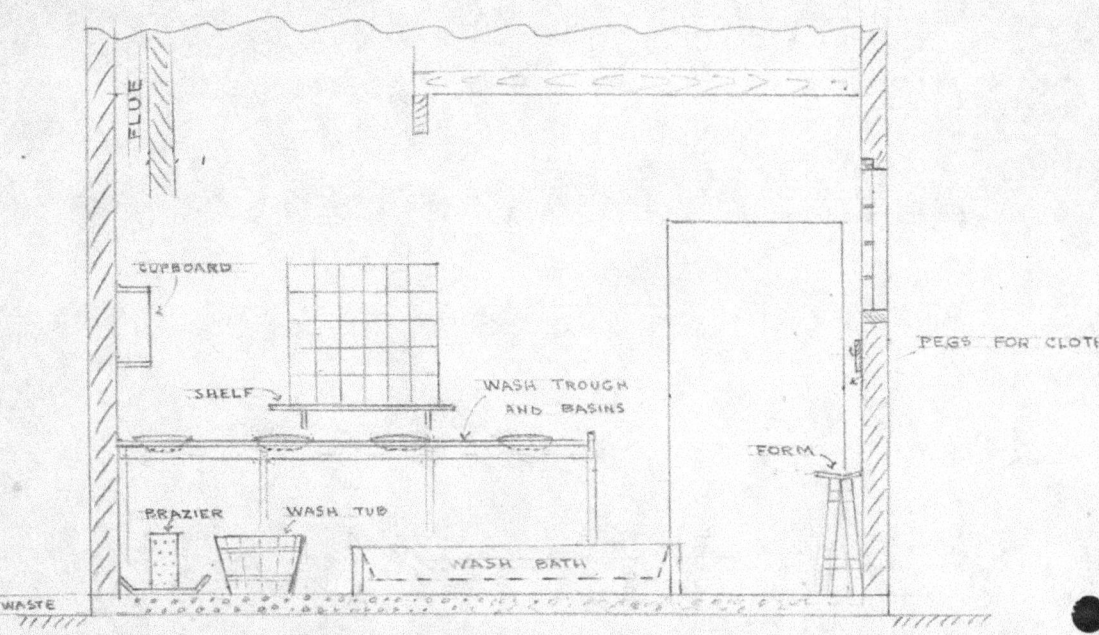

SECTION A B

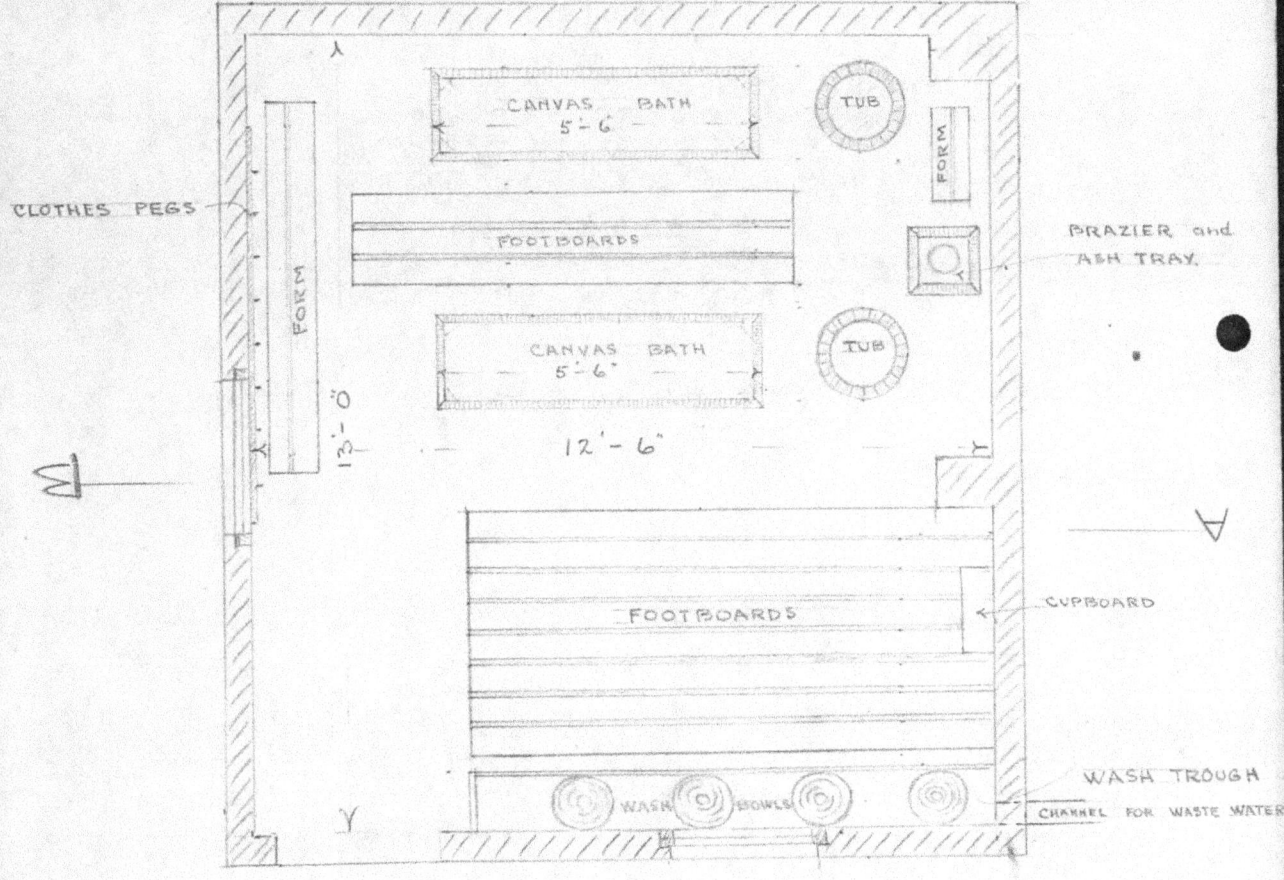

PLAN

47th (CA)
Field Ambulance

CHIPILLY.

INCINERATOR
HALF INCH SCALE

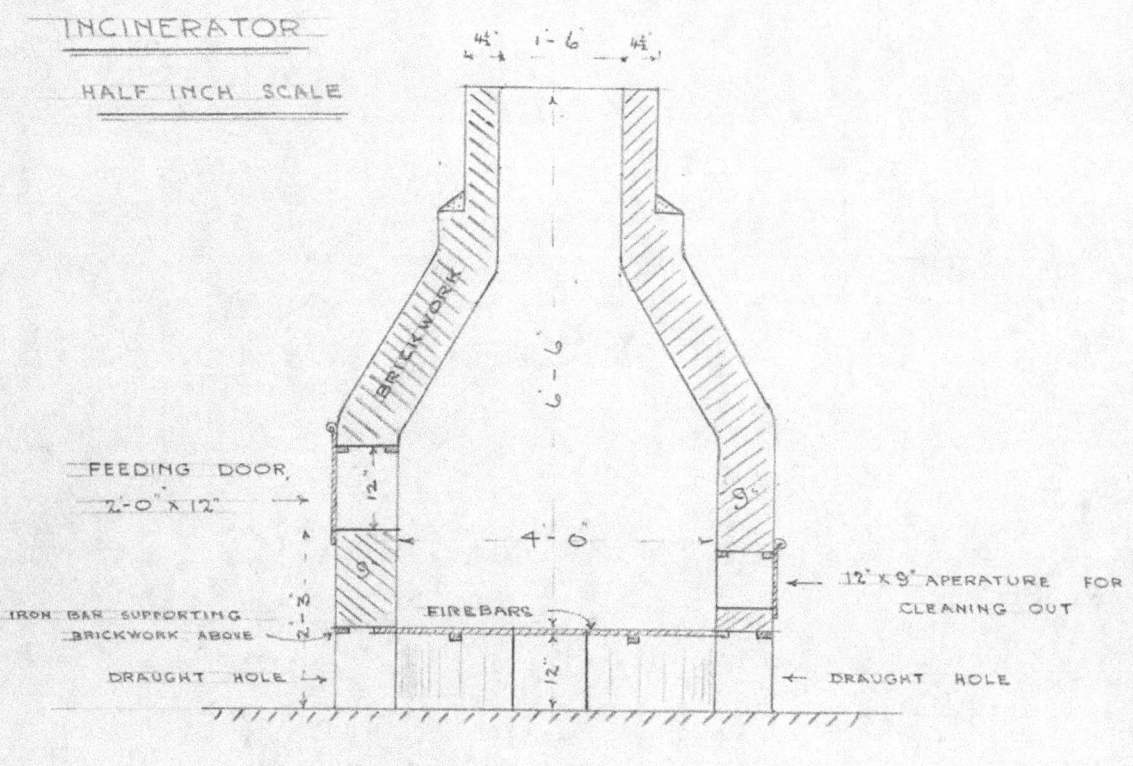

SECTION THRO CENTRE

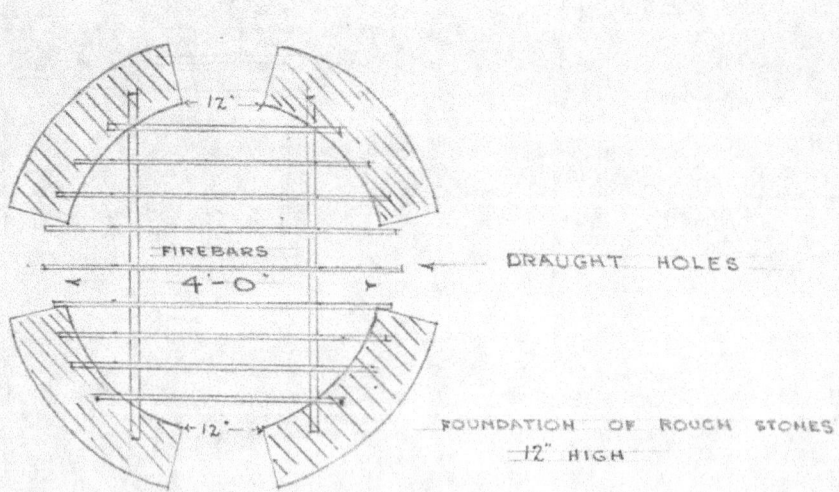

PLAN OF FIREBOTTOM

Feb 21st 1916
Maids

94th Field Ambulance

97ᵗʰ 7a.
vol: 4

97 Field
Amb
Vol 5

WAR DIARY
or
INTELLIGENCE SUMMARY
(Erase heading not required.)

Army Form C. 2118

Place	Date	Hour	Summary of Events and Information	Remarks and references to Appendices
CHIPILLY	1/2/16	10 pm	Lieut A B BATEMAN send under A.D.M.S orders to take charge of DIV Baths at Bray – Captain R.P. Lyons reports for temporary duty. Captain A.A. Fyffe now returns to unit off leave. Fine Spring Day – GCM	
CHIPILLY	2/2/16	10 pm	FINE all day – Air Baths in town are now in running order. Capt Lyons Menne is to take over as Officer in Charge on our leaving to bath the 14th Brigade who return here – GCM	
CHIPILLY	3/2/16	10 pm	A.D.M.S. arranged for car to Bray (Bull) for Revue for our Great Coats – 12 travels however return today & taken on ration strength accordingly. Fine all day – GCM	
CHIPILLY	4/2/16	10 pm	Baths Start today at 2.30 till 8.30 every day except very cold days – Rain all day – GCM	
CHIPILLY	5/2/16	10 am	Fine all day GCM	
CHIPILLY	6/2/16	10 am	Dull no rain – visit from A.D.M.S. – following reinforcements taken on strength – Ptes – Kettlewell A. – Kerr H. – Kerr J.E. – Gt ER.	
CHIPILLY	7/2/16	10 pm	Orders from A.D.M.S. that we are to proceed Lieut H.J. Torde Reeve as attached temporarily to 2nd YORKS. GCM	

Army Form C. 2118

WAR DIARY
or
INTELLIGENCE SUMMARY
(Erase heading not required.)

Instructions regarding War Diaries and Intelligence Summaries are contained in F.S. Regs., Part II. and the Staff Manual respectively. Title Pages will be prepared in manuscript.

Place	Date	Hour	Summary of Events and Information	Remarks and references to Appendices
CHIPILLY	8/2/16	10 a.m.	Fine all day. GCLM	
CHIPILLY	9/2/16	10 a.m.	Under orders ADMS sent in a report of "How legally Horses a Field Ambulance be Equipped" in code J of Order attached. GCLM Fine	
CHIPILLY	10/2/16	10 a.m.	Fine. Visit from ADMS. GCLM	
CHIPILLY	11/2/16	10 a.m.	Out of Jag Lieutenant Increase hospital at Suzanne - Kings in T faced it over to Cpl. F.A.W.D. - a new one will be erected from the same. GCLM	
CHIPILLY	12/2/16	10 p.m.	Rain. GCLM	
CHIPILLY	13/2/16	10 p.m.	Under orders ADMS fees Capt Lyons sent to carry out duties of Div Sanitary Officer who goes on leave today. Rain. GCLM	
CHIPILLY	14/2/16	10 p.m.	Sent Capt. R.H.C. Lyons Rome to replace entirely Sanitary Officer 30th Div. on leave. Rain. GCLM	
CHIPILLY	15/2/16	10 p.m.	A Divl. wishes us to find room for 20 patients to relieve congestion in Divl. Ambulance Little Altoff - form accordingly found in 25fl & Café "De heures near Dorget. Rain. GCLM	

1875 Wt. W593/826 1,000,000 4/15 J.B.C. & A. A.D.S.S./Forms/C. 2118.

Army Form C. 2118

WAR DIARY
or
INTELLIGENCE SUMMARY
(Erase heading not required.)

Instructions regarding War Diaries and Intelligence Summaries are contained in F.S. Regs., Part II. and the Staff Manual respectively. Title Pages will be prepared in manuscript.

Place	Date	Hour	Summary of Events and Information	Remarks and references to Appendices
CHIPILLY	16/2/16	10 p.m.	At present no attempt made by Turmed Troops, plan of which appeared in last week's War Journal — today's W.D. was from R.E. a Horsefall destroyed which is being put together for use in field. S.O. HIPILLY — Pte J.R. Donald a/c M.T. until 14 days leave Urgent private affairs. Fine later 9°C.M.	
CHIPILLY	17/2/16	10 a.m.	Horsefall destroyed erected and up & Clerk work this morning — Fine. 9°C.M.	
CHIPILLY	18/2/16	10 p.m.	Captain E. Hamilton Rowe sent for permanent duty with 2nd W.I.T.S.— Lieut Parker H. Game Reports for Duty — Sent for temporary duty with 3rd army F.D. Wilks.— Fine. 9°C.M.	
CHIPILLY	19/2/16	10 a.m.	Reinforcement a/c M.T. new to Parka 9— Personnel. Fine. 9°C.M.	
CHIPILLY	20/2/16	10 a.m.	Reinforcement Price, Pte Stevenson F. — Fine. 9°C.M.	
CHIPILLY	21/2/16	10 p.m.	Sent 15 men fatigue Party for Duty at Laundry of Cavalry — A.D.V.S. goes on leave — Fine. 9°C.M.	

WAR DIARY
or
INTELLIGENCE SUMMARY

Army Form C. 2118

(Erase heading not required.)

Instructions regarding War Diaries and Intelligence Summaries are contained in F. S. Regs., Part II. and the Staff Manual respectively. Title Pages will be prepared in manuscript.

Place	Date	Hour	Summary of Events and Information	Remarks and references to Appendices
CHIPILLY	22/2/16	10 p.m.	Re Destruction - The Horsfall system in all used 17th without - 9pri w/ complete an arch for the wire, & got received up to date - until 30 s/m compare favourably with our own. Road No 20 Destructor - experiments Copy which is 12 frames. fired. GSOff	
CHIPILLY	23/2/16	10 p.m.	Lieut G.F.P. Heathcote Amme Sent for Camp Duty 18th M.C.H.R.S. Heavy Frost fine. GSOff	
CHIPILLY	24/2/16	10 p.m.	Lieut J. Parker Amme for Camp Duty 18 to L.POSTS - Capt R.H.C. L yons leave Reports for Duty from Sanitary Safar - Capt L yons leave sent for Camp Duty 3rd Camp Florida. Frost fine Singst Drill. GSOff	
CHIPILLY	25/2/16	10 p.m.	Casualties - MT ASC Pierced sinews J & Pontes Res. I M.T. Depot poso - Heavy [crossed out] - Frost - Dull - Heavy frost & snow. GSOff	
CHIPILLY	26/2/16	10 p.m.	Casualties - 1st Lieut J.M. Kingsmith admitted 98th F.A. Evacuates to J.C.S. Corbie - 1 merged of Cavalry Res - Pruck Poole w/s for Returning Duty 12th wing D.F.C. Sent to USA M RGO J Rankes Leave 28-2-16 - 4-3-16 Wilber Henry Ross J Cavalry - 9 Staff	

Army Form C. 2118

WAR DIARY
or
INTELLIGENCE SUMMARY
(Erase heading not required.)

Instructions regarding War Diaries and Intelligence Summaries are contained in F. S. Regs., Part II. and the Staff Manual respectively. Title Pages will be prepared in manuscript.

Place	Date	Hour	Summary of Events and Information	Remarks and references to Appendices
CHIPILLY	27/2/16	10 pm	Thaw. G.C.M.	
CHIPILLY	28/2/16	10 am	Lieut F.E. Thompson Reve'd for temporary duty in Charge B Dn. Laundry of Corps — (later) — fine cold day. G.C.M.	
CHIPILLY	29/2/16	10 pm	Duel Drizzle G.C.M.	

Army Form C. 2118

97 Jan.

WAR DIARY
or
INTELLIGENCE SUMMARY
(Erase heading not required.)

Instructions regarding War Diaries and Intelligence Summaries are contained in F. S. Regs., Part II. and the Staff Manual respectively. Title Pages will be prepared in manuscript.

Place	Date	Hour	Summary of Events and Information	Remarks and references to Appendices
CHIPILLY	1/3/16	1. p.m.	Evacuated by Captain A.A. FYFFE. R.A.M.C. admitted who 9 S.F. Field ambulance - forturitis - fine g.c.m.	
CHIPILLY	2/3/16	10 P.M.	Visited Div Laundry afternoon will be in working order in a week - fine g.c.m.	
CHIPILLY	3/3/16	10 a.m.	Recvd orders A.D.M.S. Cmd / N.C.O. & Ten men for temporary Duty at No 3 C.C.S. CORBIE. Drizzle g.c.m.	
CHIPILLY	4/3/16	10 p.m.	Under orders A.D.M.S. Captain R.H.C. Lyon R.A.M.C. returned to Regimental Duty with 2 W.YORKS - Lieut. J.F.P. Heathcote R.A.M.C. Returns from temp. Duty 18th Y&H's. Snow later drizzle g.c.m.	
CHIPILLY	5/3/16	10 P.M.	Lieut J.F.P. Heathcote Party sent to W.O. 30 other ranks K Dicks for temp Duty - fine all day - g.c.m.	
CHIPILLY	6/3/16	10 p.m.	Recvd W.O. - Secret - Lacrimous gases	
CHIPILLY	7/3/16	10 am	Corporal Rutherford Leave sent to HeadQrs for 3 Day Sunshine in Gas & Gas Helmets - HardFrost last night - Springlike Day -	

1875 Wt. W593/826 1,000,000 4/15 J.B.C.&A. A.D.S.S./Forms/C. 2118.

WAR DIARY
or
INTELLIGENCE SUMMARY

Army Form C. 2118

Place	Date	Hour	Summary of Events and Information	Remarks and references to Appendices
CHIPILLY	8/3/16	10 p.m.	Visit from A.D.M.S. 38th Div - inspected laundry & all wheels. Staff working today - Pnr Stronghom all day. Goch	
CHIPILLY	9/3/16	10 p.m.	Captain Stronghom David. Report for duty - Inspected A.D.M.S. (off Stronghom done) Lieut Thompson 9.25 moor to Advanced Dressing Station of Seay — I am personally bent in charge of Dr Laundry — Pnr on duty Goch Pnr on duty Goch	
CHIPILLY	10/3/16	10 a.m.		
CHIPILLY	11/3/16	10 p.m.	Lukas is Laundry - Boles visit today all north Sphns J. Inspection today by Surgeon General of 4th ARMY - Very successful Expressed himself delighted with All arrangements for Baths which was the best he had seen — Pnr Tathunght - Fned G.CH.	

WAR DIARY
or
INTELLIGENCE SUMMARY
(Erase heading not required.)

Army Form C. 2118

Place	Date	Hour	Summary of Events and Information	Remarks and references to Appendices
CHIPILLY	14/3/16	10am	Fine all day – Recd. Order ADMS Fourth Army Parker Reuss from 3rd ANZ.B. FLOTILLA to supervise feeding station at Bray – GKett	
CHIPILLY	15/3/16	10am	Fine all day GKett	
CHIPILLY	14/3/16	10pm	Fine all day. Order from A.D.M.S. ALLONVILLE on the 18th/3-/16 GKett	
CHIPILLY	15/3/16	10pm	Visits D.W. REST STATION. ALLONVILLE. FIELD AMBULANCE. phoned on 16-3-16 – Lieut J.E. Thompson reports for duty from A.D.S. BRAY – Fine all day – GKett. Lieut J.S. Thompson R.amc. reports for duty tonight from MARICOURT – GKett	

WAR DIARY
or
INTELLIGENCE SUMMARY
(Erase heading not required.)

Army Form C. 2118

Place	Date	Hour	Summary of Events and Information	Remarks and references to Appendices
O.P.I.D, LA BOISSELLE	17/3/16	10 am	Orders to interpret D.R.S. at ALLONVILLE on 18-3-16 - Tomorrow Lieut N. MACFARLANE and Corpl Keehir D.F. AMBULANCE proceedo via Corbie where they will pick up 1 NCO & 10 MEN Stretchers Ambulance (on percs) to ALLONVILLE to report D.R.S from 5th to Field Ambulance 18th DIV - Fine cold day - 5°F.M.	
F.H. p.b.g	17/3/16	10 pm	Lieut Macfarlane & Corpl Heathcote & complete section Reform Regt today to take over D. R. S at ALLONVILLE at 8 A.M. Busy day handing over kits & equipment to 56 F.A. who are coming in - Advance party under Capt. M c ADAM arrives this morning - Kit Alarms against this unit berthed by each in each Mess 9) Felds - Fine all day -	

C.W.P

WAR DIARY
or
INTELLIGENCE SUMMARY

(Erase heading not required.)

Army Form C. 2118

Instructions regarding War Diaries and Intelligence Summaries are contained in F. S. Regs., Part II. and the Staff Manual respectively. Title Pages will be prepared in manuscript.

Place	Date	Hour	Summary of Events and Information	Remarks and references to Appendices
Happy/18/ ALLONVILLE /16	18/3/16	10 p.m.	Field Ambulance left CHIPILLY 8.30 p.m. arrived ALLONVILLE 4.30 p.m. Distance 18 miles – with over Div. R.S. from 3-5 th F.A. – D.R.S. in Chateau – Fine all day. Sd/OR.	
ALLONVILLE	19/3/16	11 a.m.	Relieved A.D.M.S. 98th F.A. in guarantine so we have to run Field Ambulances as well as Div. R.S. Handed over to Capt. J. S. Somerville A.M.C. Command 17 F.A. & D.R.S. placed in our quarantine. FINE. Sd/OR.	
ALLONVILLE	20/3/16	10 a.m.	Command of Officer kept. Lt. E. Keyes left this morning on leave. The A.D.M.S. visited D.R.S. & F.A. to-day. Lieut. J.E. Hooper reported for duty from Div-country at Berry. You [signature]	

WAR DIARY
or
INTELLIGENCE SUMMARY

(Erase heading not required.)

Army Form C. 2118

Instructions regarding War Diaries and Intelligence Summaries are contained in F. S. Regs., Part II. and the Staff Manual respectively. Title Pages will be prepared in manuscript.

Place	Date	Hour	Summary of Events and Information	Remarks and references to Appendices
ALLONVILLE	21.3.16	10 pm	Nothing to report. Weather fine.	
ALLONVILLE	22.3.16	10 pm	Lieut Bateman R.A.M.C. left this morning for temporary duty at D.W.S. Lt-Col Howse Spry visited D.R.S. this afternoon. Weather cloudy with little rain.	
ALLONVILLE	23.3.16	10 pm	Usual issue of personnel detailed for fatigue work in ALLONVILLE & went with R.E. Weather very cold. Some snow.	
ALLONVILLE	24.3.16	pm	A.D.M.S. 2nd Div't Lt-Col Alleyne RAMC visited D.R.S. & Y.A. this morning. Six men of personnel detailed for duty at Div'l Laundry at Query. Weather dem though cold.	

1875 Wt. W503/826 1,000,000 4/15 J.B.C. & A. A.D.S.S./Forms/C. 2118.

Army Form C. 2118

WAR DIARY
or
INTELLIGENCE SUMMARY

(Erase heading not required.)

Instructions regarding War Diaries and Intelligence Summaries are contained in F.S. Regs., Part II. and the Staff Manual respectively. Title Pages will be prepared in manuscript.

Place	Date	Hour	Summary of Events and Information	Remarks and references to Appendices
ALLONVILLE	25.3.16	10pm	Nothing to report. Weather cold & showery.	
ALLONVILLE	26.3.16	Noon	RAMC. Cpl Henderson 74981 allowed extra 2 days for temp? 2 Batty with O/C 2nd Bath. Weather cold & showery	
ALLONVILLE	27.3.16	Noon	Nothing to report. Weather remains cold and variable	
ALLONVILLE	28.3.16	10pm	DDMS XVII. Corps visited DRS this morning. CD	

WAR DIARY
or
INTELLIGENCE SUMMARY

Army Form C. 2118

Place	Date	Hour	Summary of Events and Information	Remarks and references to Appendices
ALLONVILLE	29.3.16	10pm	ADMS & ADVS visited ARS 15-Divn. Weather very cold : some snow in evening.	
ALLONVILLE	30.3.16	10pm	Lieut J Porter RAMC reported for duty 15-divn from 11th K Liverpool Regt acting DADMS. Visited ARS this afternoon. Weather fine but rather cold.	
ALLONVILLE	31.3.16	10pm	Nothing to report. Weather fine.	
ALLONVILLE	1.4.16	10pm	Major J.S.C. Hughes RAMC returns from leave this afternoon. ADMS 1st Div't and Sanitary Officer 3rd Div't visited ARS F.Day. Weather extremely fine.	

30th Div

No. 97 F. Amb

April 1915.

COMMITTEE FOR THE
MEDICAL HISTORY OF THE WAR
Date 9 - JUN. 1915

Army Form C. 2118

WAR DIARY
or
INTELLIGENCE SUMMARY
(Erase heading not required.)

97 7 Amb Vol 6

Instructions regarding War Diaries and Intelligence Summaries are contained in F.S. Regs., Part II. and the Staff Manual respectively. Title Pages will be prepared in manuscript.

Place	Date	Hour	Summary of Events and Information	Remarks and references to Appendices
ALLONVILLE	1/9/16	10 pm	Passive from Leave 9 Eleven Crummell today G.O.C. 1st of Patients in Div REST Station recovery today 111 — No of Patients in Field Ambulance recovery today 6 — Fine SSM —	
"	2/9/16	10.30am	Under instructions ADMS Lent Lieut N. MACFARLAND RAMC to temp duty with 18th M.G.R. Reg — FINE No of patients recovery in DIV. REST. today 103. No of patients recovery in Field Ambulance today 10 —	
"	3/9/16	10 am.	G.O.C. Temporarily Lieut G. F.P. Heathcote RAMC joined unit at H.A.C.S. 11th between Luzeval — No of patients recovery in D.R.S. today 84. No of patients recovery in F.A.M.D. day 13. Fine GOC	
"	4/9/16	10 AM	A.D.M.S. inspected today expressed himself satisfied — No of patients recovery in D.R.S. today 63 No of patients recovery in F.A.M. today 12 Dull Col Roy G.S.M.	
"	5/9/16	10 pm	Gas Demonstration by Gas Expert Arnis — No of patients recovery in D.R.S. today 81 No of patients recovery in Field Ambulance 4 Duce CSO Day G.O.C.	

Army Form C. 2118

WAR DIARY
or
INTELLIGENCE SUMMARY
(Erase heading not required.)

Instructions regarding War Diaries and Intelligence Summaries are contained in F.S. Regs., Part II. and the Staff Manual respectively. Title Pages will be prepared in manuscript.

Place	Date	Hour	Summary of Events and Information	Remarks and references to Appendices
ALLONVILLE	6/4/16	10/30am	No. of patients remaining in D.R.S. today 71. No. of patients remaining in F.A. today 10. Duel very cold East wind. G.E.R.	
ALLONVILLE	7/4/16	10.30am	No. of patients remaining in D.R.S. today 69. No. of patients remaining in F.Amb today 8. Fine but cold East wind. G.E.R.	
ALLONVILLE	8/4/16	10.30am	No. of patients remaining in D.R.S. today 68. No. of patients remaining with A.mb today 6. Snow cold East wind. G.E.R.	
"	9/4/16	10.30am	No. of patients in D.R.S. remaining today 64. No. of patients in F.Amb remaining today 12. Fine sunny cold NE wind. G.E.R.	
"	10/4/16	10.30am	G.O.C. 30th Div. inspected today with A.D.M.S. — reviewing round — G.O.C. expressed himself very well satisfied & especially pleased with the present order for troops made up of weeks of oil frieure — Sergt Wakehouse Lewis Lumberow. No. of patients in D.R.S. remaining today 71. No. of patients with F.Amb remaining today 19. Fine cold NE wind. G.E.R.	

1875 Wt. W593/826 1,000,000 4/15 J.B.C. & A. A.D.S.S./Forms/C. 2118.

WAR DIARY
or
INTELLIGENCE SUMMARY
(Erase heading not required.)

Army Form C. 2118

Place	Date	Hour	Summary of Events and Information	Remarks and references to Appendices
ALLONVILLE	11/4/16	10.30am	Sergt WATERHOUSE. W.P. goes on leave today — No. of patients remaining in D.R.S today 72 No. of patients remaining in F.A.N.S.R. May 15 — Rain increasing fine in afternoon. Old NE wind	
	12/4/16	10 pm	Sent TOOHER F.W. experts for party today folk Visit from D.A.D.M.S. — No of patients remaining in D.R.S 77 No of patients remaining in F.A. 23 Rain all day. Self.	
	13/4/16	10 pm	Visit from D.A.A. & Q.M.G. who apparently wished to see our sleeping tents — very well placed states see G.O.C. wishes all tents on this division to copy it — No of patients remaining in D.R.S 89 No of patients remaining in F.A. 20 Rain in morning fine in afternoon. Self.	
	14/4/16	10 pm	No of patients remaining in D.R.S 95 No of patients remaining in F.A. 5 (called) Great interest in numbers 15th in D.R.S. F.A.	

WAR DIARY
or
INTELLIGENCE SUMMARY

Army Form C. 2118

Place	Date	Hour	Summary of Events and Information	Remarks and references to Appendices
ALLONVILLE	14/5/16	10pm	For last few days it has been raining hard. 3 days of have transferred all cases refs to march to D.R.S. & F Auth. D.R.O. by G.O.C. 30th Div no. 14-19 of 13-4-16. "It is the wish of the Corps Commander that all units should make every effort for comfort & welfare of Company as they are greatly to the comfort & welfare of the men. Officers ready to be held responsible that either come to understand by the C.O.'s in the Regiment & cadre of the appendix of an 18th sheet. A very good type can also be made with helps & ord. Drums. A gathering this rather type can always be seen at 97 to C.P. Field Ambulance at ALLONVILLE." Row in teaching lorry in afternoon. J.W.W.	
ALLONVILLE	15/5/16	10pm	Number of sporocyst learning in DPD Mary 85 Number of sporocyst learning in Z. Anchorus thing to zinc — oTo NEwrew — G.R.N.	

Army Form C. 2118

WAR DIARY
or
INTELLIGENCE SUMMARY
(Erase heading not required.)

Instructions regarding War Diaries and Intelligence Summaries are contained in F. S. Regs., Part II. and the Staff Manual respectively. Title Pages will be prepared in manuscript.

Place	Date	Hour	Summary of Events and Information	Remarks and references to Appendices
ALLONVILLE	16/9/16	9 am	Visit from OC 98th Field Ambulance to arrange a Coy R. w. Men. Patients remaining in D.R.S. today 80. Patients remaining in F Amb. " 4. Fine all day. J.E.M.	
ALLONVILLE	17/9/16	11am	OC. 30th Div D.A.C. visited us & took a Coy of our men - gave him a plan. Did very well pleased — Patients remaining in D.R.S. today 74. Patients remaining in F Amb. " 2. Rain all day. Col. A N Ebden G.F.G.A.	
ALLONVILLE	18/9/16	10pm	Lieut J. W. TOOHER R.A.M.C. undecorated A.D.M.S. sent for keeps duty 19th L POOLS — Patients remaining in D.R.S. today 65. Patients remaining in F Amb. " 5. Showers - very cold. Lt. Col. Permain J.E.M.	
ALLONVILLE	19/9/16	12 pm	Patients remaining in D.R.S. today 86. Patients remaining in F Amb. today 5. Rain - Col. N E wind J.E.M.	
ALLONVILLE	20/9/16	10 am	Surprise visit 1.10 pm today by Corps Commander General Congreve & 25th Div Commander — was 2 hours with fund	

WAR DIARY
or
INTELLIGENCE SUMMARY

(Erase heading not required.)

Army Form C. 2118

Instructions regarding War Diaries and Intelligence Summaries are contained in F. S. Regs., Part II. and the Staff Manual respectively. Title Pages will be prepared in manuscript.

Place	Date	Hour	Summary of Events and Information	Remarks and references to Appendices
ALLONVILLE	21/4/16	10 p.m.	Lofler Cruwnder expressed himself very well pleased — Serj.t W.P. WATERHOUSE R.A.M.C. reports today off leave — Patients remaining in D.R.S. 59. Patients leaving in 7 Aut 3. Fine — showery in afternoon. After N.E. wind soft. Visit from A.D.M.S. yesterday after [?] General inspection expressed himself well pleased — Patients remaining in D.R.S. today 52. Patients leaving in 7 Aut today 3. Fine in morning warm — Later.. rain [?] N.E. wind soft.	
ALLONVILLE	22/4/16	10 p.m.	Patients remaining in D.R.S. today 43. Patients leaving in 7 Aut today 5 — Fine warm — G.C.M.	
ALLONVILLE	23/4/16	10 p.m.	Patients remaining in D.R.S. today 41. Patients leaving in 7 Aut today 2. Fine warm. G.C.M.	

Army Form C. 2118

WAR DIARY
or
INTELLIGENCE SUMMARY
(Erase heading not required.)

Place	Date	Hour	Summary of Events and Information	Remarks and references to Appendices
ALLONVILLE	24/3/16	10pm	Patients remaining in D.R.S. today 29. Patients remaining in F.A. today 6. Fine very warm. R.C.M.	
ALLONVILLE	25/3/16	10pm	Patients remaining in D.R.S. today 15. Patients remaining in F.A. today 10. Fine. R.C.M.	
ALLONVILLE	26/3/16	10pm	Visit from A.D.M.S. – Lieut W Parker R.A.M.C. underorders A.D.M.S. sent for duty. Andy to D.I.V. Laundry at Cerisy. Patients remaining in D.R.S. today 17. Patients remaining in F.A. today 3. Fine. Hot. R.C.M.	
ALLONVILLE	27/3/16	10pm	Received A.D.M.S. today March Table April 30th – 97th F.A. from ALLONVILLE to Sailly-Laurette	

WAR DIARY
or
INTELLIGENCE SUMMARY

Army Form C. 2118

Place	Date	Hour	Summary of Events and Information	Remarks and references to Appendices
ALLONVILLE	27/9/16	10 pm	Patients remaining in D.R.S. today 13 Patients remaining in F.A. today 2 Fine. A.D.S.M.S. Lieut PARKER.W. displaced Div Lorry 19 gone.	
ALLONVILLE	28/9/16	10 pm	Patients remaining in D.R.S. today 12. Patients remaining in F.A. today 2. Fine & cold. A.D.M.S.	
ALLONVILLE	29/9/16	10 pm	Received today following [?] to B — shifted 97th F.A. to SAILLY LAURETTE — 97th F.A. will remain closed while at SAILLY LAURETTE — PATIENTS remaining in D.R.S. today 4 Patients remaining in F.A. today nil Fine —	
SAILLY LAURETTE	30/9/16	10 am	Marched here via CORBIE. Start 9 A.M. arrive 2.30 pm 17 miles. No news yet on march. Lieut TOOHER G.W. reports for duty —	

Army Form C. 2118

WAR DIARY
or
INTELLIGENCE SUMMARY
(Erase heading not required.)

Instructions regarding War Diaries and Intelligence Summaries are contained in F. S. Regs., Part II. and the Staff Manual respectively. Title Pages will be prepared in manuscript.

Place	Date	Hour	Summary of Events and Information	Remarks and references to Appendices

Patients remaining in DRS today 3 transferred to 96th FA.
Patients remaining in F.A. nil.
Patients admitted to DRS during April
Officers 3 — Evacuated to CCS. 2
OtherRanks 138 — evacuated to CCS 8
Patients admitted to F.A. during April
Officers 6 evacuated to CCS 3
OtherRanks 134 evacuated to CCS 19 this includes 6 men suffering from German measles.
Prevailing disease during month Influenza.

Fini G.L.H.

30th FD.

No. 97 F. Amb.

May 1915.

COMMITTEE FOR THE
MEDICAL HISTORY OF THE WAR
Date 26 JUN 1915

94(CD) Jackson
SC 7

WAR DIARY
or
INTELLIGENCE SUMMARY.
(Erase heading not required.)

Army Form C. 2118.

Place	Date	Hour	Summary of Events and Information	Remarks and references to Appendices
SAILLY-	1/6/16	10 PM	Our position as before approx —	
LAURETTE			Lieut TOCHER J.P. R.A.M.C. Efficiency again from leave duty yesterday under orders ADMS. Lieut TOCHER & Lieut WILLIAM & 16 Field Amb proceed + INNOCENT to BRONFAY FERME to return to A.D.S. 9th F.A. at BRAY — FINE GREF	
DITTO	2/6/16	10 pm	Lieut Lieut R. Henderson G.Z.R.	
DITTO	3/6/16	10 pm	Undressed ADMS Lieut Capt SOMMERVILLE & Lieut HEATHCOTE and 47 personnel to help 91st F.A. in their ADS at BRAY. Lieut N. MACFARLANE & Sergt Inge in YEATMAN proceed on leave today — FINE GREF	
DITTO	4/5/16	10 pm	VISIT ADS BRAY today. Fine Gref	
DITTO	5/6/16	9 pm	No remarks. Dull very hot. Gref	
DITTO	6/6/16	10 pm	Under order ADMS to hire small field & from a Certain J.F.A. in tents to treat ophthalmia cases D Two Division D. from Major to arrange keep of new field about 1/16 to D unable —	

Army Form C. 2118.

WAR DIARY
or
INTELLIGENCE SUMMARY.

(Erase heading not required.)

Instructions regarding War Diaries and Intelligence Summaries are contained in F. S. Regs., Part II. and the Staff Manual respectively. Title pages will be prepared in manuscript.

Place	Date	Hour	Summary of Events and Information	Remarks and references to Appendices
SAILLY LAURETTE	6/5/16	10am	Busy arranging discovery of sectors on Field. Fine still weather. Died - Lt-Col Andrews Glos.	
DITTO	7/5/16	10am		
DITTO	8/5/16		LIEUT J.E. THOMSON RAMC made orders A.D.M.S. yesterday for course of instruction at PONT NOYELLES in Gas appliances. G.E.M.	
SAILLY LAURETTE	9/5/16	10pm	LIEUT BATEMAN RAMC. Leaves read today led contract heavy suffering - Capt. FIELD Ambulance to take in cases of Sunburn in tents on the arrival of sound - take over Sheerfield Downs from 96th F.A. Cases of Sunburn occurring in F.A. today 8. 070 - Hga kings Glos.	
"	9/5/16	10pm	Cases occurring in F.A. today Sunburn 14. 6 crushed toes. 070 - Shriveled Glos.	
"	10/5/16	10pm	LIEUT J.E. THOMSON made reports from current Gas School. 17 cases of Sunburn receiving in Field Ambulance today - 7 w.o - 6To wnds G.E.M.	

Army Form C. 2118.

WAR DIARY
or
INTELLIGENCE SUMMARY.
(Erase heading not required.)

Instructions regarding War Diaries and Intelligence Summaries are contained in F.S. Regs., Part II. and the Staff Manual respectively. Title pages will be prepared in manuscript.

Place	Date	Hour	Summary of Events and Information	Remarks and references to Appendices
SAILLY-LAURETTE	11/5/16	10 pm	1 N.C.O. & 14 men report for duty from DIV. LAUNDRY where they have been doing duty since FEBRUARY. Lot of patients remaining in FIELD AMBULANCE today 19 — Fine — warmer — G.E.B.	
"	12/5/16	10 am	Nr.1) Patients remaining n.A.L today 27 — Accompanied A.D.M.S. to Brigdy FERME & from Divine Road trenches to Road outside MARICOURT & back & Brigdy F&2.R.M.C. Fine all Day. G.E.B.	
"	13/5/16	10 pm	Nr.1) Patients remaining in F.A. today 27 — Sent Sergt REID & 8 Stretcher bearers to report to Capt Sunderland Brig? & proceed to Brigdy FERME to relieve Corps Bearers & 8 Stretcher bearers on relief Corps Parties & Stretcher bearers to return to Sailly Laurette. Under orders A.D.M.S. send 2 non. Corp M.A.C.L.S. & Corp Butterworth & 6 men for duty at Divine Rain. Sailly Laurette Barge — Corps Wms. G.E.B.	

T2134. Wt. W708—776. 50000. 4/15. Sir J.C. & S.

WAR DIARY or INTELLIGENCE SUMMARY

Army Form C. 2118.

Place	Date	Hour	Summary of Events and Information	Remarks and references to Appendices
Sailly-Laurette	14/5/16	10am	Under orders of Divs. Sand 1 NCO & 49 men (for Res) prepared – Orders from A Div. to take Dret Field Ambulance A. Dressing Station at Bray from 9th F.A. – visit A.D.S. at Bray – Fine. Gen	
Loyelyn Bayonvillers ?	15/5/16	10pm	Today bethe over men Dressing Station at Sailly & Vauvillers & ADS from 9th to F.A. also attending posts at Bonfay F.A. Run & Sup ones – also posts at MAR COURT – visited A.D.S. Bray – & Bronfay F.A. Run. – Cas. F.C. A; I New reports from public the day. To Dr over from 9th F.A. 15th A. Today 13th & Receiving sick in F.A. today 17 & Receiving wounded in F.A. today 8. Fine. Geoff	

Army Form C. 2118.

WAR DIARY
or
INTELLIGENCE SUMMARY.
(Erase heading not required.)

Instructions regarding War Diaries and Intelligence Summaries are contained in F. S. Regs., Part II. and the Staff Manual respectively. Title pages will be prepared in manuscript.

Place	Date	Hour	Summary of Events and Information	Remarks and references to Appendices
SAILLY LABRETTE	10/5/16	18hr	Relieved Lieut TOOHER at Bercifay F.A. went with 4/o Lieut N. MACFARLANE — reached A.D.S & Bercifay to day — Remaining in F.A. today sick 15. 0 (Remaining in F.A. today wounded) 1. 0 Fine	
"	11/5/16	10pm.	Attacked & referred ADMS. Office today at JENWAM - LIEUT HALL R.A.M.C. Report for duty to day — Remaining in F.A today sick 13 # (Remaining in F.A today wounded) 1 # — Fine	S.E.H.

WAR DIARY
or
INTELLIGENCE SUMMARY.
(Erase heading not required.)

Army Form C. 2118.

Place	Date	Hour	Summary of Events and Information	Remarks and references to Appendices
SAILLY LAURETTE	18/5/16	10pm	Visit BROMFAY FARM try shells burning M 3 Endwalked — LIEUT. MACFARLANE slight. Went to Bray by M.D.S. — LIEUT Thompson & E. BASNYC leaves for short tour. Staff Sergt Kerr leaves leave for short leave. Running sick in FIELD Ambulance today /29 Serving wounded in field Ambulance /2. Fine.	[signature]
"	19/5/16	10pm	Visit Bray A.D. Shannon this afternoon believe leave party at MARICOURT at Suzanne & Bray & the personnel of the Gp of F.A. & send up to believe them; two NCOs & 35 men — Running sick in F.A. today 133 Runners wounded in F.A. today 9 — Fine	[signature]

Army Form C. 2118.

WAR DIARY
or
INTELLIGENCE SUMMARY.
(Erase heading not required.)

Instructions regarding War Diaries and Intelligence Summaries are contained in F. S. Regs., Part II. and the Staff Manual respectively. Title pages will be prepared in manuscript.

Place	Date	Hour	Summary of Events and Information	Remarks and references to Appendices
SAILLY LAURETTE	20/6	10pm	Lieut Porter J. R.A.M.C. attached at A.D.M.S. office at 9 a.m. with Asst Divn R.A.M.C. Major Hayes evacuated sick to 31st C.C.S., A.D.M.S. visited F.A. 16. Day Sick returned to F.A. 113: Wounded 9. Weather fine.	
"	21/6	10pm	Capt. Shaw P.D. R.A.M.C. reports for duty from 96th F.A. to take over temporary command of H.Q. of F.A. Capt. Herron W. G. R.A.M.C. reports for duty. Sick returned to F.A. 125: wounded 10, Horse ambulance destroyed by shell fire at Bray. Driver wounded severely neck, at duty. Weather fine	
"	22/6	10pm	Nothing to relate. Weather variable. Sick returned to F.A. 114: wounded 12.	
"	23/6	10pm	Lieut Hall J R R.A.M.C. reports for duty at A.D.S. Lieut Foster J W. reports for duty at H.Q. from A.D.S. Capt Sommerville J.S. attached to temporary command of F.A. by A.D.M.S. 3rd Divn. Sick returned to F.A. 16A: wounded 4. Weather fine	

Army Form C. 2118.

WAR DIARY
or
INTELLIGENCE SUMMARY.
(Erase heading not required.)

Instructions regarding War Diaries and Intelligence Summaries are contained in F. S. Regs., Part II. and the Staff Manual respectively. Title pages will be prepared in manuscript.

Place	Date	Hour	Summary of Events and Information	Remarks and references to Appendices
SAILLY LAURETTE	24/6/16	10 p.m.	Cpl. Crowe E.J. M.T. A.S.C. att'd. Qr. to-day for Base with motor cycle. Sick remained in F.A. 16H. : wounded 7. weather fine.	
"	25/6/16	11.15 a.m.	A.D.M.S. visited F.A. this morning. Allowed conference at A.D.M.S. Office at 3 p.m. Lieut. Parker W. R.A.M.C. started for duty from 50th Div Batts. first Reg. was E.B., Q.M. started for duty from ack leave — 3 months. Under new rota transmit Sergt. Gee W. A.S.C. 4T. left for Base Depot for duty. Horse Ambulance arrived & repres was destroyed by shell-fire on 21/5/16. Sick remained 151: wounded 6. weather fine.	
"	26/6/16	10 p.m.	Lieut. Porter J. R.A.M.C. left to-day for duty of A.D.S. Lieut. McFarlane K. R.A.M.C. started for duty from A.D.S. Pte Morgan J., Edwards W. c. out sick 17., sent to H.Q. S.P. H.A. Group. Sick remained in F.A. 121: wounded 7. Weather showery.	

Army Form C. 2118.

WAR DIARY
or
INTELLIGENCE SUMMARY.
(Erase heading not required.)

Place	Date	Hour	Summary of Events and Information	Remarks and references to Appendices
SAILLY LAURETTE	27/10	10 p.m.	Nothing to relate. Sick removed to F.A. 100; wounded 7. Weather fine.	
"	28/10	10 p.m.	Nothing to relate. Sick removed to F.A. 96; wounded 13. Weather variable.	
"	29/10	10 p.m.	Nothing to relate. Sick removed to F.A. 98; wounded 12. Some rain.	
"	30/10	10 p.m.	Visit by A.D.M.S. Sick removed to F.A. 95; wounded 14. Fine. Wire from Lieut. Thompson J.E. Detained at Southampton Rest Camp for 16 days.	
"	31/10	10 p.m.	Nothing 16 relate. Sick removed to F.A. 91; wounded 8. Weather fine.	

140/9.9

30th Div—

9th Field Ambulance

June 1916

COMMITTEE FOR THE
MEDICAL HISTORY OF THE WAR
Date 17 MAY 1917

Army Form C. 2118.

WAR DIARY
or
INTELLIGENCE SUMMARY.
(Erase heading not required.)

of OC 97 (c) Fd Amb Force

Sheet 1 June 1916

Instructions regarding War Diaries and Intelligence Summaries are contained in F. S. Regs., Part II. and the Staff Manual respectively. Title pages will be prepared in manuscript.

Place	Date	Hour	Summary of Events and Information	Remarks and references to Appendices
SAILLY				
LAORETTE	1/6/16	10 a.m.	FA visited by O.C. 39th Division. Sick evacuated F.A. 101 wounded 10. Weather fine.	
"	2/6/16	10 a.m.	Attack on Vimy in evening. Sick remained in FA. Very little remained in FA. 111 wounded 11. Weather showery	
"	3/6/16	10 a.m.	Nothing to relate. Sick remained in FA 118, wounded 12. Weather fine but rather cold.	
"	4/6/16	10 p.m.	Nothing to relate. Sick remained on FA 82, wounded on FA 14. Weather fine	
"	5/6/16	10 a.m.	Instructions from 33rd Division that Major G.S.C. HAYES R.A.M.C. knowing men evacuated to the Rear should be struck off strength of FA from 2.3.16. Sick remained in FA 82, wounded 12. Weather rather cold. Showery	
"	6/6/16	10 a.m.	33rd Division visited FA to day. Sick remained in FA 89 wounded 11. Weather cold, showery	
"	7/6		Major B.B. BURNE D.S.O. R.A.M.C. reported his arrival assumed command of 97th Fd Amb. Evacuating to FA Sick 86 wounded 9	
"	8/6		Major G.S.C. HAYES R.A.M.C. evacuated Sick on 5/6. Evacuating to FA Amb 85 wounded 9. Nothing of note to report	
"	9/6		Sick remaining at FA Amb. Renewing on F. Amb Sick 28 wounded 7. 13th & 30th Divisions visited FA Amb.	

Army Form C. 2118.

WAR DIARY
or
INTELLIGENCE SUMMARY.
(Erase heading not required.)

a. 9r. 7p. Ambce

Sheet 2 June 1916

Place	Date	Hour	Summary of Events and Information	Remarks and references to Appendices
SAILLY LAURETTE	10th		Remaining in Wood Sick 50 wounded 9	
"	11th		Remaining in Wood. Sick 29, wounded 16. Weather cold, showery	
"	12.		Issued 30 stretchers to Field. Corps L.D. SHAW RAMC Posted to Mobile Section at H. Ander. M.E. THOMPSON RAMC transferred from 97 Fd Amb to 98 Fd Amb	
			Remaining in Wood Sick 12 wounded.	
"	13th		Noted all "dug outs" & trenches which are being constructed for the coming offensive. Wounded a	
			officer & collecting data in view of an expected offensive.	
			Conference at R.A.M.C office re H. Dr. Remaining Wood Sick 17 Wounded.	
"	14th		Verbal orders received from 2nd that to close H. Amb at SAILLY LAURETTE on 15th to Evacuate all sick that will not be well in three days to go H. Amb. & also all wounded. Remainder to be evacuated. Instructions regarding medical arrangements for coming offensive received & preliminary arrangements to open	
			Remaining Sick 23, wounded 26.	
"	15		Closed Fd. Amb at SAILLY LAURETTE. Remaining Sick 14 Wounded 5	
BRAY	16		A Sec 97 Fd Amb moved to A.D.S. BRAY. All equipment required for	

WAR DIARY
or
INTELLIGENCE SUMMARY

Army Form C. 2118.

L.o.C. 97th Fd. Amb. (?)

Sheet 3 JUNE 1916

Place	Date	Hour	Summary of Events and Information	Remarks and references to Appendices
BRAY	16th		(cont'd) 1st Aug Bde forming Adv Dressing Stn at BILLON Fm & Bug bts 259 Collecting Posts in Bug outs at THALUS Pt. h.9.5 WEST PERONNE A.30 & 9.8 MARICOURT A.21.h.4.8 CAMBRIDGE COPSE A.15 b.2.8 was allocated & taken.	ALBERT Cambridge Sheet 57cSW
"	17th		Visited A.D.S. & collecting posts. Work not nearly completed. Handed over from 1 Fd. Amb. & Bde. to open A.D.S. BILLON Fm. at 12 noon 17th LT. J.E. THOMPSON reported event A.D.S. BRAY to 98 Fd. Amb. at 12 noon 17th "C" Section closed A.D.S. BRAY & handed over to 98 Fd. Amb. at 12 Noon. "A" Section proceeded to BILLON Bug outs & opened A.D.S. at 12 noon. "B" Section 2nd Lieut. Jon proceeded to MARICOURT Bug outs. Visited all Collecting Posts with Estimates accommodation which had to be completed so as at each Collecting Post 150 at 258.	
"	18th		Instructions received re proceeding stretchers took on Collecting Posts much delayed owing to fall of earth. Thats low & Sn. taveth repaired. Notification rec'd of movement of Division received. Mil. police working parties of 30 to come under my Command.	
"	19th		Moved my D. Qrs. to A.D.S. BILLON trigbrls Inspected all Collecting Posts Incomes at THALUS & IN PERONNE Alow.	

T2131. Wt. W708–770. 500,000. 4/15. Sh. J.C. & S.

Army Form C. 2118.

WAR DIARY
or
INTELLIGENCE SUMMARY.

of O.C 97 (Co) 7th R.W.F

(Erase heading not required.)

Rec'd 4 June 1916

Instructions regarding War Diaries and Intelligence Summaries are contained in F. S. Regs., Part II. and the Staff Manual respectively. Title pages will be prepared in manuscript.

Place	Date	Hour	Summary of Events and Information	Remarks and references to Appendices
Bois Français & Billon Copse	20		Inspected all Collecting Posts. TALUS + PERONNE not completed yet. Refreshment of officers has been a great boon. Reconnaissance of trenches + Battery positions made Bof to TALUS + CAMBRIDGE + to PERONNE Collecting Posts which are being provided with 100 gall tanks at Aerial Office + apparatus for water to be laid from mains on to TALUS + CAMBRIDGE + PERONNE Collecting Posts. Arrangements inspected by 2nd Army 2nd and XIII Corps. Interior Ecch House — Reservoirs + Pumps + Latrines have been dug at each Post by my personnel. Cart Shed protection approved for + will be completed shortly.	
"	21		Work progressing at Collecting Post + RAP. The latter place as well as Collecting Post at MARICOURT + CAMBRIDGE COPSE being opened + receiving wounded	
"	22	10 am	Enemy hit 6 shells 100 yards N of POS. Billon. Inspected trenches in front of CAMBRIDGE C.P. as to best method of getting wounded back. Better arrangements for Scarlet Posts appear to have been made by units at present holding the line. Issued to 2nd Div orders all Posts + R3H	
		5.30	R.A.P. Billon again shelled but nothing fell nearer than 50 yards, no damage done.	

WAR DIARY or INTELLIGENCE SUMMARY

Army Form C. 2118.

of OC 97 (?) Fd Amb.
Dec 15 June 1916.

Place	Date	Hour	Summary of Events and Information	Remarks and references to Appendices
Bois des S. Billon Dug Out	23"	1 P.M	R.A.M.C. Operation Order received. "T" Stays to day. A.D.S. shelled this morning — again from 3 P.M to 5 P.M this afternoon — working parties got under cover — no casualties occurred. Was a conference with O.C B.C B'ers & collected plan of operations & general scheme of evacuation. Commenced construction of small posts for bearers at N26 a.53 pt 103. The posts will collect from R.A. aid posts by wheeled stretchers & will work Tramway running from about A20.d.27 to A.26.a. Thence through Billon Wood to Bromfay Fm F29.b.17. I have obtained one of the Tramway from A20.d.27 to A.25.a during the day. Have 2 trolley places at A30.d.57. Can use empty returning munition trucks during night to run wounded. Dressing Heavy wounded in at ETINEHEM	
"	24"	6 am	"U" Day. Bombardment commenced. Wheeled Trans Bois Collecting Post & Billon W.OO.Po. of 21st Inf. Brigade. Sunset Shelham Café Post" reported at ADS which	
"	25"	"	"V" Day. Heavy bombardment during night. Casualties few mostly from premature bursts. Bombardment continues. NODAL Post at A21 a.53 shows severe stretcher cases brought in by Tramway lights etc.	

WAR DIARY
or INTELLIGENCE SUMMARY

Army Form C. 2118.

of O.C. 97th (E) Field Ambulance

Sheet 6. June 1916

Place	Date	Hour	Summary of Events and Information	Remarks and references to Appendices
A.25.	25th	(continued)	MARICOURT to PERONNE 2.P.S. Reports at 2 P.M. R.O. + M.O. established. All medical arrangements taken to early information to be transmitted to one receiving Casualties.	
"	26.		"W" day. Bombardment has commenced day & night. Sent 30 k. Wounded at Collecting Posts at "North" we "Noon" B.C. working well at Z.IR.11.d.4. R.D.M.C. put X of the post to day.	
		5 P.M.	Several enemy shrapnel burst over A.D.S. 21 bde 13 bde have put up flag on road close to A.D.S. that may account to shrapnel. Aske to the flag to be placed on a lower level. Weather cold & showery.	
"	27.	6 a.m.	"X" day one dugout at A.D.S hit by whiz-bang during night. No damage done. Stewards of 99 Casualties thro' A.D.S. since 9am. All arrangements working smoothly. Wired to send one receiver Bearer Sub to report here at 7.30 P.M. to reinforce XIII Corps Commander A.D.M.S. wishes A.D.S. also (A.D.M.S.) 30 Division. Heavy bombardment continues. Shrapnel bursting over A.D.S. No damage. Weather showery & cool.	

WAR DIARY of OC 97(?) Fd Amb(?) Ac United Army Form C. 2118.

or

INTELLIGENCE SUMMARY. Sheet 7 June 1916.

(Erase heading not required.)

Place	Date	Hour	Summary of Events and Information	Remarks and references to Appendices
A.A.J.	28th		"Y" day. Weather cool with heavy rain. Evacuation of wounded from "MODEL Post" Tramway by wheeled stretchers so difficult on account of state of road thro' BILLON WOOD	
		3.30 pm	Bearer sub. of 98 Fd Amb & 2 Officers reported. Directed "A" Section Bearer sub division 98 Fd Amb to proceed to CAMBRIDGE COPSE collecting post & "C" Section Bearer sub division 98 Fd Amb to TOTUS BOYSE C.P. releaving "B" Section here in reserve	
		4 pm	Wired xx D informing me that operations were postponed for 48 hours & directing me to return Bearer Stl of 98 Fd Amb to GROVE TOWN CAMP (north of MO?) This was acted upon at once. MV Dressing Stn shelled at intervals during the day, no direct hits	
"	29	2 pm	Weather cold & overcast but dry. Visited all collecting posts. "MODEL Post" Tramway occupied by ammunition supplies so all cases were brought by wheeled stretcher from W. PERONNE ROAD Post visited by 4th Army Commander & XIII Corps Commander.	
		5 pm	"MODEL Post shelled & tear shells. MO & Lt HALL R.A.M.C. suffered from effects of	

Army Form C. 2118.

WAR DIARY
or
INTELLIGENCE SUMMARY.

OC 27/(a) Field Ambulance Australian

(Erase heading not required.)

Sheet 6 June 1916

Place	Date	Hour	Summary of Events and Information	Remarks and references to Appendices
A.D.S.	29.	5pm	(continued) of gas & shock. Brought him back to A.D.S. for a rest.	
"		9pm	Usual shelling of road by A.D.S. No damage to dug outs or personnel.	
"	30		Lt. HALL R.A.M.C. evacuated to M.D.S. Owing to suffering from effects of inhalatory gas attack. Took over all collecting posts & A.D.S. below.	
		4pm	Bearer division 98th Amb reported. Disposed of as follows.	
			"D" Bearer sub-division to CAMBRIDGE Collecting Post	
			"C" Bearer sub-division to TALUS Collecting Post "B" sub-division A.D.S.	

R.M.G.d.
Commanding 27 (C.P.) Field Ambulance

W109/3

5.

To ADMS
 30 Division

Ref. preceding minutes

The War Diary of this Field Ambulance for June 1916 was despatched to the DAG 3rd Echelon Base early in July of that year. The duplicate copy has also been sent to Officer i/c of RAMC Records, Base.

27/3/17   A.B. Forbes
                              Capt. RAMC
                              OC 97 (S) F. Amb.

6.

DDMS VII Corps.

Please see minute 5.

                              W.H. Alderton Capt
28-3-17   Ju ADMS 30th Divs.

11

To A.D.M.S
30 Division.

Herewith copy of war diary of this Unit for JUNE 1916, for transmission to D.A.G. Base.

6/5/1917.

SDShaw Lt Col. RAMC.
OC. 97th (c1) Fld Ambulance

12

D.A.G.
3rd Echelon G.H.Q

Herewith duplicate of War Diary of 97 Field Ambulance for the month of June 1916. as per Minute 8.

May. 7/17

R Alexander
Capt. Col.
for A.D.M.S 30th Division.

> DIRECTOR
> MEDICAL SERVICES,
> THIRD ARMY.
>
> No. 1730/23

7.

The D.M.S.,
Third Army.

    Forwarded.

                                  Captain, R.A.M.C.
29/3/17.   for D.D.M.S., VII Corps.

-8-

The D.D.M.S.,
   VII Corps.

    As the diary has apparently been lost in transit the duplicate copy should be obtained from Officer i/c Records and another copy made out for despatch to War Office through D.A.G., 3rd Echelon.

                                    Surgeon General,
Headquarters,   D.M.S.
Third Army,
30.3.1917.

9.

The A.D.M.S.,
30th Division.

    For your information and action.

    Please report when the diary has been despatched to the D.A.G.

                                    Captain, R.A.M.C.
1/4/17.   For D.D.M.S., VII Corps.

10.

O.C. 97 Field Ambulance.

    Forwarded for necessary action & report.

                              Capt.
2-4-17   For A.D.M.S. 30th Div.

DG 250/4.

D.M.S.,

    Third Army.

    The attached list of outstanding War Diaries from Medical Units serving under your administration, is forwarded for your information.

    The War Office is pressing for these Diaries - will you please hasten ?

G.H.Q.,   (sd) F.J.Martin Major,
2nd Echelon   for D.G.M.S.
20.3.1917.

-2-

The D.D.M.S.,

    V11   Corps.

    For necessary action.

    Please report when the diaries referred to have been despatched.

Headquarters,   Surgeon General,
Third Army,   D.M.S.
21.3.1917.

                     3.

The O.C., 97th Field Ambulance,

u/c A.D.M.S., 30th Division.

                     For your necessary action.

                            Captain, R.A.M.C.
22/3/17.   for D.D.M.S., V11 Corps.

O.C. 97 Field Ambulance.
    For necessary action & report please

                            W.Aldeth Capt
                            for A.D.M.S. 30 Div

30th Division

No. 97 Field Ambulance

July 1916

Army Form C. 2118

WAR DIARY or INTELLIGENCE SUMMARY

(Erase heading not required.)

O.C. 97 (2) Field Ambulance   July 1916   Sheet 1

Instructions regarding War Diaries and Intelligence Summaries are contained in F.S. Regs., Part II. and the Staff Manual respectively. Title Pages will be prepared in manuscript.

Place	Date	Hour	Summary of Events and Information	Remarks and references to Appendices
A.D.S.	1st	4 A.M.	M.O. H.Q. from A.D.M.S. 30th Div. received notifying me to send a Medical Officer RAMC. with 17th Liverpool Regt., who in another capacity, Lt. MacFarlane "B" Section was detailed & proceeded at once to report to 89th Inf. Bde H.Q.	Ref. map ALBERT. Confirmed sheet 1/40000
		5 A.M.	Lt. J.C. Robinson RAMC 98th F.A. Amb. reported for duty & was sent to "B" Section for duty at CAMBRIDGE COPSE Bearer Collecting Post.	
		6 A.M.	Medical situation is as follows for forward area.	
			A.D.S. BILLON FM Dugouts. H.Q. 97 F.A. & "A" Section 97 F.A. two personnel, NODAL POST (F.24.b + 30.a Thistle.8.) "NODAL" POST "B" Bearer Sub Div 98 F.A. two 1 N.C.O. 42 Guards (A.26.a.5.2.) 1 N.C.O. + 2 Bearer Squads 97 F.A. "A" Sec. 1 N.C.O. + the "B" Sec Bearer 98 F.A. 3 labelled thistle corner.	
			Collecting Posts. CAMBRIDGE COPSE → "B" Sec. 97 F.A. A.15.a.6.3 3 M.O.'s & Tnt. Sub. Div. + MARICOURT 9 Bearer Squads A.21.a.10.8. TALUS BOIS → "C" Sec. 97 F.A. A.15.a.2.2 2 M.O.'s Tnt Sub Div + West PERONNE 9 Bearer Squads A.26 & 9.8 → "C" Sec Bearer 98 F.A. (1 M.O. + 8 Squads) → "C" Sec Bearer 98 F.A. (1 M.O. + 8 Squads)	
			Bearer Divisn 98 F.A. Amb. 4 Nursing Section at GROVETOWN. (L.8.)	
		7.30 A.M.	Infantry attack launched.	
		8 A.M.	Walking wounded begin to dribble up to A.D.S. & were passed thro' Rest Post, manned by Lieut SMITH, Sergt. C.F. Solfn, 1 Nursing Orderly + 2 O.R. where thin

WAR DIARY
or
INTELLIGENCE SUMMARY

Army Form C. 2118

97-2nd F.A.

July 1916   Sheet 2

Place	Date	Hour	Summary of Events and Information	Remarks and references to Appendices
A.D.S.	1st		Barrages were reported. Quantity of ammunition & They used a Monday water & a cigarette before being moved further in. Cases made to put any further in which regt re-covery being sent to A.D.	
		11:30AM	Wheat & Morris put in establishment in the open. Stretcher cases began to arrive by Railway & carried to A.D.S. in which carried via NOAH POST.	
		12 Noon	CARNOY post reports passable, many to walking. Motor Ambulances sent to PERONNE Rd. & Cross-roads sw of Wheeled Cross. Motor Ambulances sent to clear MARICOURT C.P. & WEST PERONNE C.P.	
		12-45PM	Wired A.D.M.S. for Rapid Bearer Div. 96 F.A. to move to BILLON FM. Report for CAMBRIDGE COPSE C.P. that all was well.	
		4:30PM	Had frequently to send a guide with Motor Amb. Cars as Drivers did not know collecting posts. "A" Sect Bearer 96 F.H. reported & went out to TALUS BOIS C.P. Large number of walking cases being passed on, & sitting cases & stretcher cases being cleared.	
		5PM	Lt PITTER RAMC reported & was sent to relieve A.O. i/c 2nd Reg Into Force reported wounded.	
			"B" Sect Bearers 96 F.A. reported & were sent to TALUS BOIS, as informed there two were there.	
		9-50PM	That majority of casualties over on left of Line. "C" Sect Bearers 96 F.A. sent to TALUS BOIS. This joins 1½ Reserve Div. on left of line.	
	2nd		& 2 Fd. Div g Bearers on night of line. 2 Fd. Div. & reserves sent to A.D. & NOAH POST. Report for CAMBRIDGE COPSE all well. Have had Wagons out Tow & TALUS C.P. road not for the return that yet. A.D.S. being cleared well.	
		2 AM.	A.D.S. clear for the moment. M.O's returned to bel them a rest in low shifts. Information recd that 12 D'ports had been rec'd members of wounded. SL 472 Returned, A.D.M.S. H457/1	
		7.30AM		

WAR DIARY or INTELLIGENCE SUMMARY

Army Form C. 2118

of 97 L.C.P.F Ambulance

July 16. Sheet 3.

Place	Date	Hour	Summary of Events and Information	Remarks and references to Appendices
A.D.S.	2nd	8.30 AM	"B" Section Bearers 97 F.A. sent to TALUS ROIS to assist in clearing BLATZ Redoubt. Sent by Motor Amb. Which for then successfully. A steady service was now established to TALUS C.P.	
		10.30 AM	A.D.M.S. 30 Div. called & discussed the possibility of establishing a more forward C.P. MARICOURT – MONTAUBAN road not passable for ambulances of any sort yet. Had there been a strong counter-attack on MONTAUBAN during the night that there were a considerable number of casualties.	
		11.30 AM	Request for TALUS C.P. for more stretchers & dressings. Sent 25 stretchers & ample supply of dressings by Motor Amb. Closed up NODAL Post & detached Bearers. Ordered D.T. "B" section to unit & Lt. ROBINSON R.A.M.C to assist at TALUS C.P.	
		1 P.M	Request rec'd for TALUS for extra Motor Amb. Sent up all available cars at once & arranged with D.T. Transport for more.	
		3 P.M	A.D.S. comparatively clear. What proved to TALUS ROIS C.P. Found some confusion as wounded were being brought in faster than they could be evacuated. This C.P. has become the A.D.S. to all intents & purposes. Closed up WEST PERDONN C.P. & ordered personnel (abs. 1 N.CO & 4 OR) to TALUS ROIS. D.T. 'C' section to evolve evacuation. Arranged for 10 Motor Amb cars to him & be sent up.	
		3.45 P.M	Proceeded with Lt. KELLY 96 F.A. to mountain most content— & of officers as regards the possibility of establishing a more forward post for collecting wounded. On returning from here just behind MONTAUBAN, heavy shelling began & Lt. KELLY R.A.M.C was killed by my side in SILESIA SUPPORT Trench. Left his body i/c of Machine Gun by of N.C.I. Strong Point. So returned.	

Army Form C. 2118

WAR DIARY
or
INTELLIGENCE SUMMARY of No. 47 (C.P.) F.A.

Visit H. July 16

Place	Date	Hour	Summary of Events and Information	Remarks and references to Appendices
A.D.S.	2nd		to TALUS BUIS C.P. Sent party up to bring in empty. Also despatched Reams & Mt into Trucks to R.A.P's in MONTAUBAN. Saw the party up & Lt O'DONNELL & 98 F.A. coming into heavy shell fire but Lt O'DONNELL took 2 squads forward with great courage & succeeded in getting into MONTAUBAN. We are now in touch with all R.A's and P.O.B.	
		6-30 PM	Returned to A.D.S. & reported to A.D.M.S. re O'KELLY's death & progress of clearing field. Front is practically clear except for good cases & MONTAUBAN.	
		7-30 PM	O.A.D.M.S. 30 Div visited A.D.S.	
		8 P.M	TALUS BUIS C.P. reported clear of wounded. Nothing further of note received during my stay.	
	3rd	7 A.M.	South African F.A. Reams 98 Div moved up during the night to near & C.A. Sq. P.S. to left of line. I ordered 98 F.A. Reams Div truck to W. PERONNE Dry Dock for rest, also 98 F.A. Blonde Div (Also A. Dublin.)	
		10 A.M	Visited all collecting Posts, everything quiet & proceeding smoothly. A battery of 60 lb. guns has been established close to TALUS Bq.Dr.E. & there is some difficulty in getting Amb. Cars to the C.P. Battery has to cease fire to allow them to pass. A forward dump for wounded has been established by "B" Lot 97 F.A. on MARICOURT - MONTAUBAN Rd. A.D. BILLON Fm two practically ceased to exist as an A.D.S. except for dead & walking wounded.	
	4th	10 A.M.	Visited all C.P's & arranged for material etc. to convert 2 large shell-holes near "B" Lot 97 F.A. dump on MARICOURT - MONTAUBAN Rd. into dug-out shelter for wounded. Orders Res. Col. Bri. 98 F.A. to carry out this work.	
"		3 P.M.	Very heavy thunderstorm & rain. Dry dock at BILLON Fm flooded out.	

WAR DIARY or INTELLIGENCE SUMMARY

Army Form C. 2118

B Pt 4y (C.P) F.A.

July/16. Sheet 5

Place	Date	Hour	Summary of Events and Information	Remarks and references to Appendices
A.D.S.	4th		Arranged for service of FORD Amb. Cars between MARICOURT CP & Dumps in MARICOURT–MONTAUBAN Rd. Road to TALUS CP impossible for Motor Amb. after rain. Sent up Horse Amb. Wagons.	
		5 P.M.	Heard that 9th Div F.A. would take over A.D.S. & CPs at 10 A.M. St Wast "B" & "C" sections 97 F.A. to be ready to hand over.	
	5th	1 A.M.	A.D.M.S. M Sec/7 9th D/M rect. Orders to hand over A.D.S. & CPs to 28 F.A. 9th Div by 10 A.M. + subsequently move to DIVE COPSE. Orders received to GC "B" & "C" sections 97 F.A. to rendezvous at BILLON FM A.D.S. at 9 A.M., subject to rendezvous being rect for them inspection D.C.S. Bearer Div of 97 F.A. to proceed to BOIS de TAILLES. Bearer Div of 97 F.A. to 9.9 by RB	RB
		3 P.M.	Test Div 97 F.A. left BILLON FM for BOIS de TAILLES.	
		3.30 P.M.	Capt SOMERVILLE R.A.M.C. moved up for BILLON FM for DIVE COPSE	
		6 P.M.	" " " arrived at DIVE COPSE	
	6th	2.45 P.M.	Dispatched two Motor Amb. Cars, 3 Dis, 3 dispatched 2 Missis, 2 NCOs & 15 O.R. J Test Div to 45 C.C.S. VECQUEMONT for duty.	RB
	7th		Nothing to note except that 2/Lt A.H.B. PEARCE & 2/Lt JC McMILLAN R.A.M.C. reported for duty.	
	8th	10.30 A.M.	Proceeded c A.D.M.S. 30 Div to survey possible sites for A.D.S. for 30 Div phase of battle.	RB
		4 P.M.	Arranged for surplus equipment to be picked up & sent to Group CORBIE	
		10 P.M.	Orders rect for Unit (less Bearer Div) to proceed to BILLON FM to rendezvous somewhere from here.	

Army Form C. 2118

WAR DIARY
or
INTELLIGENCE SUMMARY

3 DC 97 (C.P.) F.A. Amb.

(Erase heading not required.)

July 1916

Place	Date	Hour	Summary of Events and Information	Remarks and references to Appendices
DIVE CORPS BILLON F.m	9th	10.30AM	That Div & HQ 6th 91 FA left for BILLON F.m	
BILLON F.m		2 PM	That Div & HQ 6th 97 FA arrived at BILLON F.m & pitched tent.	
		4 PM	I proceeded to MARICOURT to localise likely places for forming A.D.S. forgot.	
		7 PM	Detailed Lt TOCHER 1 NCO & 3 OR to proceed to MARICOURT from small carrying Par to keep in touch with Bearer Div 96 FA working along MARICOURT–MONTAUBAN Rd.	
		10 PM	Visited 97 FA Bearer Div installed at CEYLON WOOD. Div that evening off to MARICOURT & also B 99 & 97 RB 2L McMILLAN could not remember work. ADMS informed.	
BILLON F.m	10th		Little going on until a few yds beyond for the tire about mid-day.	
			Made reconnaissance of MARICOURT–BRIQUETERIE Rd to see if Bank could be cut & worked about it. Found road & general condition of the hung shelled.	
		3 PM	Bearer Div 97 FA & MARICOURT moves up & took behind P.Q. & 97 DS & night & relieve Bearer Div 96 FA at 9 PM at 90 & 97 RB	
		6 PM	Under instruction from ADMS 3rd Div I detached Capt SHAW RAMC "B" sect to form ADS & Regt aid Post Party not & MARICOURT to night, ammunition Lt Lyon & men Lt TOCHER proceed to Bearer Div via 2S McMILLAN conveyance visit	
		7 PM	Capt REES RAMC to reported for duty. Heavy bombardment N.J. ALBERT visible	
	11th	5.30 AM	ADS. open at Hy 2E MARICOURT. Bearer Div moved up & established tents on the MARICOURT–BRIQUETERIE Rd into the S.E. BRIQUETERIE. 89 Inf Bd's been established.	
			TRONES WOOD.	
		10.30AM	Visited ADS & dumps to MARICOURT and of BRIQUETERIE Rd, Bosrapt reserve & comf. Cars between dumps & ADS. Rail transport to Rlwn Div 97 FA that is now in touch with	

WAR DIARY
or
INTELLIGENCE SUMMARY

(Erase heading not required.)

Army Form C. 2118

6C 97(C.P) F¹ Amb.

July 1916 Sheet 1.

Place	Date	Hour	Summary of Events and Information	Remarks and references to Appendices
BILLON FME	11ᵗʰ	11 P.M.	Evacuation has proceeded satisfactorily all day. A.D.M.S. 30 Div visited Bearer Div post at BRIQUETERIE Trnch.	AL
"	12ᵗʰ	2 p.m.	Visited BRIQUETERIE Trnch & Bearer Div. All arrangements working well. A Battery of Field Artillery in MARICOURT-BRIQUETERIE prevents Ford Cars being run to Bearer Dump near BRIQUETERIE. So it goes shortly across the road. Dr Bearer Div reports that No 67391 Pte URMSON.W & No 67238 Pte TANNER J.H are missing & believed to been killed in TRONES WOOD. Reported to A.D.M.J.	AL
		9 P.M	Orders recd from A.D.M.J. 30 Div that 5ᵗʰ F.A. Ambt would take over A.D.S. Hosp. in MARICOURT at 10 A.M. That Div 97 FA to return to Div'e Corps. that 30ᵗʰ Div is being relieved by 18ᵗʰ Div	AL
	13ᵗʰ	10.30 A.M	That Div 97FA moved to Div'e Corps & arrived there at 1 P.M.	BB
		2 M/s & 6 Nursing Orderlies detained for duty with 96FA	
	14ᵗʰ	9 A.M.	Visit (from Bearer Div) of Div'e Corps	
		7 P.M	Orders recd from A.D.M.S. 30 Div that That Div was to proceed to CORBIE & billet there on 15ᵗʰ.	
	15ᵗʰ	10.30 A.M	That Div moved to CORBIE	CC
		12.30 P.M	" " arrived at CORBIE. Bearer Div rejoined HQRs Unit in billets.	
CORBIE	16ᵗʰ		Church Parade & Battery Parade.	AL
	17ᵗʰ		Parades, cleaning & checking equipment. Re-organisation of Bearer Div to open commence & march with 89ᵗʰ Inf Bde to which Unit is affiliated.	AL

WAR DIARY or INTELLIGENCE SUMMARY

Army Form C. 2118

O.C. 97 (C.P.) F.A.

July 1916   Sheet 8.

Place	Date	Hour	Summary of Events and Information	Remarks and references to Appendices
CORBIE	18"	9AM	Unit Parades & Training.	
		11AM	Orders rec'd from ADMS 30th Div. for That Div. (less personnel at 45 C.C.S. & with Reserves) to take over Corps Rest Station CORBIE CHATEAU.	AB
"	19"	2PM	Recon. Div. march off with 89th Inf. Bde to Forward Area.	
		7PM	That Div. took over Corps Rest Station CORBIE from 105th F. Amb.	
			That Div. 97th F. Amb. reported for duty at Corps Rest Station & Took over from 105 F.Amb.	AB
"	20"		Re-organization of Corps Rest Station. D.D.M.S. XIII Corps visited Rest St.	AB
"	21"		Routine Duty XIII Corps Rest Station.	AB
"	22"		Period 12 noon 21" to 12 noon 22"	AB
			Admitted Off. OR
			7 - 164
			Evacuated 5 - 63
			To Duty 2 - 81
			Remaining 8 - 250.	
"	23"		Period 12 noon 22" to 12 noon 23"	AB
			Admitted Off. OR
			5 - 79
			Evacuated - - 115
			To Duty - - 127
			Remaining 7 - 227
			Nothing further of note to report.	
"	24"		Period 12 noon 23" to 12 noon 24"	AB
			Admitted Off. OR
			3 - 119
			Evacuated 2 - 57
			To Duty 1 - 43
			Remaining 9 - 269
			Nothing of note to report.	AB

WAR DIARY
or
INTELLIGENCE SUMMARY

(Erase heading not required.)

Army Form C. 2118

b DC 97 (LR) Fd Ambc.

Feb 1916   Sheet 9

Place	Date	Hour	Summary of Events and Information	Remarks and references to Appendices
CORBIE. XIII Corps Rest St.	25th		Admitted O. OR 7 - 111 Evacuated 4 - 46 Revert to 12 non. To Duty - - 28 Remaining 12 - 306	
,,	26th		Routine. Recce Rive with Pg & J 8th & HAPPY VALLEY. Admitted O. OR 9 - 145 Evacuated 6 - 60 To Duty 1 - 18 Remaining 14 - 203	NS

,,	27th		Routine O - OR
			                Admitted
			                Evacuated
			                Duty
			                Remaining
				NS

,,	28th		Routine Admitted O - OR
			                      7 - 144
			          Evacuated 1 - 83
			          Duty - 73
			          Remaining 15 - 280
				NS

,,	29th		Admitted O - OR 6 - 193 Evacuated 8 - 61 Duty 1 - 35 Remaining 12 - 377	NS

WAR DIARY
or
INTELLIGENCE SUMMARY

Army Form C. 2118

OC 97 (SP) FC Amb

July 1916 Sheet 10

(Erase heading not required.)

Place	Date	Hour	Summary of Events and Information	Remarks and references to Appendices
CORBIE	30		Routine. Report recd from 5th Res. Brd. Hut 6 OR Kitchen wounded. Admitted O - 108, 1 - 1455, 2 - 122, 3 - 66, 4 - 334, Remaining 12 - 334	
"	31st		Orders recd to hand over Camp Hut 15 & 73 F.A. 24th Div to morrow (1st) at 12 noon.	

30th Division "A"

Herewith War Diary from 97 Field Ambulance for the month of July 1916.

8/8/16.

M. Alexander
Colonel
ADMS 30th Div

Secret

War Diary
of
97th (C.P.) Field Ambulance.
R.A.M.C
for the month of August. 1916
Volume 10

WAR DIARY
or
INTELLIGENCE SUMMARY

Army Form C. 2118

1 RC 97 (CP) F. Amb.

August 1916 Sheet 1

Place	Date	Hour	Summary of Events and Information	Remarks and references to Appendices
CORBIE	1st	12 noon	Handed over XIIIth Corps Rest Stn. to 73rd Fd. Amb. 24th Divn.	
"		4 P.M.	Transport & Tent Divn. moved off to join Transport of 98th Inf. Bde. at CARDONETTE	
"	2nd	10.15 A.M.	Personnel & Tent Divn. marched off to MERICOURT to entrain for LONGPRÉ	
HUPPY	3rd	1. A.M.	Transport & Tent Divn. + Bearer Divn. arrived HUPPY	
"		4.30 A.M.	Bearer + Tent Divn. arrived HUPPY	
"		12 noon	Orders recd. from 98th Inf. Bde. for Unit to entrain at PONT REMY for MERVILLE at 2.58. P.M. (4th)	
"	4th	9 A.M.	Unit marched out of HUPPY for PONT REMY & entrained.	
"		10.14 P.M.	Unit detrained at MERVILLE & marched to CALONNE SUR LA LYS.	
CALONNE SUR LA LYS.	5th		In Billets. A.D.M.S. 30 Divn. visited HQrs.	
"	6th		Routine.	
"	7th		Attended Conference at A.D.M.S. Office & then proceeded to HQrs 134th Fd. Amb. ANNEZIN. with refr. to taking over from that unit. R.A.M.C. g/s Order No. 141. rec'd.	F.S. Central BETHUNE
"	8th		Capt L.O. SHAW + Personnel for adv. Dressg. Stn. MARAIS marched to that place. Took over A.D.S. of 134th Fd. Amb.	1/40000
"	9th		"C" Section moved to ANNEZIN. Capt R L CRABB reported for duty	
ANNEZIN	10th		HQrs & "A" Section moved to ANNEZIN. Took over [illeg.] MAIN Dressg. Stn. B	1/40000
"	11th	9 A.M.	134th Fd. Amb. [illeg.] Sect. Personnel Field Amb. Offr. 1 OR 67. Wounded OR 4.	

WAR DIARY or INTELLIGENCE SUMMARY

Army Form C. 2118

8 OT 91 (CP) Fd Amb.

August 1916

Place	Date	Hour	Summary of Events and Information	Remarks and references to Appendices
ANNEZIN	12th		Visited Rehn Dressing Stn & Relay Post. Remaining i Fd Amb. OR sick 62 wounded 4.	App
"	13th		Remaining i Fd Amb. OR sick 53 Wounded 4. A Dms 3W Div inspected mens dinners. JS	App
"	14th		Remaining i F.A. OR sick 40 Wounded 6. "A" Section examined i Training Course. BO RT Corps inspected C.O. mens dinners P.S.	App
"	15th		Remaining i F.A. OR sick 36 wounded 3.	App
"	16th		Remaining i F.A. OR sick 28 wounded 7.	App
"	17th		Remaining i F.A. Off sick 1. OR sick 16 wounded 5.	App
"	18th		Remaining i F.A. OR sick 17 wounded 5. Acting on ADms for Establishments Rtrns in leave.	App
"	19th		Remaining i F.A. OR sick 21 wounded 2. Off sick 1. "A" Section Training Course completed. Capt Little and 4 Officers & RAMC visited.	App
"	20th		"A" Section returned "C" Section at Motor Ambcy Stn. Remaining i F.A. Off sick 1. OR sick 24. not OR wounded 5.	App
"	21st		"C" Section commenced Training Course. Remaining i Fd Amb. Off wounded 2. OR w: 19 OR sick 21.	App
"	22nd		Remaining i F.A. OR sick 24 wounded 10.	App
"	23rd		Remaining i Fd Amb. Off sick 1. OR sick 32. OR wounded 2. Reinforcements 11 OR joined.	App
"	24th		Remaining i Fd Amb. OR sick 30.	App

WAR DIARY or INTELLIGENCE SUMMARY

Army Form C. 2118

1 Pt 47 (1P) 1st Sprt.

August 1916

Place	Date	Hour	Summary of Events and Information	Remarks and references to Appendices
ANNEZIN	25th		Visited A.D.S. & Trenches. ADRes returned from leave & resumed command vice Lt. GYMA. Remaining in Field. OR sick 29 Wounded 2.	
"	26th		"C" Section employed burying. Capt SOMERVILLE RAMC admitted sick. P.U.O. Remaining in Field. Off sick 1. OR sick 26. Wounded 4.	
"	27th		"C" Section personnel for A.D.S. proceeded to MARAIS (F.S.64212) to relieve "B" Section personnel. Remaining in Field. Off sick 2. OR sick 33 Wounded 2.	
"	28th		Remaining in Field. Off sick 1. OR sick 26. Wounded 2.	
"	29th	9 a.m.	"C" Section relieved "B" Section & took over A.Ds. Remaining in Field. Officers sick 1. OR sick 19.	
		12 noon	"B" Section personnel rejoined H.Q.e.	
"	30th		Remaining in Field. Off sick 1. wounded 1. OR sick 24.	
"	31st		30e. 30CDiv inspected Field Ambulance. Remaining OR sick 25 wounded 3	

RABrown
Lt Col RAMC
OC 47 (IP) Field Amb.

Secret

War Diary
of
97th (C.P.) Field Ambulance
for the month of
September 1916

———"———

Volume XI

COMMITTEE FOR THE
MEDICAL HISTORY OF THE WAR
Date 30 OCT. 1916

WAR DIARY or INTELLIGENCE SUMMARY

Army Form C. 2118

2 ot 97 Fl Amb

September 1916   Sheet 1

Place	Date	Hour	Summary of Events and Information	Remarks and references to Appendices
ANNEZIN	1st		Capt SOMERVILLE sent for Temporary duty at Divl. Bombing School vice Lt PARKER who returns to H.Q. R.E. Remaining at Fl Amb. Officers sick 1 O.R. sick 22.	
"	2nd		Under instructions from ADMS 30th Divn. Lt J.E. THOMPSON RAMC is attached for duty with 18t Kings Liverpool Regt + is struck off the strength of this Unit. Remaining at Fl. Amb. Off sick 2 O.R. sick 18 visited A.B.S.	
"	3rd		Under instructions from ADMS 30th Divn I handed over Girls School to 92nd Fl Amb. 32nd Divn. in Annezin. Boys School for the Unit. Remaining at Fl Amb. Off sick 2 O.R. sick 25.	
"	4th		Remaining at Fl Amb. Off sick 1 O.R. sick 14 Visited A.D.S.	
"	5th		Under instructions from ADMS 30th Divn a party of 2 NCO's + 22 O.R. proceeded to ADS for fatigue work under R.E. Remaining at F.A. Off sick 1 O.R. sick 16. "B" Section completed work Bonney's new magazine.	
"	6th		Under instructions from ADMS 30th Divn a party of 1 NCO + 24 O.R. was detached to report to Lt Colonel Lancs Regt. (Pioneers) for fatigue duty. Remaining at Fl Amb. Off sick 1 O.R. sick 21.	
"	7th		Remaining at Fl Amb. Officers sick 0 O.R. sick 17.	
"	8th		Visited A.D.S. Remaining at Fl Amb. Officers sick 0 O.R. sick 12 wounded 1.	
"	9th		Under orders from ADMS Lt PARKER Returned for Temp duty + 20th King's Liverpool Regt 30th Divn relieved 2. Remaining at Fl Amb. OR sick 9 wounded 2.	

WAR DIARY or INTELLIGENCE SUMMARY

8 or 9? Field Amb. September 1916 Sheet 2

(Erase heading not required.)

Instructions regarding War Diaries and Intelligence Summaries are contained in F.S. Regs., Part II. and the Staff Manual respectively. Title Pages will be prepared in manuscript.

Place	Date	Hour	Summary of Events and Information	Remarks and references to Appendices
ANNEZIN	10th		Capt SOMERVILLE returned from Tempy duty at Div School. Remainder of F/Amb. OR sick 10. wounded 3.	Ref. App.
"	11th		Majr SOMERVILLE A.D.S. Remaining & F/Amb. OR sick 10. wounded 9. Capt WILSON returned from A.D.S. & was relieved for Temp duty & 150 Field R.F.A.	Ref. App. HAZEBROUCK Sheet S.A.
"	12th		Remaining & F/Amb. OR sick 10. Wounded 2. "A" Section personnel relieved "C" Sect personnel at Adv. Dressg. Stn. MARAIS.	R.B.
"	13th		A.D.M.S. 30th Div inspected F/Amb.	R.B.
"	14th		Routine. Remaining & F/Amb. Sick Officers 1. OR 19. wounded. OR 1.	R.B.
"	15th	12:30pm	R.A.M.C. OR. Pte No.15 Field Amb. Sick OR 14 Wounded OR 1.	R.B.
"	16th	5 pm	Adv. party of 9 OR 2nd F/Amb arrived at Erak new School ANNEZIN. Capt AO FORBES reported to A.D. Medical Sces for duty. Remaining & F/Amb.	R.B.
"	17th	6 pm	Unit marched to billets in BUSNES area. Orders recd to entrain at LILLERS at 2/57am	R.B.
BUSNES	18th		Billets at BUSNES. Lt Col HANSON reported for duty & was attached for rations & Capt WARING proceeded to 7 Som Yeo. for duty. Infantry Bgde & Army to contract notice of moveft. Unit left BUSNES at 9-30 pm.	
BEZAINCOURT	19th	2:57 am	Train left LILLERS, entraining was completed in 1½ hrs	Ref. App. HAZEBROUCK Sheet S.A.
		7 am	Arrived DOULLENS & detrained.	
		9 am	Marched to BEZAINCOURT. Billets. A.D.M.S. 30th Div. Visited Unit.	Ref App LEMS II.
"	20th		Billets at BEZAINCOURT.	R.B.

WAR DIARY
or
INTELLIGENCE SUMMARY

(Erase heading not required.)

Army Form C. 2118

B Dr. 97 (CD) Fd. Amb.

September 1916   Sheet 7

Place	Date	Hour	Summary of Events and Information	Remarks and references to Appendices
DILLINCOURT	21	9.25AM	Unit marched out of GEZAINCOURT to rear of Regt. Inf. Hdqrs.	
		2.45PM	Unit arrived at DILLINCOURT Chateau & billetted there. Accommodation for 30 sick & Officers Adv. Dg. Hosp.	Adv. Dg. Hosp. LIENS II.
"	22nd		A.D.M.S. 30th Div. visited Unit. Lt. PARKER reported from temporary duty c 20th Kings Liverpool Regt.	N.S.
"	23rd		Routine. Motor Amb. Cars joined Unit from 24th Div. Supply Column.	N.S.
"	24th		Routine. Duties in training.	N.S.
"	25th		Routine " "	N.S.
"	26th		Routine " "	N.S.
"	27th		Routine " "	N.S.
"	28th		Routine " "	N.S.
"	29th		Routine " "	N.S.
"	30th		A.D.M.S. held a Conference of Fd. Amb. Commanders & Regt. M.O.'s	N.S.

R.O.Rose
Lt. Col. R.A.M.C.
O.C 67 F.A.

Secret

War Diary
of 97 Field Ambulance
for the month
of October 1916
Volume XII

COMMITTEE FOR THE
MEDICAL HISTORY OF THE WAR
Date -9 DEC. 1916

Army Form C. 2118

WAR DIARY
or
INTELLIGENCE SUMMARY
(Erase heading not required.)

3 Oct 94 Fd Amb.

October 1916   Sheet 1

Place	Date	Hour	Summary of Events and Information	Remarks and references to Appendices
OLLINCOURT	1st		Routine Drills & Training	NB
"	2nd		Routine do. Recd. orders for Transport to proceed to ALLONVILLE.	NB
"	3rd		Lt. & Q.M. at RINGROVE attended to hosp. kits & transferred to No. 1 New Zealand Stat. Hosp. AMIENS. Transport moved to ALLONVILLE under Lt. PARKER en route for DERNANCOURT.	NB
"	4th	9.30AM	Personnel of Fd. Amb. entrained & proceed to DERNANCOURT with 8 & 2 Inf. Bde.	E&a D.9
DERNANCOURT		6 PM.	Arrived DERNANCOURT. took over working of A.D.M.S. Capt SOMERVILLE & 7 O.R detailed to report to 38 C.C.S for temporary duty. Lt TOCHER & "C" det Tent sub. Division detailed to proceed to XV Corps Brain Dressing Sta.	Agg attd Conbu sheet
BECORDEL	5th	2.PM	9 Fd. Amb. (Coo. & tent sub. plus 2 jeeps Bus) proceeded to BECORDEL & took over XV Corps Collecting Station for lightly wounded from New Zealand F.A.	F.9 6.8. 2
"	6 "		Capt WILSON returned from temp duty e RFA Bde. & proceeded to 38 CCS in acting of Capt SOMERVILLE proceeding to U.K. Contract expired. Brain Div with 9 9 Inf. Bde.	NB
"	7 "	1-USPM	Capt SOMERVILLE motored thro XV Corps to St. Vaast.	NB
"	8 "	12 Non	823 Wounded passed thro XV Corps Coll. 15 since 12 noon yesterday	NB
"	9 "		Routine. RAMC Op. Order No. 17 recd. Bearer Div. moved to 89 Inf. Bde & proceeded to Green Dump without they came into the orders 6 Oct. 98 F.C. Amb.	022.6.2.9.
"	10th		Others not to hand one XV Corps Collecting 6.15 & Fd Amb. 24 S. Div. 9 proceeded to Bechuel Dump.	NB
Medical Dump 11th			Arrived our XV Corps Collecting Sta. & proceed to Bechuel Dump. 1 R(?) & 6 Nursing orderlies	X.29. d.3.2
X.29.d.32			Capt FORBES & Capt CRABB & Capt CRABB detailed for temp duty e 98th Fd Amb. detailed for temp duty e 98th Fd. Amb.	NB

Army Form C. 2118

WAR DIARY
or
INTELLIGENCE SUMMARY of 8 97 (2/1) F.Amb.
Oct/Nov 1916 Sheet 2.

(Erase heading not required.)

Instructions regarding War Diaries and Intelligence Summaries are contained in F.S. Regs., Part II. and the Staff Manual respectively. Title Pages will be prepared in manuscript.

Place	Date	Hour	Summary of Events and Information	Remarks and references to Appendices
MEDICAL DUMP X 29d 3.2.	12th		Hd. Qrs. & 8 F.Amb. is now in rooms at Medical Dump. All Officers except O.C. & three NCOs & men are detached for Temp. duty elsewhere. Attack by 39th & 49th Inf. Bde	Ref. Instr. attached
"	13th		Lt. HANSON R.A.M.C. detached from Beaver Div. & posted to take charge 8 19th Kings 2 Bn. R.D.F. under instructions from A.D.M.S. 30th Div.	BB
"	14th		Lt. Q.M. RINGROSE reported for duty on discharge from Hospital.	BB
"	15th		2 Sergt. Clerks R.A.M.C. detailed for duty (Temporary) c/o 98th F.Amb.	BB
"	16th		Lt. PARKER admitted to F.Amb. for Beaver Div. (S.C.T. feet)	BB
"	17th		Capt. SHAW (OC Beaver Div.) admitted to F.Amb. (MUD). Capt FORBES attached as OC Beaver Div. Capt. J. NYE R.A.M.C. & Capt FENWICK R.A.M.C. reported for duty & were attached to 98th F.Amb. & 97th F.Amb. Beaver Div respectively.	BB BB
"	18th		Attack by 21st & 23rd Bdes. Weather cold & wet.	BB
"	19th		Heavy rain during night.	BB
"	20th		Orders rec'd. from A.D.M.S. 30th Div. That 97 F.A. (Hdq & Beaver Div.) will proceed to BECORDEL to morrow.	BB
BECORDEL	21st		Took over Sr. Corps Main Dressing St. Took over Sr. Corps Main Dressing St. That Div. promised attached to 98 F.A. returned. A.D.M.S. 30th Div. 2 Tent Sub.Div. 8 98th F.Amb. reported for duty. R.A.M.C. Bearer NCO rec'd.	BB
"	22		Lt. TOCHER R.A.M.C. detached to report to A.D.M.S. 29th Div. to eliminate & instructions from Tent Div. 8 15th Australian F.Amb. appointed for duty on XI Corps Main Dressing St.	BB
"	23rd		Beaver Div. regained Hd.Qrs. at BECORDEL. Orders rec'd. to send one Sr. Offr. A.D. & 15 Australian F.Amb. & 2 NCOs & orderlies NCO & Btn. at BUIRE.	BB

1875 Wt. W503/826 1,000,000 4/15 J.B.C. & A. A.D.S.S./Forms/C. 2118.

WAR DIARY or INTELLIGENCE SUMMARY

Army Form C. 2118

Unit: 2/2 OC 97 (CCS) Fld Amb.

Month and Year: October 1916 — Sheet 3

Place	Date	Hour	Summary of Events and Information	Remarks and references to Appendices
BUIRE	24th		Handed over to Capt. M.D.S. to O.C. 15th Ano Fishian Fd Amb. & proceeded to Unit at BUIRE reporting arrival to 89th Fd Amb. Went allernoons Notel & Tents as Fd Capos Road JE Orders recd from 89th Fd Amb. for Transport to proceed at 7AM 25t to LUCHEAUX own under orders of 89th Fd Transport Officer.	Ref. Appx. ALBERT contoured sheet 1/40000
"	25th	7. AM	Transport left for LUCHEAUX area. 89th Fd Amb. also nil. Personnel to proceed to LUCHEAUX area by bus on 26th. Embassy on BUIRE-RIBEMONT road at 9.30 A.M. 26th Capt. WILSON & party reported for 38 CCS.	"
"	26th		Emboneing Orders cancelled. Personnel & tnsnt. will entrain at 12 p.m. to Pg 27 Fd Amb at EDGE HILL siding.	
"	27th		Proceeded to GREVAS at 6 p.m. by J.F. with 83 Personnel arrived at 9 AM. having retained at DOULLENS Marched to GREVAS. Billets & Chateau. Attended conference at ADMS Office & was told Just Take over 3rd N MIDLAND Fd Amb (46 Div) at LAHERLIERE.	Ref. Appx. LENS Sheet 11.
"	28th			
"	29th		Proceeded to LAHERLIERE & made arrangements for Taking over Jul. 3 N M Fld Amb. ADMS & RAMC Of 46th Div NESS 2nd & 1st Fd Amb D.O. N21 wrud at 10 p.m. 29th "c" Section marched to BERLES & "B" Sec. Tnsf Lub.Div & LAHERLIERE respectively (4.H Central)	do
"	30th		HqOs "A" Sec & "B" Sec Reserve Lub.Div marched to LAHERLIERE ADS. LAHERLIERE Fd Amb. O.O. 2 issued. (4.H Central)	do
"	31st		Visited Regtl Aid Post & Bearer Relay line & ADS BERLES	do

Appendix A

No 1

OPERATION ORDERS BY LIEUT.COL. B.B.BURKE, D.S.O.
COMMANDING 27th(O.P.) FIELD AMBULANCE, R.A.M.C.

Map Reference LENS Sheet 11.

October 28th 1916

1. "C" Section with full equipment will fall in at 8-15 a.m. and proceed at 8-30 a.m. October 29th 1916 to take over the Advanced Dressing Station at NEULME-AU-BOIS with Collecting Post at SIENVILLERS.

2. The Bearers of "C" Section will work with the Bearers of the outgoing Field Ambulance on the night of 29th-30th, the relief to be completed on the morning of the 30th inst.

3. When the necessary "C" Section equipment has been unloaded from the wagons, the remainder of the equipment with transport-less one Water Cart and one pair of horses- will be returned to the Main Dressing Station at LA HERLIERE.

4. Five wheeled stretchers will accompany "C" Section.

5. Capt.C.D.Shaw, R.A.M.C. with "B" Section Tent Sub-Division and "B" Section equipment will fall in at 8-15 a.m. and proceed at 8-30 a.m. October 29th 1916 to the Main Dressing Station at LA HERLIERE. They will march with "C" Section.

6. O.C."B" Section will arrange to replace the equipment of the outgoing Field Ambulance at LA HERLIERE – Main Dressing Station – on the morning of the 30th inst.

7. The Transport of "B" Section, with the Transport returned from "C" Section, will be parked, under arrangements to be made with the outgoing Field Ambulance at LA HERLIERE.

8. Sergt.J.Frisby, A.S.C. will be in charge of the Transport of "B" and "C" Sections.

9. Lieut.C.S.Ringrose, R.A.M.C., accompanied by one cook, will proceed by Motor Ambulance in advance with the rations of these parties and report to the Quartermaster of the outgoing Field Ambulance at LA HERLIERE. He will return to Headquarters at GREMAS on completion of arrangements for taking over on the 30th inst.

10. Sergt.J.J.O'Sullivan with the undermentioned men of "A" Section – one of whom must be able to cook – will proceed with "B" and "C" Sections to LA CAUCHIE to take over the Disinfecting Station. He will report to the N.C.O. in charge and obtain all necessary details as to the working of the Station.

11. The necessary arrangements for rationing "B" and "C" Sections will be made by the Quartermaster.

The following men are detailed as per No.10:-
67298 Pte Hewitt, J.   67448 Pte.Beardwood, J.
67410 "   Walsh, C.   67453 "   Boreman, F.L.
67641 "   Rosbottom, S.B.   77508 "   Tattersall, S.

29:10:16   (Sd) B.B.Burke.   Lieut.Col.R.A.M.C.
                              Commanding 27th (O.P.) F.A.

OPERATION ORDERS BY LIEUT.COL.B.B.BURKE, D.S.O.
COMMANDING 97th (C.P.) FIELD AMBULANCE, R.A.M.C.

1. "A" Section complete with transport and the Bearer Sub-Division of "B" Section will proceed to the Main Dressing Station at LA HERLIERE on Monday the 30th inst.

    Parade...... 8-30 a.m.   March off....... 8-45 a.m.
    Dress. Full marching order with steel helmets. Great coats will be packed and carried in the haversack.
    All personnel blankets will be collected and packed by 8 a.m. and placed in the horsed ambulance wagons.

2. The Transport of "A" Section will form up facing north on the road by the horse lines.

29:10:16

Lieut.Col. R.A.M.C.
Commanding 97th (C.P.) F.A.

Secret. Vol 13

War Diary
of
97 Field Ambulance
for the month
of
November 1916

Volume XIII.

COMMITTEE FOR THE
MEDICAL HISTORY OF THE WAR
Date -3 JAN. 1917

Army Form C. 2118

WAR DIARY
or
INTELLIGENCE SUMMARY   of O.C. 97 (C.P.) Field Ambulance
(Erase heading not required.)

NOVEMBER 1916   Sheet 1.

Place	Date	Hour	Summary of Events and Information	Remarks and references to Appendices
LA HERLIÈRE	1st		Capt. S. FENWICK detailed for temporary duty with 2nd Bedford Regt.	Ref. Map LENS. Sheet 11.
"	2nd	about 4.30pm	Motor Ambulance Car (Ford. No. 15653) of 97 F.A. collided with and injured a French soldier cyclist at NUNCQ. Car containing Capt. L.D. SHAW returning from duty at No. 12 Stationary Hosp. at St. Pol.	
"		2.30pm	Court of Inquiry assembled to enquire into circumstances of patients' accident. President, Capt. L.J.J. NYE, Members Capt. E.A. WILSON and Capt. R.L. CRABB. Capt. S. FENWICK reported for duty having completed temporary duty with 2nd Bedfords. Capt. E.A. WILSON detailed for daily attendance at P.O.W. Camp No. 31 at LA BAZEQUE.	
"	3rd		2 NCOs and 7 Stretcher Squads detailed to deal with a gas emergency. Capt. S. FENWICK M.O. I/C. Capt. S. FENWICK and above 2 NCOs detailed to make themselves acquainted with the area for which they are responsible for evacuating.	
"	4th		Capt. L.D. SHAW and Capt. L.J.J. NYE detailed to acquaint themselves with evacuation area from Advanced Dressing Station forwards.	
"	5th			
"	6th		Capt. L.J.J. NYE evacuated to No. 43 C.C.S. (appendicitis)	
"	7th	3pm	Head quarters, hospital etc. visited by Col. SHAW, A.M.S., D.D.M.S. VII Corps. Lt.-Col. B.B. BURKE. D.S.O. on leave for ten days from this date. Capt. L.D. SHAW acting O.C. of 97 F.A. Capt. R.L. CRABB detailed to attend a demonstration on anti gas measures at 3rd Army H.Q. St. Pol. Headquarters, hospital etc inspected by Surg-Gen. MURRAY IRWIN D.M.S. 3rd Army.	
"	8th		Relays of Emergency bearers commence visiting evacuation area.	

WAR DIARY or INTELLIGENCE SUMMARY

Army Form C. 2118.

97 C.P.H.Bank November 1916 Sheet 1

Place	Date	Hour	Summary of Events and Information	Remarks and references to Appendices
LA HERLIÈRE	Nov. 9		Capt. SHAW and Capt. CRABB visit NCO I/c park at BENVILLERS and B. Reg'l Aid Post and area for which they are responsible. Disinfecting Station at LA CAUCHIE also inspected. Gas alarm 6.30pm Capt. FENWICK despatched with emergency party with 1/4 hour. Alarm ultimately false, party return. Capt. CRABB admitted to F.A.(R.U.O)	
	10	7.30pm	Air raid on R.E. Dump by horse lines. 6 Deaths and 8 severely injured. All taken in F.A.	
	11		Col. SWAN D.D.M.S. VII Corps visited Advanced Dressing Station at BERLES.	
	12		Capt. FENWICK and half 'B' Section proceed to A.D.S. at BERLES. Lieut. PARKER and half 'C' Section report at Headquarters from A.D.S. BERLES.	
	13	3 am	Capt. FORSYTH and remainder Gas attack along selected areas of 30th Divisional front by Gas Company 1 Divisional R.E. Emergency party Lieut. PARKER i/c & dispatched. 16 Casualties taken at A.D.S.	
			Capt. FORBES and remainder of 'C' Section reported at Headquarters. Capt. WILSON and remainder of 'B' completes the relief of 'C' Section at A.D.S. BERLES.	
			Lieut. PARKER and 1 NCO and 8 men detailed for duty at No 43 C.C.S.	
	14		Capt. CRABB returns to duty.	

Army Form C. 2118.

WAR DIARY O.C. 97 (CP) Fd Amb
or
INTELLIGENCE SUMMARY.
(Erase heading not required.)

November 1916

Instructions regarding War Diaries and Intelligence Summaries are contained in F. S. Regs., Part II. and the Staff Manual respectively. Title pages will be prepared in manuscript.

Place	Date	Hour	Summary of Events and Information	Remarks and references to Appendices
LA HERLIERE	15		Capt. A. St. JOHNSTON, R.A.M.C. reports for duty.	
	16		Capt. S. FENNICK details for duty with 19th Manchester Regt. Capt. St JOHNSTON proceeded to A.D.M. BERLES. Capt. WILSON has O.O. at BERLES.	
	17		Capt. SHAW to BENVILLERS with Lt. Col. McKINNON O.C. West Riding Fd. Amb. to take over his post.	
	18		Lt. Col. BURKE D.S.O. returned from leave & reassumes command of the unit.	
	19		Capt. FORBES reports sick (P.U.O.) admitted to F.d. Amb.	
	20		Capt. CRABB detailed to attend a course of instruction at 3rd Army HQ. St POL commencing today. Lt. PARKER & party rejoined from temp. duty at 43 CCS.	
	21		Corps Commander O/C Corps inspected Fd. Amb. arrangements.	
	22		Attended conference at A.D.M.S. office. Lt. ORR R.A.M.C. (att 2/0 y/c 17 K.L.Rgt) landed over under escort to me for safe custody by Lt. 1/2 K.L.R. with instructions for H.Q. 49th Div. Visited A.D.S. BERLES.	
	23rd		Heavy rain	
	24th		Capt. Crabb returned to duty from gas class	
	25th		Lt. Col. Burke took over duties as A.D.M.S. Capt. Shaw as Tony O.C. 97th F.A.	
	26th			

Army Form C. 2118.

WAR DIARY
or
INTELLIGENCE SUMMARY.
(Erase heading not required.)

Instructions regarding War Diaries and Intelligence Summaries are contained in F. S. Regs., Part II. and the Staff Manual respectively. Title pages will be prepared in manuscript.

Place	Date	Hour	Summary of Events and Information	Remarks and references to Appendices
	27th		The relief of A.D.S. Beuk was completed. The teams of "A" section & the 1st subdivision M.C. relieved the personnel of "B". Lt. Parker left for England.	
	28th		Reinforcements sent to A.D.S. Beuk in motor lorry. 1 gas attack which did not warrant...	
	29th		Capt Finlare reported from D.R.S. A.D.S. visited	
	30		Lt. Dr Rowe left in charge of convoy. Inquiry held at Beuk & returned. Stuff in rear event.	

Secret

140/903
Vol 14

War Diary of
97 Field Ambulance.
for the month of
December 1916.

Volume XIV

Dec 1916

> COMMITTEE FOR THE
> MEDICAL HISTORY OF THE WAR
> Date -1 JAN. 1917

Army Form C. 2118.

WAR DIARY of OC. 97 F. Amb
INTELLIGENCE SUMMARY.
(Erase heading not required.)

December 1916.   Sheet 1

Place	Date	Hour	Summary of Events and Information	Remarks and references to Appendices
La Herlière	1st Dec		Routine	
"	2nd		Capt Gadd given 2 days leave to see procured at HQ. Capt M. Ladlan acting for Gadd	
"	3rd		St. Sergts commanding VII Corps imm. F.A. ambulance	
"	4th		Capt M. Ladlan admits Capt St John Im. at ADS Berles. Capt Gadd taking over command	
"	5th		Routine	
"	6th		Capt Vasey up for duty. Lt Col B B Bruce returning to ambulance	
"	7th		Capt L D Shaw. & Capt Forbes proceeded on leave.	88
"	8th		Visited A.D.S.	
"	9th		Routine. RAMC Gp. Order Nº 24 recd.	88
"	10th		VII Corps Commander inspected Hospital. ADS in accordance with O.O. 24.	89
"	11th		Capt Vasey + 5 Bearer Squad sent to A.D. Visited ADS a respected all arrangements (medical) for embarkment of Monchy Salient. ADMS. & AA+QMS inspected Hospital at MDS	69

Army Form C. 2118.

WAR DIARY of OC 91 (CP) FL Amb.
or
INTELLIGENCE SUMMARY.
(Erase heading not required.)

December 1916 / Kent 77

Instructions regarding War Diaries and Intelligence Summaries are contained in F. S. Regs., Part II. and the Staff Manual respectively. Title pages will be prepared in manuscript.

Place	Date	Hour	Summary of Events and Information	Remarks and references to Appendices
LAHERLIERE	12th		DDMS VII Corps inspected Main Dressing Station.	1
		9am	Enemy shelled RE Dump LAHERLIERE & obtained a direct hit on 2nd pull of man. M.O. & Bearer squads sent to Dump & 22 casualties brought to M.D.S.	
"	13th		G.O.C. 30th Div. inspected Main Dressing Station. Heavy bombardment of enemy lines & MONCHY Salient	
		8.20pm	Enemy shelled SAULTY - LABRET Station. M.O & Bearer Squads sent to render assistance. No casualties.	
"	14th	2pm	Enemy shelled WARLINCOURT.	
"	15th		"B" Section returns. "A" Tut. and Div. & Relief teams in A.D.S. Capt VASEY assumes command of A.D.S. vice Capt CRABBE returning to HQ.	
"	16th		Visited A.D.S. & arranged for extra accommodation to be provided by means of bombing or shelter huts. Capt CRABBE returned to temp. duty at Div. HQ as a/DADMS.	
"	17th		VII Corps Commander visited Main Dressing Stn. Enemy shelled SAULTY by 5.9.	
"	18th		Routine.	

Army Form C. 2118.

WAR DIARY 3 OC 97 (CP) Fd Amb.
or
INTELLIGENCE SUMMARY.
(Erase heading not required.)

December 1916. Sheet 3.

Instructions regarding War Diaries and Intelligence Summaries are contained in F. S. Regs., Part II. and the Staff Manual respectively. Title pages will be prepared in manuscript.

Place	Date	Hour	Summary of Events and Information	Remarks and references to Appendices
LAHERLIERE	19th		Visited 3rd Army School of Sanitation. Routine.	M.
"	20th		Visited A.D.S. in conjunction with O.C. 2nd Fd. Amb. R.E., selected site for bivouac, Fd. Amb. collecting Post nr W. 16 Central. Work to begin at once.	R.S. Appendix Sheet S.E.
"	21st		Routine	
"	22nd		Enemy shelled LAHERLIERE in the vicinity of Main Dressing Station, the roofs of several huts being damaged. All patients were placed in safety in a large cave, in accordance with pre-arranged scheme. No casualties occurred. A.D.M.S. 2nd Div informed. Capt J.M. SETTLESON reported for duty.	M.
"	23rd		A.D.M.S 30 Div visited M.D.S. Another L.D. brother had died near attached to 9th Fd Amb. No more sick as to be admitted to M.D.S. for the present. Routine. Capt WILSON RAME left yesterday to report to A.D.M.S. CALAIS for duty. Capt FORBES returned from leave.	M.
"	24th		Xmas Day. Nothing of note to report. Capt SETTLESON proceeded on leave.	M.
"	25th		Enemy shelled SAPPY LARRET Station. No casualties.	M.
"	26th		Capt R. CLACHLAN proceeded on leave. Capt SETTLESON proceeded to A.D.S. for duty.	M.
"	27th		Capt J. JOHNSTONE detailed for temporary duty at Divisional School.	M.
"	28th		Capt CRAGSE detailed for temporary duty at Div R.E. H.Q.	M.

Army Form C. 2118.

WAR DIARY
of
INTELLIGENCE SUMMARY

(Erase heading not required.)

8 OC 97 (CP) Field Amb.

December 1916.   Sheet 4.

Place	Date	Hour	Summary of Events and Information	Remarks and references to Appendices
LAHERLIERE	29		No. 76790 Pte SANDERS. V. RAMC was killed to-day by a shell whilst on duty	
			"B" No 8's WACK Tank.	
		10ᵃ	Proceeded to "C" Section relieved "B" Section at A.D.S.	
			Enemy shelled LAHERLIERE, no Casualties. All personnel & cost accommodated in Caves.	
		3ᵖ	Capt A.D. ETRNES a visit hut with dugouts. ADMS visits A.D.S.	
"			Routine.	

M. Mulholland
Lieut-Col.
OC 97 (CP) Field Amb.

Secret. Vol 15

War Diary
of
97 Field Ambulance
for the month of
January 1917.
Volume XV

Army Form C. 2118.

WAR DIARY
or
INTELLIGENCE SUMMARY.
(Erase heading not required.)

3 OC 97 (UP) Fl. Amb.

January 1917 Sheet 1

Place	Date	Hour	Summary of Events and Information	Remarks and references to Appendices
LAHERLIERE	1st		Routine	
"	2nd		R.A.M.C. Op. order No 2 issued ref. move of Div. & relief by 49th Div.	
"	3rd		Genero visit Capt. visited M.D.S. visited A.D.S. BERLES with OC 1st/2nd S. Midland Ft. Amb. re/H. taking over A2S by that unit	
"	4th		Enemy shells LAHERLIERE, no casualties.	
"	5th	1.30 P.M.	"B" Section proceeded to MONDICOURT as advance party to Path no. 12 Amb. Site from 1st West Riding Ft. Amb. 49th Div. 1st/2nd West Riding arrived.	
"	6th	7.15AM	1st/2nd 1st W.R. Ft. Amb. proceeded from LAHERLIERE to BERLES & took over A.D.S. During Night Tham from "C" Sect 97F.A. "C" Sect proceeded to MONDICOURT.	
MONDICOURT	7th		"A" Sect & H.Qrs. proceeded to MONDICOURT & took 3 movement command & Ft. Amb. site at MONDICOURT.	
"	8th		A.D.M.S. 30th Div. visited Ft. Amb.	
"	9th		Routine	
"	10th		Routine	
"	11th		Capt. SETTLESTONE R.A.M.C. returned from temporary duty at R.E. H.Qrs.	
"	12th		Routine	

WAR DIARY or INTELLIGENCE SUMMARY

Army Form C. 2118.

9 OC 97 (CO) F.Amb.

January 1917 Sheet 2.

Place	Date	Hour	Summary of Events and Information	Remarks and references to Appendices
MONDICOURT	13th		Recd orders to proceed to No 12 Stationary Hospital & assume command forthwith.	
	14th		Capt L.D. SHAW RAMC (T) appointed to command 97 F.Amb.	M2
			DDMS VII Corps visited.	
	15th		Handed over to Capt L.D. SHAW. RAMC (T) he being junior	M2
	16th		Assumed command of 97th F.A. SdS	SdS
			Capt VAISEY returned to F.A. from Temporary duty with the 50th N.L.R. Capt T.	SdS
			SETTLESON returned from Temporary duty with the 3rd Bat/E.R.	SdS
	16th		ADMS visited F.A.	SdS
	17th		Routine	SdS
	18th		Capt LITTHON took over medical charge of RAFFIN CAMP	SdS
			Capt McLAUGHLAN returned from leave	SdS
	19th		Capt St JOHNSTON evacuated sick to 19th C.C.S.	SdS
	20th		Capt McCUBBIN reported for duty from 43 C.C.S.	SdS
	23rd		Capt McCUBBIN reported for duty with 149 Bde R.F.A. - vice a Trench with Capt Creagh provided him to	SdS
			arrest in charge of Ambulances	
			on y and 23/1/17 - 2/3/17	

WAR DIARY
or
INTELLIGENCE SUMMARY.

(Erase heading not required.)

Army Form C. 2118.

Place	Date	Hour	Summary of Events and Information	Remarks and references to Appendices
	24th		Capt Littleton w/ATA for Embarg. duty with 17 K.L.R. Capt Forbes took over charge of Kaffir Camp. Sent A Newton Brady w/ATA for duty	See
	25th		ROUTINE. Investigation of charge against Capt McCubbin, application made for a Court martial to be convened.	See
	26th		ROUTINE.	See
	27th		Further evidence in charge against Capt McCubbin taken	See
	28th		Capt Littleton w/ATA for duty from 17 K.L.R. ADMS. relieves FA	See
	29th		ROUTINE	See
	30th		Capt McLaughlan takes over duty from Capt	See
	31st		ROUTINE.	See

Secret

War Diary
of
97 Field Ambulance
for the month of
February 1917
Volume XVI

COMMITTEE FOR THE
MEDICAL HISTORY OF THE WAR
Date 4.—APR.1917

WAR DIARY
or
INTELLIGENCE SUMMARY.

(Erase heading not required.)

Army Form C. 2118.

1 Oc. 97th F.A. Etaney

Place	Date	Hour	Summary of Events and Information	Remarks and references to Appendices
Hardium	1		Routine	
	2		Capt Cadman Tch from leave	
	3		Capt McLachlan discharged from hospital	
	4		Routine	
	5		Capt McLachlan detailed for Temporary duty with 86th Div Depot	
	6		Routine	
	7		Capt J. Johnson detailed Temporary duty with 17th Manchester Regt	
	8		Lieut Brady Dental Team & detld to 15th F.A.	
	9		A.D.M.S. visited Rest Station & F.A.	
	10		Routine	
	11		Sr. St. arrived in T.S.D. Snow commanding VIIth Corps inspected F.A. & A.D.S. A.D.M.S. inspected F.A. & D.R.S. Capt J. Johnson detailed for permanent duty with 17th Manchester Regt. Sch. of dinner from the services war production Fn. – Capt M. Curtin sent to England.	
	12		Routine	

WAR DIARY
or
INTELLIGENCE SUMMARY.
(Erase heading not required.)

Army Form C. 2118.

Instructions regarding War Diaries and Intelligence Summaries are contained in F. S. Regs., Part II. and the Staff Manual respectively. Title pages will be prepared in manuscript.

Place	Date	Hour	Summary of Events and Information	Remarks and references to Appendices
	13		Routine. Sgt O'Sullivan SB proceeded to England on promotion for commission	See
	14		ADMS visited FA and DRS	See
	15		Sgt Brady RAMC to TA for leave	See
	16		Routine. 11 mo ambulance in traffic inspected	See
	17		Routine	See
	18		S/Sgt Glenn SB proceeded to 3rd Field Ambce as on probation. Conference at A.D.M.S.	See
	19		Routine	See
	20		ADMS 20th Div had a medical board at FA + inspected hospital	See
	21		Col Swan DDMS VII Corps visited FA + DRS	See
	22		Routine	See
	23		Capt C.W. Bond rejoined for duty	See
	24		Sgt Brady RAMC rejoined for duty from leave. A/Sgt visited the 30th Div RE	See
	25		Routine	See
	26		Routine	
	27		ADMS held no med board. DADMS III Army inspected FA + DRS	See
	28		Sgt Brady RAMC to duty from 30 Div R.E.	See 4th FA

Secret

Vol 17

140/2042

32nd Div

War Diary
of
97 Field Ambulance
for the month
of
March 1917
Volume XVII

COMMITTEE FOR THE
MEDICAL HISTORY OF THE WAR
Date 11 MAY. 1917

51

Army Form C. 2118.

WAR DIARY
or
INTELLIGENCE SUMMARY.
(Erase heading not required.)

Place	Date	Hour	Summary of Events and Information	Remarks and references to Appendices
Moislains	1st		Capt M.R. M'Kay RAMC. unfit for duty	
	2nd		Capt C.N. Faber was in Amb (eyelid) from 3.3.17 till 16 & 17	
	3rd		Col. Swan DDMS. VIII Corps visits F.A. – Rly Station	
	4th		Capt M.R. M'Kay proceeds for duty with 146 Bde R.F.A.	
	5th		Routine	
	6th		DADMS 30th Div visits F.A. ward round in Lud	
	7th		Routine	
	8th		3 NCO's + 47 men unfit for duty with O.C. 96th F.A. at Beaumont	
	9th		Routine	
	10th		Routine	
	11th		Routine	
	12th		Routine	
	13th		ADiv. 30th Div visits F.A. + met Station + Adv. overhead board	
	14th		Full guard controverted with Lt Orr RAMC. Act M.O. 17th KLR	
	15th		attendance conference of field ambulance commanders at Beauvillé	
	16th		Visits 96th /3rd F.A. Beaumont	

Army Form C. 2118.

WAR DIARY
or
INTELLIGENCE SUMMARY.
(Erase heading not required.)

Instructions regarding War Diaries and Intelligence Summaries are contained in F. S. Regs., Part II. and the Staff Manual respectively. Title pages will be prepared in manuscript.

Place	Date	Hour	Summary of Events and Information	Remarks and references to Appendices
Bradinont	August 17th		Visits selected posts as inspected and posts in 30th Div front	
	18th		Routine	
	19th		Routine	
	20th		A.D.M.S. 30th Div visited F.A. field medical board	
	21st		Lt Newton Brady joined head qtrs. attached 96th F.A.	
	22nd		Routine	
	23rd		Capt M'Lachlan (N.L. proceed to England on intimation of contract	
			Lt Col L.D. Shaw. South African on half leave from 24.3.17 to 7.4.17	
			Capt A.D. Forbes. brown assumed command of 97th F.A.	
	24th		Capt A.D. Forbes assumed command of 97th F.A.	
	25th		Routine	
	26th		Routine	
	27th		A.D.M.S. 30 + Div visited F.A. field medical board	
	28th		Routine	
	29th		Capt C.N. Hussey R.A.M.C. reported for duty	
	30th		Routine	
	31st		Attended Conference A.D.M.S. 30th Div Bradinont	

Confidential.

War Diary
of
97th Field Ambulance
for the month of
April. 1917.

Volume. XVIII

Army Form C. 2118.

WAR DIARY
or
INTELLIGENCE SUMMARY.
(Erase heading not required.)

Instructions regarding War Diaries and Intelligence Summaries are contained in F. S. Regs., Part II. and the Staff Manual respectively. Title pages will be prepared in manuscript.

Place	Date	Hour	Summary of Events and Information	Remarks and references to Appendices
Montrécourt	April 2nd		Took over from ADMS 30th Div. Advanced party proceeded to Bavincourt to take over ambulances	Apx
			Set from 2/3 London FA. 56th Div	
Montrécourt	April 3rd		The rest of Ambulance, less 1 Tent Sub-Div left behind at Montrécourt proceeded to Bavincourt	Apx
			completed relieving 2/3 London FA	
Bavincourt	April 3rd		ADMS 30th Division paid visit. He gave out the same day	Apx
Bavincourt	April 4th		That the Bavincourt Division H-Prs/Farm alys in FA.	
			Bavincourt under Capt Brown RAMC. The rest of Bavin. Div equipment went to with the part	Apx
Bavincourt	April 6th		First from ADMS 30th Div. The visiting half Bavin Div, as 1 up to 95 1/2 A, again impects Reserve Div.	
	7th		as waiting for 1 officer. Lt Col. L. D. Shaw returned from leave	Apx
	8		St Col S D Shaw assumed command of 1/3rd FA	L/S
			Capt Forbes proceeded to England on termination of short. Lt Dl Davies	L/S
			arrived for duty & was also on Sick leave Lt 1/3rd FA. Lt DL Davies	
			reported for temporary duty with the 96 FA. Col Swan DDMS VII Corps	
	9th		Routine	£28
	10		Routine	£28
				£20

Army Form C. 2118.

WAR DIARY
or
INTELLIGENCE SUMMARY.
(Erase heading not required.)

Instructions regarding War Diaries and Intelligence Summaries are contained in F.S. Regs., Part II. and the Staff Manual respectively. Title pages will be prepared in manuscript.

Place	Date	Hour	Summary of Events and Information	Remarks and references to Appendices
Beaumont	11th		Routine	SOS
	12th		Routine	SOS
	13th		St DL Dawson reported for duty from 96th FA	SOS
	14th		Brian Dawson reported 97th FA & was attached to So Hadden L/cpl J Forsyth proceeded to England on Probation for an commission SOS	SOS
	15th		Lieut Allyand ADMS visited Hosptal	SOS
	16th		Routine	SOS
	17th		Col T & S Walsh – Sur T & Maitland reported at 1st Ant 97th FA Left Bavincourt & took over ADS in Neuville Vitasse from 2/3 City of London FA at 4pm. Horse lines & horse not camped when established on Neuville Vitasse- Beaurains road in N 18 a 2 8	SOS
	18th		The horse lines of 96th FA & 95th FA was attached to 97th FA	SOS
	19th		A collecting post was established in N 22 d 7 8 & horse squads were attached to each regiment and post – a system of horse relays was arranged to carry to N 20 B 4 8 when horse ambulances of 3rd Corps were STretched & evacuated to ADS in N 19 & 9. Wounded thump ADS till 7pm & other sends SOS

WAR DIARY or INTELLIGENCE SUMMARY

Army Form C. 2118.

Place	Date	Hour	Summary of Events and Information	Remarks and references to Appendices
Neuville-Vitasse	April 20th		Work was started to increase the sleeping accommodation for women at ADS + to erect a splint [shed?] & examining room at subs[?] post No 2 & 51. A car anteroom was established at N19 a 4.5. On Being[?] division was found insufficient to take the sim & the others with in [?] human camp. Wounded through to ADS. Two 7pm 1 off. an 31 O.R. Casualties	
	21st		in human division Cpt Byrne 98th FA + Pte Bryan 147th subdivision 97th FA SDS. Construction work continued at ADS. Wounded Two 7pm 5 off. an 26 O.R. SDS	
	22nd		Work completed at ADS. Slim quarry arrangement started for Shelter for 27 stretcher cases. Splint shed at No 2 & 51 was also completed. SDS + [?] on an examining room. Wounded Two 7pm 1 off an 16 O.R.	
	23rd		Construction of the ADS, the arrangements for Shelter wounded men [?] the Field [?] the stretcher cases ready [?] were two hour division [?] in it was [?]. Two hours after zero the [?] of the Shelter ever so what & was found possible to send the ambulance & let cars farther up to the line chains from N31 a 5.9. Two rest stations also [?] with Inns & [?] were also used & proved very serviceable	

Army Form C. 2118.

WAR DIARY
or
INTELLIGENCE SUMMARY.
(Erase heading not required.)

Instructions regarding War Diaries and Intelligence Summaries are contained in F. S. Regs., Part II. and the Staff Manual respectively. Title pages will be prepared in manuscript.

Place	Date	Hour	Summary of Events and Information	Remarks and references to Appendices
Manville Place	April 23		Wounded through ADS Tui 7pm 15 o/r and 132 OR Summers & Casualties	SDR
	24th		In forenoon dept of A TURNER 98 FA advanced in vicinity of mechanism to arr for ADS was advised in N28c 6.6 and collecting station in N30 a i.4 and work of construction started. Wounded through ADS Tui 7pm 12 o/r and OR 195 Summers 10	SDS
	25		Work completed in ADS + collecting post. Evacuation camp established N30c90. Ambulance car unloading established HENIN N32a7.8. Wounded through ADS 24 o/r and 57 OR.	SDS
	26th		During night 25th-26th both ADS's were kept busy treatment of wounded. During morning ADS Neuville Vitasse was evacuated. Wounded through ADS Tui 7pm 1 o/r and 160 R.	SDS SDS
	27th		Wounded through ADS Tui 7pm 9 OR.	SDS
	28.		97th FA was relieved by 54th FA at 5¹m wounded admitted by 54th FA up to 2pm 17 OR. The 97th FA on relief marched to New Drouay SE'n S3905	SDS
	29th		97 FA marched to AVESNES le COMTE	SDS
	30		97 FA marched to FRAMECOURT + opened for receiving of sick and wounded	SDS S⁹fFA

B.E.F.

SUMMARY OF MEDICAL WAR DIARIES FOR 97th F.A. 30th Divn. 7th Corps, 3rd Army

18th Corps from 12/4/17.
7th   "   " 18/4/17.
19th   "   " 29/4/17.

2nd Army 11th Corps from 20/5/17.

WESTERN FRONT. April- May. '17.

O.C. Lt. Col. L.D. Shaw.

SUMMARISED UNDER THE FOLLOWING HEADINGS.
Phase "B" Battle of Arras- April- May. 1917.
1st Period Attack on Vimy Ridge April. '17.
2nd Period Capture of Siegfried Line May.

B.E.F.

97th F.A. 30th Divn. 7th Corps 3rd Army.   WESTERN FRONT.
O.C. Lt. Col. L.D. Shaw.   April. '17.
18th Corps from 12/4/17.

Phase "B" Battle of Arras- April- May. '17.
1st Period Attack on Vimy Ridge April.

1917.	Headquarters. at MONDICOURT.
April. 2nd.	Moves: To Bavincourt (Less 1 T.S.D. at Bavincourt) and relieved 2/3rd London Field Ambulance. F.A.
4th.	Moves Detachment: Half B.D. relieved remaining half at 98th/
6th.	Moved Detachment: Half B.D. that had been resting moved to 98th Field Ambulance making complete Br. Divn. attached
12th.	Transfer. To 18th Corps.

B.E.F.

97th F.A. 30th Divn. 18th Corps 3rd Army.   WESTERN FRONT.
O.C. Lt. Col. L.D. Shaw.   April. '17.
7th Corps from 18/4/17.

Phase "B" Battle of Arras- April- May.
1st Period Attack on Vimt Ridge April.

1917.
April. 12th.   Transfer.   18th Corps.
       14th.   B.D. rejoined Unit from 98th Field Ambulance.
       18th.   Transfer.   To 7th Corps.

B.E.F. 3.

97th F.A. 30th Divn. 7th Corps 3rd Army.   WESTERN FRONT.
O.C. Lt. Col. L.D. Shaw.   April. '17.

Phase "B" Battle of Arras- April- May. '17.
1st Period Attack on Vimy Ridge April.

1917.

April. 18th. **Transfer.** To 7th Corps.

19th. **Moves:** To Neuville Vitasse and took over A.D.S. from 2/3rd London Field Ambulance.

Medical Arrangements: Horse Lines and Br. Camp, N.18.a.2.8.

Brs. of 96th and 98th Field Ambulances attached to 97th Field Ambulance.

Coll. Post established at N.22.d.7.8.

Br. Squads attached to each R.A.P.

Evacuation: By Br. relays to N.20.B.4.8. thence by Horse Ambulance and Fords to A.D.S. N.19.b.8.9.

Casualties. 0 and 8 through A.D.S.

20th. **Medical Arrangements: Accommodation:** Shell-proof accommodation for wounded increased at A.D.S. and Relay Post N.22.a.5.1.

Car rendez-vous N.19.a.4.3.

Casualties. 1 and 31 wounded.

Casualties R.A.M.C. 0 and 1 wounded 98th Field Ambulance. 0 and 1 wounded 97th Field Ambulance.

21st. **Casualties.**   5 and 26 wounded

22nd.   "   1 and 18   "

23rd. **Medical Arrangements:** 2 Br. Ds. in line, 1 in reserve.

Operations. Attack- (No details)

Casualties: Evacuation: first wounded arrived 2 hours after zero. H. Amb.& Fords cleared from N.21.a.5.9. 2 wh. Strs. with horse Attachments also used 15 & 134 W.Br. 8 W. Ger.

B.E.F. 4.

97th F.A. 30th Divn. 7th Corps. 3rd Army.   WESTERN FRONT
O.C. Lt. Col. L.D.Shaw.   April. '17.
19th Corps from 29/4/17.

Phase "B" cont.

1st Period cont.

Q
1917.

23rd cont.   Casualties R.A.M.C.   0 and 1 W. 98th F.A.

April. 24th:-   Evacuation: Medical Arrangements:-

New route owing to advance.
A.D.S.- N.28.c.6.6.

Coll. Stn.- N.30.a.1.4.

Casualties. 14 and 192 wounded Br. 10 wounded Germans.

25th.   Medical Arrangements:-

Br. Rest Camp = N.20.c.9.0.

Horse Lines and Rendez-vous = Henin N.32.d.7.8.

Casualties. 2 and 57 wounded.

26th.   Medical Arrangements: A.D.S. Neuville Vitasse closed.

Casualties:-

1 and 16 wounded.

27th.   0 " 9 "

28th.   Moves: To M.D.S. S.3.a.0.5. on relief by 54th Field Ambulance.

29th.   Moves and Transfer. To Avesnes Le Comte and 19th Corps.

97th F.A. 30th Divn. 19th Corps 3rd. Army.   WESTERN FRONT.
O.C. Lt. Col. L.D. Shaw.   April. '17.

Phase "B" Battle of Arras- April- May. '17.
1st Period Attack on Vimy Ridge April.

1917.
April. 29th.   Moves and Transfer. To Avesnes Le Comte and 19th Corps.
     30th.   Moves To Framecourt and opened for sick.

B.E.F.

<u>97th F.A. 30th Divn. 7th Corps 3rd Army.</u>   <u>WESTERN FRONT.</u>
<u>O.C. Lt. Col. L.D. Shaw.</u>   <u>April. '17.</u>
<u>18th Corps from 12/4/17.</u>

<u>Phase "B" Battle of Arras- April- May. '17.</u>
<u>1st Period Attack on Vimy Ridge April.</u>

1917.	<u>Headquarters.</u> at MONDICOURT.
April. 2nd.	<u>Moves:</u> To Bavincourt (Less 1 T.S.D. at Bavincourt) and relieved 2/3rd London Field Ambulance. F.A.
4th.	<u>Moves Detachment:</u> Half B.D. relieved remaining half at 98th/
6th.	<u>Moved Detachment:</u> Half B.D. that had been resting moved to 98th Field Ambulance making complete Br. Divn. attached
12th.	<u>Transfer.</u> To 18th Corps.

B.E.F.

97th F.A. 30th Divn. 18th Corps 3rd Army.   WESTERN FRONT.
O.C. Lt. Col. L.D. Shaw.   April. '17.
7th Corps from 18/4/17.

Phase "B" Battle of Arras- April- May.
1st Period Attack on Vimt Ridge April.

1917.
April. 12th.   Transfer.   18th Corps.
       14th.   B.D. rejoined Unit from 98th Field Ambulance.
       18th.   Transfer.   To 7th Corps.

B.E.F. 3.

97th F.A. 30th Divn. 7th Corps 3rd Army.   WESTERN FRONT.
O.C. Lt. Col. L.D. Shaw.   April. '17.

Phase "B" Battle of Arras- April- May. '17.
1st Period Attack on Vimy Ridge April.

1917.

April. 18th.   Transfer. To 7th Corps.

19th.   Moves: To Neuville Vitasse and took over A.D.S. from
2/3rd London Field Ambulance.
Medical Arrangements: Horse Lines and Br. Camp,
N.18.a.2.8.
Brs. of 96th and 98th Field Ambulances attached to
97th Field Ambulance.
Coll. Post established at N.22.d.7.8.
Br. Squads attached to each R.A.P.
Evacuation: By Br. relays to N.20. B.4.8. thence by
Horse Ambulance and Fords to A.D.S. N.19.b.8.9.
Casualties. 0 and 8 through A.D.S.

20th.   Medical Arrangements: Accommodation: Shell proof
accommodation for wounded increased at A.D.S. and Relay
Post N.22.a.5.1.
Car rendez vous N.19.a.4.3.
Casualties. 1 and 31 wounded.
Casualties R.A.M.C. 0 and 1 wounded 98th Field
Ambulance.   0 and 1 wounded 97th Field Ambulance.

21st.   Casualties.   5 and 26 wounded

22nd.   "   1 and 18   "

23rd.   Medical Arrangements: 2 Br. Dc. in line 1 in reserve.
Operations. Attack- (No details)
Casualties: Evacuation: first wounded arrived 2 hours
after zero. H. Amb. & Fords cleared from N.21.a.5.9. 2 wh.
strs. with horse Attachments also used 15 & 134 W. Br.
18 W.Ger.   3.

B.E.F. 4.

97th F.A. 30th Divn. 7th Corps. 3rd Army.   WESTERN FRONT
O.C. Lt. Col. L.D.Shaw.   April. '17.
19th Corps from 29/4/17.

Phase "B" cont.
1st Period cont.

1917.

23rd. cont.   Casualties R.A.M.C.   0 and 1 W. 98th F.A.

April. 24th   Evacuation: Medical Arrangements.
              New route owing to advance.
              A.D.S.- N.28.c.6.6.
              Coll. Stn.- N.30.a.1.4.
              Casualties. 14 and 192 wounded Br.   10 wounded Germans.

25th.   Medical Arrangements:-

                        Br. Rest Camp = N.20.c.9.0.

                        Horse Lines and Rendez vous = Henin N.32.d.7.8.
              Casualties. 2 and 57 wounded.

26th.   Medical Arrangements: A.D.S. Neuville Vitasse closed.
              Casualties:-
              1 and 16 wounded.

27th.   0 " 9 "

28th.   Moves: To M.D.S. S.3.a.0.5. on relief by 54th Field
              Ambulance.

29th.   Moves and Transfer. To Avesnes Le Comte and 19th Corps.

B.E.F.

97th F.A. 30th Divn. 19th Corps 3rd.Army.   WESTERN FRONT.
O.C. Lt. Col. L.D. Shaw.   April. '17.

Phase "B" Battle of Arras- April- May. '17.
1st Period Attack on Vimy Ridge April.

1917.
April. 29th.   Moves and Transfer. To Avesnes Le Comte and 19th Corps.
       30th.   Moves To Framecourt and opened for sick.

Secret

War Diary
of
97th Field Ambulance
for the month of
May. 1917
Volume XIX.

Army Form C. 2118.

WAR DIARY
or
INTELLIGENCE SUMMARY.

(Erase heading not required.)

of O.C. 97 (C.P.) Field Ambulance
May 1917. Sheet 1

Place	Date	Hour	Summary of Events and Information	Remarks and references to Appendices
FRANCECOURT	1	3pm	ADMS visits F.A. Brigade Sick to be accommodated in tents. Village un- suitable for F.A. site.	SDS
	2		Capt. R.L. CRABB. RAMC appointed 2nd i/c 97th F.A.	SDS
	3	1.30pm	F.A. leaves FRANCECOURT and follows 89th Brigade. Proceed to BACHIMONT and Chateau in the village taken over as hospital site.	SDS
BACHIMONT	4	1 pm	ADMS visits F.A. Site. Accommodation to be extended to take 150 patients by means of tents.	SDS
	5		Work on Sanitation, Cookhouse, Erection of tents etc. Capt. J.J. WALSH. RAMC attended Town Major of BACHIMONT.	SDS
	6		Further improvements. Sick accommodation in chateau now amounts to 3 off 59 O.R.	SDS
	7		C.O. taken (Capt C.N. VAISEY. RAMC, Capt CM BOND RAMC. Lieut. A.NEWTON-BRADY RAMC) Lieut. A.NEWTON-BRADY RAMC appointed Sanitary Officer.	SDS
	8		Routine improvement.	SDS
	9		Routine improvements.	SDS
	10	3pm	O.C. and Capt. CRABB attend a Conference of O.C. F.d Amb's Col. will the	SDS

Army Form C. 2118.

of O.C. 97"(C.P.) Field Ambulance

WAR DIARY
or
INTELLIGENCE SUMMARY.
(Erase heading not required.)

May 1917, Sheet II

Instructions regarding War Diaries and Intelligence Summaries are contained in F.S. Regs., Part II. and the Staff Manual respectively. Title pages will be prepared in manuscript.

Place	Date	Hour	Summary of Events and Information	Remarks and references to Appendices
BACHIMONT	10	3/pm	Lieut Secombe in Command, Proceeds on leave to the A.D.M.S.	2 Ds.
	11	-	Routine	S.O.S
	12	3/pm	Concluded 1 week's training by 'C' Section. Section inspected by C.O.	S.O.S
	13	7 pm	C Section relieves B Section in Fd Amb.ce Hospital.	S.O.S
	14		B Section commence training.	S.O.S
	15	9 am	Lieut. D.L. DAVIES detailed for temporary duty with Divisional Train. F.A. visited by MAJ-GEN. WILLIAMS, G.O.C. 30th Div.n	S.O.S
	16	11 am	A.D.M.S. visits Fd Amb.ce Capt. C.W. BOND, R.A.M.C. departed for England on contract leave	S.O.S
	17	4.45pm	Fd Amb.ce visited by Col. O.R.A. JULIAN, A.M.S., D.D.M.S. XIX Corps and A.D.M.S. 30th Div.n	3 Ds. S.C. 2 Ds. A.C. 2 Ds.
	18		Routine	
	19		Routine	
ECOIVRES	20	9 am	Fd Amb.ce moved via Rougefay, Conchy, Avrochet, Flers to ECOIVRES	S.O.S
CONTEVILLE	21	8.30 am	Fd Amb.ce moved via Francourt, St Pol to CONTEVILLE. Capt. J.J. WALSH, R.A.M.C. departed to report to A.D.M.S. 29th Div.n for duty.	
LESPESSES		8.30 am	Fd Amb.ce moved via Pernes, Rocklingham, Fontay to LESPESSES. Unit in Billets.	2 Ds.

Army Form C. 2118.

WAR DIARY
or
INTELLIGENCE SUMMARY.
(Erase heading not required.)

Instructions regarding War Diaries and Intelligence Summaries are contained in F.S. Regs., Part II. and the Staff Manual respectively. Title pages will be prepared in manuscript.

of O.C. 97°(C.P.) Field Ambulance

MAY 1917 Sheet 111

Place	Date	Hour	Summary of Events and Information	Remarks and references to Appendices
LESPESSES	MAY 22		en route by the Secretary of State for War - LORD DERBY.	SDS
	23.		Lieut. A. NEWTON-BRADY and two NCOs proceeded to CAESTRE area in advance billeting party. Lieut. D. COZLAN, R.A.M.C. reports for duty.	SDS
THIENNES	24		Fd Ambe proceeded via St Hilaire, Norrent-Fontes, Lambres to THIENNES.	SDS
ROUGE CROIX Sheet 27. 1 in 40000 NQ 27.7.	25	7.10am	Fd Ambe proceeded via Steenbecque, Morbecque, Hazebrouck, Caestre to ROUGE CROIX	SDS
BEAUVOORDE FARM Sheet 27 1 in 40000 K.34.c.8.9.	26		Lieut. NEWTON-BRADY rejoined the unit BEAUVOORDE FARM. Fd Ambe proceeded via Steenvoorde to XENEY Officers of the unit inspected by Sir Claud Jacob. K.C.B. G.O.C. II corps. Lieut. COZLAN R.A.M.C. reports for duty at 2nd BEDFORD REGt	SDS
	27		Two ambulances inspection & gas drill by whole unit	SDS
	28	9 am	Capt. R.L.CRABB. R.A.M.C. and B section tent subdivision proceeded to BRANDHOEK to ad- vance front to take over from 72nd Fd Amb a (24th Div.) the site selected as ad corps main dressing station for lightly wounded walking cases.	SDS
BRANDHOEK Sheet 28 1 in 40000 G.6.D.4.O.	29		Fd Ambe less B section tent subdivision proceeded to BRANDHOEK. Work proceeded with to complete Dressing Station	SDS
	30		Tents erected & general progress with Dressing Station. Capt. C.M.RAISEY R.A.M.C. admitted to 30th DivL Rest Station.	SDS
	31		General progress & improvement. Main Dressing Station visited by D.S.M.S. II Corps. Lieut. D.L.DAVIES. R.A.M.C. reports completion of his CPS at BAILLEUL rejoined duty with Divisional train.	SDS A.Newton Brady Lt O.C. 97 (CF) F.A.

B.E.F.

SUMMARY OF MEDICAL WAR DIARIES FOR 97th F.A. 30th Divn. 7th Corps, 3rd Army
18th Corps from 12/4/17.
7th   "   " 18/4/17.
19th   "   " 29/4/17.

2nd Army 11th Corps from 20/5/17.

WESTERN FRONT. April- May. '17.

O.C. Lt. Col. L.D. Shaw.

SUMMARISED UNDER THE FOLLOWING HEADINGS.
Phase "B" Battle of Arras- April- May. 1917.
1st Period Attack on Vimy Ridge April. '17.
2nd Period Capture of Siegfried Line May.

97th F.A. 30th Divn. 19th Corps. 3rd Army.   WESTERN FRONT.
O.C. Lt. Col. L.D. Shaw.   May. '17.
11th Corps, 2nd Army from 20/5/17.

Phase "B" Battle of Arras April- May. '17.
2nd Period Capture of Siegfried Line May:

1917.

May. 3rd.   Moves: To Bachimont with 89th Bde.
              Accommodation: In Chateau for 3 and 59 sick.
4th- 19th.   Operations R.A.M.C. Nothing of note. Routine.
  20th.   Moves and Transfer. To Ecoivres en route for 2nd Army Area, 11th Corps.

97th F.A. 30th Divn. 19th Corps. 3rd Army.   WESTERN FRONT.
O.C. Lt. Col. L.D. Shaw.   May. '17.
11th Corps, 2nd Army from 20/5/17.

Phase "B" Battle of Arras April- May. '17.
2nd Period Capture of Siegfried Line May:

1917.

May. 3rd.	Moves:	To Bachimont with 89th Bde.
	Accommodation:	In Chateau for 3 and 59 sick.
4th- 19th.	Operations R.A.M.C.	Nothing of note. Routine.
20th.	Moves and Transfer.	To Ecoivres en route for 2nd Army Area, 11th Corps.

Secret.

War Diary
of
97th Field Ambulance
for the month of
June, 1917.

Volume XX.

Army Form C. 2118.

WAR DIARY
or
INTELLIGENCE SUMMARY.

(Erase heading not required.)

of O.C. 97 (C.P.) Field Ambulance

JUNE 1917 Sheet 1

Instructions regarding War Diaries and Intelligence Summaries are contained in F.S. Regs., Part II. and the Staff Manual respectively. Title pages will be prepared in manuscript.

Place	Date	Hour	Summary of Events and Information	Remarks and references to Appendices
BRANDHOEK Sheet 28 1 in 40000 G.6.D.4.0.	June 1	4 a.m.	Officers & Senior NCOs of Bearer Subdivision proceed to YPRES Salient to learn Divisional route of Evacuation of wounded. Further improvement in X corps M.D.S. for walking wounded.	SOS
	2	3 p.m.	hn in Dressing Station visited by Col. S.Guise Moores, D.D.M.S. II corps and ADMS 30. Div.	SOS
		8 p.m.	Capt. C.N.BOND, R.A.M.C. reports for duty on return from contract course Corps X corps	SOS
	3	10 a.m.	Improvements. Col. HERGOD, A.M.S. visited M.D.S.	SOS
	4	11 a.m.	Improvements. Surg. Genl R. PORTER, D.M.S. 2nd Army visited M.D.S.	SOS
	5		Lt. Col. L.D.SHAW, R.A.M.C., O.C. 97 (C.P.) Fd. Amb &, awarded a D.S.O. in H.M. the KING'S Birthday Honours. D.A.D.M.S. II corps visited M.D.S.	SOS
	6	9 a.m.	Capt. C.N.BOND details for temp' duty as M.O. to 30th Div'n Amm'n Column.	
		9 a.m.	Lieut. A. Newton Brady and 6 bearer Squads from C Section reports for duty to O.C. 96 Fd Amb & co at Wamsfling KeMill. Capt. T.BADGER, R.A.M.C. (110 to 30 Div Train) reports for temp' duty S.B.	
	7	3.30 a.m.	X corps M.D.S. opened for the reception of wounded ("Wrecking"). Numbers passing through up to 12 noon — Officers 8 O.R. 346 P.O.W. O.R. 6 Lieut. A.L.DAVIES, R.A.M.C. and 7 bearer Squads reported for duty to O.C. 96 Fd Amb. Capt. D. CAMERON, R.A.M.C.(T.F.) reports for duty from the Base.	SOS

WAR DIARY or INTELLIGENCE SUMMARY.

Army Form C. 2118.

of OC. 97"(C.P.)F.A.Auds
June Sheet II

Place	Date	Hour	Summary of Events and Information	Remarks and references to Appendices
BRANDHOEK Sheet 28 1 in 40000 G.6.D.4.0	June 8		Wounded passing through MDS from 12 noon June 7 to 12 noon June 8. Officers 40 O.R. 1382 P.O.W. O.R. 3	SD8
	9		Wounded passed through MDS from 12 noon June 8 to 12 noon June 9. Officers 4 O.R. 340 P.O.W. O.R. 74. Mr. ORR. Began the division 97 F.A. arrived	SD8
	10		Wounded passed through from 12 noon June 9 to 12 noon June 10. Officers 4 O.R. 121 P.O.W. 0. Lt. MAY relieved by Sir A. SLOGGETT, D.G.M.S.	SD8
	11		Wounded passed through from 12 noon June 10 to 12 noon June 11. Officers 4 O.R. 125 P.O.W. 0. Capt. T. BRIDGER, RAMC returned to Division	SD8
	12		Wounded passed through from 12 noon June 11 to 12 noon June 12. Officers 2 O.R. 75 P.O.W 0	SD8
		3 a.m.	Temp MDS for lightly wounded closed at 3 a.m.	
		6 f'noon	Capt. R.L. CRABB, RAMC with 1 N.C.O proceeded to 47" Division Rest Station at REMY SIDING to take over from 6th London F.A. Amb Co.	
BRANDHOEK Sheet 28 1 in 40000 G.12.6.5.7	13	2 pm	97 F.D. Amb Co. took over I Corps MDS for seriously wounded, BRANDHOEK.	SD8
	14	11 am	Capt. R.L. CRABB, RAMC, and party reported for duty on handing over 47 D.R.S. at REMY SIDING to 26" F.A., 6th Division. Major G. NICARD reported for duty with 97 F.A.	SD8

WAR DIARY
or
INTELLIGENCE SUMMARY.
(Erase heading not required.)

of O.C. 97 (C.P.) Field Ambulance
June 1917. Sheet III.

Army Form C. 2118.

Place	Date	Hour	Summary of Events and Information	Remarks and references to Appendices
BRANDHOEK Sheet 28 1:40,000 S.6,X,11,12,13 2.13.C.5.g	15		From 30 Div HQ. Wounded passed through from 12 noon June 14 to 12 noon June 15:- Off 2. O.R. 100	SSL
	16		Attended conference of F.A. commanders at A.D.M.S. office. Wounded passed through from 12 noon June 15 to 12 noon June 16. Off 1. O.R. 63	SSL
	17		Wounded passed through 12 noon June 16 – 12 noon June 17. Off 2. O.R. 54. Lieut. A. NEWTON-BRADY R.A.M.C. returned for duty c 2nd Bedfords Regt.	SSL
	18		Wounded through – June 17 – June 18. Off 4. O.R. 112. Capt. ON BOND R.A.M.C. reports from leave? on S.S. sick 30". D.A.O.	SSL
	19		Wounded through June 18 – June 19 Off 6. O.R. 86. Capt. D. CAYGOON R.A.M.C. t 2 N.C.O.'s proceeded to take over a site for a Divisional Rest Station at WIPPENHOEK Sheet 27. L	SSL
	20		Wounded through June 19 – June 20 Off 5– O.R. 26. Lieut. T. GWYNNE-MAITLAND R.A.M.C. proceeded on Special leave to England. Capt. S. CAYGOON R.A.M.C. reports for duty. from A.R.S. WIPPENHOEK leaving 2 N.C.O.'s party holding the site. Capt. ON BOND R.A.M.C.	

Army Form C. 2118.

WAR DIARY
or
INTELLIGENCE SUMMARY.
(Erase heading not required.)

O.C. 97 (CO) Field Ambulance
June 1917   Sheet IV

Instructions regarding War Diaries and Intelligence Summaries are contained in F. S. Regs., Part II. and the Staff M. mud respectively. Title pages will be prepared in manuscript.

Place	Date	Hour	Summary of Events and Information	Remarks and references to Appendices
BRANDHOEK Sheet 28 I 44000 O.R. S.S. 9	20		with 2 NCOs and a fair sprinkling of bearers proceeded to report to O.C. 96 F.A. at DICKEBUSCH Lieut. D.L. DAVIES, RAMC reported at Headquarters with 2 NCOs & bearer Section. Visit by Capt. BOYDS party. a/Sergt. P. PINDER, RAMC 97 F.A. awarded a bar to the Military Medal to gallantry in the field.	
	21		wounded forces through from the now June 20 6-13 noon June 21 of 6. O.R. 118 " " " " 21 " 2 pm " 0 - 10 2h.m. h.Q.D.S. for evening wounded closed. Capt. D. CAMERON, RAMC.T ans ambulance subdivision proceeded to TOURNEHEM to F.d. Amb o/c for the reception of sick of 90th Infantry Bgde training in that area.	
WIPPENHOEK Sheet 27 L.44000 L26 d47	22	11.30am	97 Fd Amb. ce proceeded to WIPPENHOEK and took over the Divisional Rest Station Recently occupied by 139 F.d Amb ce	
	23	10am	A.D.M.S. 30 L. Dur visited D.R.S.	
	24	10pm 3pm	Capt. A. CHEPBURN, RAMC.T reported for duty. A.D.M.S. II Corps visited D.R.S. Sergt Archibald a/a 13 bearers reported from 96 F.A. ce being relieved by Capt. Corbett a/a 13 bearers.	

Army Form C. 2118.

WAR DIARY
or
INTELLIGENCE SUMMARY
O.C. 97 (C.P.) Pros Ambulance
June 1917 Sheet V

(Erase heading not required.)

Instructions regarding War Diaries and Intelligence Summaries are contained in F. S. Regs., Part II. and the Staff Manual respectively. Title Pages will be prepared in manuscript.

Place	Date	Hour	Summary of Events and Information	Remarks and references to Appendices
WIPPENHOEK Sheet 27 I 20 40000 L 28 D 4.7	25		Improvement	SOS
	26		Visited Test Battalion at TOURNEHEM.	SOS
	27		Improvement.	
	28		Attended Conference of F. Ambce commanders at office of ADMS 30 Div. Capt. R.L. CRABB RAMC detailed to Company attd to 2/3 Pris 30 Div.	SOS
	29		Routine & improvement	SOS
	30		Routine & improvement	SOS

S D Shaw
Lt Col
O.C. 97 FA

Vol 21

Secret.

War Diary of
97th Field Ambulance
for the month of
July. 1917.

Volume XXI

WAR DIARY
or
INTELLIGENCE SUMMARY

(Erase heading not required.)

Army Form C. 2118.

Place	Date	Hour	Summary of Events and Information	Remarks and references to Appendices
Wippenhoek L.4432.c	July 1		Routine + improvements	SDS
	2		75013 Pte Gibson + 81303 Pte H.J. Fieldman were killed in action. 67431 Pte Wheatley H + 67441 Pte L.S. Roebuck were wounded	SDS
	3		Lt + 2m E&S Rangers RAMC yester leave from 3/7/17 to 13/7/17. Lt T. Grogan Maitland RAMC rptd to duty from leave	SDS
	4		Routine + improvements	SDS
	5		Lt D.S. David RAMC rptd to OC 17 Bn KLR for temporary duty. WO22614 Sandicar with Ambulance. Car was dis[c]h'd + put on tip action	SDS
			MP/077646 Pte A Paton on ASC(MT) Sec dismd and 67303 Pte A.W. Thompson Lt. Car to duty. Was light wounded	
	6		MP/077618 Pte G Paton ASC(MT) du't M wounded. The Divisional Rest Station at Wiltjen HQ+K were handed over to the 56 Field Ambulance	SDS
Hogeland SW754	7		The Field Ambulance moved in two parties for NOORDPEENE during the	SDS

Army Form C. 2118.

WAR DIARY
or
INTELLIGENCE SUMMARY

(Erase heading not required.)

Instructions regarding War Diaries and Intelligence Summaries are contained in F. S. Regs., Part II. and the Staff Manual respectively. Title Pages will be prepared in manuscript.

Place	Date	Hour	Summary of Events and Information	Remarks and references to Appendices
Hazebrouck Sur ISA Y100.00.	8		L/T NOORDE PEENE & turned C.T. RUMINGHEM. Temporary command hospital out CW for ord of 69 Brigade	
	9		CAPT CRABB w/p To from a.T. the S.A.D.M.S. 30th Division	S.o.S.
	10		from 9/7/17 To 23/7/17 Scheme of Tactical training of platoon outlined on the lines of J.T. Cameron - Lt Colonel 4 95th FA 65 Queens w/p To W/F duty Training started	
	11			
	12		CAPT CAMERON D RAMC w/p To to or 19th R.W.R.L.R. for Temporary duty on medical officer/in To the 2/10th RAMC w/from To w/p To for duty	S.o.S. S.o.S.
	13		Major General W.d.L. Williams D.O.E. 30th Div inspected the personnel of the Ambulance & ex-found by the A.D.M.S. 30th Div Today	
	14			S.o.S.
	15		CapT Ac Arthur To Co on O.B.S with Lt. Col C.R. Rimgar w/p To from the am	S.o.S S.o.S

2449 Wt. W14957/M90 750,000 1/16 J.B.C. & A. Forms/C.2118/12.

WAR DIARY
INTELLIGENCE SUMMARY

(Erase heading not required.)

Army Form C. 2118.

Place	Date	Hour	Summary of Events and Information	Remarks and references to Appendices
RUMINGHEM	16		Training & Church Parade. Service in Y.M.C.A. Paris.	
	17		Training Continued.	
	18		Field Ambulance, when on Inroadwance met Lt MAITLAND to lines of bidizy Brigade Sid man. proceeded by ambulance to OCHTEZEELE, MOORDEENE and billeted the night there	
OUDEZEELE	19		Lft OCHTEZEELE & proceeded by ambulance to OUDERZEELE. (amb - Inf hostels formed. That sub division formed)	
MILITAIN	20		Lft OUDERZEELE & proceeded by ambulance from RUMINGHEM ADM'd into FA train, but sub division under Lt MAITLAND to OUDERZEELE	
	21		Took over at 11 am the Sin Road Station at WIPPENHOEK from 56 Fd Amb under Lt	
	22		13 Rank and file reported after being Admitted into DRS & FA	
	23		Admitted to base of ambulance convoys at 9pm Adm'd Lt D.DAVIES RAMC returned from 17 KLR	
	24		Capt Q Cadell reported for duty - posted to report to OC 105 Consecrant Dep	

WAR DIARY
or
INTELLIGENCE SUMMARY

Army Form C. 2118.

Place	Date	Hour	Summary of Events and Information	Remarks and references to Appendices
Withernsea	25		Capt D Cameron RAMC up to TU from 19th RLR & Capt C W Bond RAMC & Lt D Cameron RAMC & Capt A C Hepburn RAMC with 3 line ambulances proceeded to up to TU to be 98th Field Ambulance for duty	
	26		Col S B Moore's DDMS II Corps & ADMS 30th Div. inspected FA & DRS	
	27		Rank: 73164 Pte Dunn was wounded	
	28		Ranks	
	29		m TU subdivision up to TU to be 96th FA	
	30		Lt Davies up to TU to 98th FA for duty with heavy of 97th FA Capt Cameron taking over charge of TU Ordnance attached to 96th FA. Capt W.S. Danks 96th FA	
	31st		up to TU for duty with 97th FA Qn Tu	

S J Shaw
Lt Col
OC 97th FA

War Diary
of
97th Field Ambulance.
for the month
of
August 1917

Volume XXII

WAR DIARY
or
INTELLIGENCE SUMMARY

Army Form C. 2118.

97th Field Ambulance
Volume XXII

Place	Date	Hour	Summary of Events and Information	Remarks and references to Appendices
Witternhoek	August 1	Night	The following proceeded of 97th FA on m/cted journey on 30.7.17. 72459 S/qt Wentworth S.S. 76815 Pt Spittlehouse C.F. 75712 Pt Monk W.G. 81482 Pt Jordan S.H. 48035 Pt Rogers E. 53261 Pt Annie A. 51811 Pt Pollard L. 67375 Pt Slaney 72455 Pt Rees H. 78667 Pt Quadrick J.E. 75114 Pt Bristol A.	S/qt
	2		67311 Corn T.S. 97th FA reported on duty recovered. 67320 Pt Robinson C. 67421 Pt Dalh. 68050 Pt Cons O m/cted recovered. Capt. D. CAMERON RAMC(T)	S/qt S/qt
	3		at Field Amb duty for Temp duty with 3rd Bd/m/A. Capt D Cameron RAMC(T) m/cted for duty to 98 FA. Capt Bond C.W. m/cted GA	S/qt
	4		Routine	S/qt
	5		Capt W.S.L. WAMBEEK m/cted for duty	S/qt
	6		Routine	S/qt
	7		Divisional Rest Station Witternhoek handed over to 2/3 Lowland F.A. 97th FA marched to OUTTERSTEENE & opened for nothing brigade with 2/3 L.F.A. subdivision under Capt Hepburn m/cted from duty with 98 F.A.	S/qt

Army Form C. 2118.

WAR DIARY
or
INTELLIGENCE SUMMARY
(Erase heading not required.)

Instructions regarding War Diaries and Intelligence Summaries are contained in F. S. Regs., Part II. and the Staff Manual respectively. Title Pages will be prepared in manuscript.

Place	Date	Hour	Summary of Events and Information	Remarks and references to Appendices
OUTTERSTEENE SH1 36A F 8 & 93	August 8		Lieut N.C. Rogers RAMC (TC) rejoined for duty	See
	9		Lieut S.W. Fredette V.S.A. Rejoined for duty	
ST JANS CAPPELL	10		Field Ambulance marched to St Jans Cappell area + opened for reception of sick at Sheet 27 X.12.d.9.9	
Sheet 27 X.12.d.9.9	11		ADMS visited FA	See
	12		Routine	See
	13		Lieut DL Davies granted leave 13/8/17 to 22/8/17	See
	14		Capt W&L Wambeek left for temporary duty with 30 K.L.R.	See
	15		Conference of Ambulance Commanders held	See
	16		Capt D Cameron detached for temporary duty with 11th South Lancs	See
	17		Routine. Training of personnel	
	18		Routine. Training of personnel. Sgt T & Maitland left for temporary duty in England on visitation of unwell	See
	19		Routine. Training of personnel	See
	20		Capt A.E. Hepburn left for temporary duty with 3rd Bedford Reg't 67349 P/Cpl ED Margrave R.P. was awarded the Military Medal for gallantry	See
	21		Routine. Training of personnel	See
	22		Routine. Training of personnel	See

Army Form C. 2118.

WAR DIARY
or
INTELLIGENCE SUMMARY
(Erase heading not required.)

Instructions regarding War Diaries and Intelligence Summaries are contained in F. S. Regs., Part II. and the Staff Manual respectively. Title Pages will be prepared in manuscript.

Place	Date	Hour	Summary of Events and Information	Remarks and references to Appendices
St Sans Cappell	August 23		Field Ambulance left St Sans Cappell am & marched to Dranoutre billet 28	
			M36 c 2.2 Taking over the main Dressing Station from the 13th Australian F.A.	
			C. de E. Lt. N.N. Saddington made the command of Lieut N.C. Rogers proceed to	
Dranoutre billet 28 M36 c 2.2	24		up to O.C. 9th F.A. 1-a-5	SDS
	25		Lieut D.L. Davies attd. C.A. from Leave. St (D. French left p/duty 5 Div In Sch. Sch Sanj	SDS
	26		Routine – no movements	SDS
	27		Routine – no movements	SDS
	28		Capt W.L. Wamberk returned to duty from 20th R.L.R	SDS
			Lieut D.L. Davies on duty of B. have sick division returned Lieut N.C. Rogers + a human ambulance staff with 96 F.A. Lieut N.C. Rogers left for temporary duty with 19th K.L.R.	SDS
	29		Lt S.D. Fredette returned from Div Gs School attd a fuller ambulance commander en route	SDS
	30		Routine – no movements	SDS
	31			SDS

L.D. Chanfeau
Lt Col
O.C. 9 F.A.

2449 Wt. W14957/M90 750,000 1/16 J.B.C. & A. Forms/C.2118/12.

Secret

War Diary

of

97th Field Ambulance

for the month of

September 1917.

Volume XXIII

Army Form C. 2118.

WAR DIARY
or
INTELLIGENCE SUMMARY of O.C. 97th (C.O.) F.A. Amb.

(Erase heading not required.)

Instructions regarding War Diaries and Intelligence Summaries are contained in F. S. Regs., Part II. and the Staff Manual respectively. Title Pages will be prepared in manuscript.

Place	Date 1917	Hour	Summary of Events and Information	Remarks and references to Appendices
DRANOUTRE	Sep 1st		Captain CAMERON R.A.M.C. returned from temporary duty with 11th Batt. S. Lancs. Capt. HEPBURN R.A.M.C. from temp duty with 2nd Batt. Bedfords, the latter officer being replaced by Capt. WOMBEEK R.A.M.C. from this F.A. Ambulance. New recourses ward of 18 beds completed ready for patients. Admitted during 24 hrs up to midday O.R. 46/5/1 w.	
"	Sep 2nd		Lt.Col. L.D. SHAW A.D.D. R.A.M.C. went on leave, handing Capt. W.S. DANKS R.A.M.C. in temporary command of the ambulance. Capt. HEPBURN also went on leave in afternoon. A bomb accident again by wounded death of one child & wounding 3 another. Admitted during 24 hrs up to midday O.R. 35/5.	
"	Sep 3rd		Visit from A.D.M.S. 3rd Division in morning. Captain WOMBEEK R.A.M.C. returned from duty with 2nd Batt Bedfords, & post with "A" Section reverse to A.D.S. Admitted during 24 hrs up to midday Off. 1 S. O.R. 25/5/2 w.	
"	Sep 4th		Lieut. DAVIE L. R.A.M.C. with "B" Section hereon returned from A.D.S. Pay of establishment. Rebuilding of cookhouse proceeding. Admitted for 24 hrs up to midday Off.2 36/5 4w.	
"	Sep 5th		Ron time work & improvements about hospital & camp. Sick officers ward now completed. Lecture to personnel on CAS by Lieut. FREDETTE U.S.A.R. M.O.R.C. Admitted during 24 hrs up to midday Off.1 S. O.R. 37/5 2w.	
"	Sep 6th		Captain WOMBEEK R.A.M.C. left ambulance for temporary duty with 17th Batt. K.L.R. Captain CAMERON R.A.M.C. proc with R.O.D., admitted to hospital. Lt. DAVIES R.A.M.C. returned from duty with heroes at A.D.S. Visit from Lt Col DIVE, acting A.D.M.S. Admitted Off. 1 S. O.R. 25/5 4w.	
"	Sep 7		Court of enquiry on death child (see Sep 2nd) returned verdict No 5. Con. not Lot. Routine work & improvements proceeding. DRAINAGE of camp commenced. Admitted Off. 1 S. O.R. 525 2w.	

Army Form C. 2118.

WAR DIARY
or
INTELLIGENCE SUMMARY of O.C. 97th (C.O.) F.A. Amb.

(Erase heading not required.)

Place	Date 1917	Hour	Summary of Events and Information	Remarks and references to Appendices
DRANOUTRE	Sep 8		Lt RINGROSE R.A.M.C. (Quartermaster) presented Canteen accounts at O.C. French Div HQ. Visit by DDMS IX Corps of inspection. "C" Section turned out to A.D.S. to relieve "B". Admitted B/B 15 2w. o.r. 33s 7w.	W/P Roberts Lieut R.A.M.C.
	Sep 9		Routine work & continuation of improvements. In evening visited collecting post, relay posts & R.A.P.s of northern brigade in line. Admitted off. 1s o.r. 39s 4w.	[sgd]
	Sep 10		Lieut D. DAVIS. U.S.A.R. reported from base for duty. In early morning visited relay posts & R.A.P.'s of southern brigade in line. Admitted o.r. 29s.	
	Sep 11		Routine work. Admitted B/B 1s o.r. 34s 1w.	
	Sep 12		Lt DAVIES R.A.M.C. to C.R.E. for temp'y duty. Visit at 2.45 p.m. by Medical Commission from England. Sir RICKMAN GODLEE, Lt Bt STYLES R.A.M.C. accompanied by DDMS IX Corps, A/ADMS 30th Division, Surg. General Sir ANTHONY BOWLBY, C/L BORCHALL, C/L GORDON WATSON, and others. Inspection. Admitted r/r 1s o.r. 41s 1w.	[sgd]
	Sep 13.		Routine work — new alterations in cookhouse completed — drainage of camp completed. S.S.M. RUMBALL A.S.C. H.T. arrived from base for duty. Admitted B/B 2s o.r. 39s.	
	Sep 14		Visited C.R.E. 30th Div & A.D.M.S. re heading of Noon Boustalls & plans for new buildings. Visit from A.D.M.S. in afternoon. Admitted B/B 1s o.r. 41s 2w.	[sgd]
	Sep 15		Routine work. Admitted B/B 2s o.r. 32s 2w.	
	Sep 16		Visit of inspection from DDMS IX Corps. Lieut T.W FREDETTE U.S.A.R. left in evening for temporary duty with 18th Batt. Manchesters. Capt HEPBURN returned from leave. Admitted B/B 3s o.r. 41s 2w.	Lieut Styles R.A.M.C. to France

2449 Wt. W14957/Mgo 750,000 1/16 J.B.C. & A. Forms/C.2118/12.

WAR DIARY
or
INTELLIGENCE SUMMARY of O.C. 97th (CD) Fld Amb

Army Form C. 2118.

(Erase heading not required.)

Place	Date 1917	Hour	Summary of Events and Information	Remarks and references to Appendices
DRANOUTRE	Sep 17		Inspection by A.D.M.S. 30th Division in afternoon.	W. Danks Des Rifle
	Sep 18		Routine work. Admitted O.R. 385. Sick.	
			Captain CAMERON R.A.M.C. of this Fld Amb. who has been a patient in it since 6th inst., suffering from P.U.O. evacuated to 1st Aust. C.C.S.	Reply Hughes
			Routine work. Admitted in 24 hrs up to midday O.R. 355 2 w.	
			Lt. Col. SHAW. D.S.O. R.A.M.C. relieved from Leave & resumed command of unit.	
	Sep 19		Capt Hughes A.C. R.A.M.C. reported for duty at 51st Field Ambulance + O.C.R.E. 30 Div	SOS
	20		A section was returned & sections of A.D.S.	SOS
	21		A.D.M.S. 30 Div visited. Capt Hughes a/c returned from 51st Field Ambulance + SOS	
	22		Sgt O.L. Brown R.A.M.C. with duty with C.R.E. 30 Div	SOS
	23		Capt D CAMERON R.A.M.C.T. washed out & was noted 11 of 11 with Y 91 FA	SOS
			from 19 Sept. Sgt Nc ROGERS R.A.M.C. returned from duty with 19 Bn Kings S'port Reg	SOS
	24		A.D.M.S. VIII Corps inspected ambulances	SOS
	25		Sgt D Davis V.S.A.R. detailed for temp duty at NO 2 Canadian C.C.S.	SOS
	26		Capt C.F. Knight R.A.M.C. reported for duty with 91st FA.	SOS
	27		Capt A.C. Hepburn R.A.M.C.T reported for duty with 96 F.A.	SOS

Army Form C. 2118.

WAR DIARY
or
INTELLIGENCE SUMMARY

(Erase heading not required.)

Instructions regarding War Diaries and Intelligence Summaries are contained in F. S. Regs., Part II. and the Staff Manual respectively. Title Pages will be prepared in manuscript.

Place	Date	Hour	Summary of Events and Information	Remarks and references to Appendices
DYANOVTRE SAT	28		Capt. W.S. DANKS Range Mgt. 1/c Paris on 7 days sick leave	SOS
	29		Routine work + improvements. Enemy a/craft active during night bombs dropped in vicinity of Ambulance	SOS
	30		ADMS visits Ambulance Lieut S.W. FREDETTE USAR. reports for duty with 18th ambulance	SOS
				SO Claude etc O.C. 4th F.A. SOS

2449 Wt. W14957/M90 750,000 1/16 J.B.C. & A. Forms/C.2118/12.

Secret

War Diary
of
97th Field Ambulance
for the month of
October 1917.

Volume XXIV

WAR DIARY
or
INTELLIGENCE SUMMARY

Army Form C. 2118.

Place	Date	Hour	Summary of Events and Information	Remarks and references to Appendices
DRANOUTRE SHEET 28 M/36 c.2.2	October 1917 1st		Routine Hospital improvement	SOS
	2nd		Routine Hospital improvement	SOS
	3rd		Baths returned to duty	SOS
	4th		Visit from DDMS VIII Corps & ADMS XXII Div. Capt Knight RAMC St Francis left for disposal H Q Unit	SOS
	5th		Routine Hospital improvement	SOS
	6th		ADMS XXV Div visited ambulance. Capt Knight - St Patrick. vt at Two frails from H Q cct	SOS
	7th		Capt Danks, vt Patt from ord dear White Lines command	SOC
	8th		Capt Hepburn was relieved from duty St D.L. Davies	
	9th		Baths returned to duty. Capt Hepburn left for Trench duty with 146th Bde R.F.A.	SOS
	10th		Capt Knight RAMC left for duty with 146th Bde R.F.A.	SOS
	11th		Routine Hospital improvement	SOS
	12th		Sgt McRogers ret'd and Lt D.L. Davies to return to duty	SOS
	13th		ADMS XXV Div visited ambulance	SOS
	14th		Lt Rimmer reported to the Ambulance	SOS
	15th		Routine Hospital improvement	SOS
	16th		Baths returned to duty Lt D Davies W.A.R. married to Base and	SOS

WAR DIARY
or
INTELLIGENCE SUMMARY

Army Form C. 2118.

Place	Date	Hour	Summary of Events and Information	Remarks and references to Appendices
Dyarbekir	October 1917			
	16th		Routine Hospital improvements	
	17th		ADMS 5th Div visits Ambulance. Capt Hepburn w/ patient draft for 16 months E. of.	see
	18th		Routine hospital improvements	
	19th		Routine hospital improvements	see
	20th		ADMS 5th Div visits Ambulance. Capt. S.S. Scott reports w/ 5th Div for duty	see
	21st			see
	22nd		Capt Hepburn returns from duty at 5th Div Rec Inf. hosp w/ men	see
	23rd		Bathing returns in full	
	24th		Routine Hospital improvements	
	25th		Routine Hospital improvements	see
	26th		Major General W. de L. Williams CMG DSO Major Gen Ambulance	see
	27th		Paid a visit of inspection & addressed by Lt General Sir Aylmer Hunter-Weston KCB DSO	see
	28th		Routine hospital improvements	see
	29th		Routine hospital improvements	
	30th		Bathing returns in full	see
	31st		Routine hosp. improvements	see

Secret.

War Diary
of
97th Field Ambulance.
for the month of
November 1917.

Volume XXV

COMMITTEE FOR THE MEDICAL HISTORY OF THE WAR
Date 17 JAN 1918

WAR DIARY
or
INTELLIGENCE SUMMARY

Army Form C. 2118.

(Erase heading not required.)

Place	Date	Hour	Summary of Events and Information	Remarks and references to Appendices
BRANDHOUTRE M36cL3	Nov	1st	Routine + Hospital improvements	
		2nd	ADMS 30th Div visited ambulance	
		3rd	Pte MARGRAVE & L/mCpl A/Sgt	
		4th	DDMS ANZAC Corps visited Hospital	
		5th	Routine + hospital improvements	
		6th	ADMS 30th Div visited ambulance. Capt AC Hepburn RAMC returned. Sent Dr Dunn for duties in the line. Conference of ambulance commanders ADMS 9/11	
		7th	Visit of inspection by GOC Anzac + GOC 30th Division	
		8th	Routine + improvements	
		9th	ADMC 10th Div visited ambulance	
		10th	Routine + improvements	
		11th	Capt S.S. Scott RAMC sent to ADMS for movement duty	
		12th	Capt AC Hepburn – duty tonight proceed to J 33 C.4.D. to take over ambulance	
		13th	Bearers + nr duty (?) relieved 96th FA returned to HeadQuarters	
		14th	Routine + improvements	

Army Form C. 2118.

WAR DIARY
or
INTELLIGENCE SUMMARY

(Erase heading not required.)

Place	Date	Hour	Summary of Events and Information	Remarks and references to Appendices
TYRONE FARM M.36.a.9.2.	15th March		Hospital at DRANOUTRE handed over to 15th Australian Field Ambulance. Ambulance moved to TYRONE FARM	SDS
	16th	Noon	Ambulance moved to OUDEZEELE. Personnel & Am. Transport Horse and	SDS
	17th		Routine & march training. Sgt S.W. FRALEY M.O.R.C. U.S.A. ½ of detachment	SDS
			of a collecting post for duty at STEENVOORDE	
	18th		Routine & march training	SDS
	19th		Sgt S.W. FRALEY M.O.R.C. left on 14 days leave for PARIS	SDS
	20th		Small Arms field of march at MAIRIE STEENVOORDE Sul[D]Davis more on duty. Sgt T.	SDS
	21st		Mr ROGERS R.A.M.C. M/att to 17th R.L.R. for temp duty as M.O.	SDS
	22nd		CAPT W.S. DANIELS now licensed on leave to SUSSEX	SDS
			ROUTINE. DE 97th F.A. and DE 33rd F.A. visited WOODCOTE HOUSE & Ambulance & reported the	SDS
	23rd		Lady 24 Donors	
			Inspector of Ambulance Commanders + arrived & remained at "A.D.M.S." office	SDS
	24th		CAPTAIN H. Dunn o ST. D. LLOYD-DAVIS in charge of A.R.P with leave proceed to	SDS
			ECOLE / PRES.	SDS

WAR DIARY
or
INTELLIGENCE SUMMARY.

Army Form C. 2118.

Place	Date	Hour	Summary of Events and Information	Remarks and references to Appendices
WOODCOTE HOUSE I30.c.4.1 Sht 28.	25th Nov		Lt Col Davis MoRC y/c L/Sit ran lines forward to École/Ypres. Lt Col Lloyd-Davis returned on leaf of leave on 27th Div in the line. A horse of 97 FA Ambulance came to Woodcote House from our 1st 152nd Field Ambulance Capt. A.C. Hepburn attached. Remnant of Horses of Sit Do in the line from. of 97 FA. The following amongst preparations of wounded man habited Main dressing Station. Woodcote House I30.c.4.2. Advance dressing Station Canada Shed I30.a.95.D. C60 Shed I31.c.5.4. R/T RAP I30.a.37. Sgt RAP I30.b.56. Sit nr RAP Sit 9.6.8.1. Ambulance lr reien was attached to all RAP's and any post established at Gordon Ho. J19.2.1.9. Tankview I30.6.91. Crematory I31.c.9.3.	S d C
	26th			S d C
	27th		A.D.M.S. 33rd Div visited Ambulance admitted Wounded Officers Mil O.R. 15 P.O.W. I	S d C
	28th		Hospital Impounds admitted Wounded Officers Nil O.R. 9.	S d C
	29th		1 Section of 97 FA Amb. was relieved in the line by 96 FA Amb. m charge	S d C
	30th		of Capt Morgan admitted wounded Officers Nil O.R. 11 1 Section of 97 FA Amb. was relieved by 1 Section of 96 FA Amb m. charge of Capt Walker. admitted wounded Officers 2 O.R. 14	S d C

S D Lloyd
D C 97 FA

Secret

War Diary
of
97th Field Ambulance
for the month of
December 1917.

Volume XXVI

Army Form C. 2118.

WAR DIARY
or
INTELLIGENCE SUMMARY

(Erase heading not required.)

97th Field Ambulance

Instructions regarding War Diaries and Intelligence Summaries are contained in F. S. Regs., Part II. and the Staff Manual respectively. Title Pages will be prepared in manuscript.

Place	Date 1917	Hour	Summary of Events and Information	Remarks and references to Appendices
WOODCOTE HOUSE. T.20.C.4.3 (Sheet 28)	Dec.1		Wounded passing through Field Ambulance during 24 hrs ending noon 1st Dec. 1917.	
			REMAINING / ADMITTED / TO C.C.S. / TO D.R.S. / TO DUTY / DIED / REMAINING	
			OFF. OR / OFF. OR / OFF. OR / OFF. OR / OFF. OR / OFF. OR / OFF. OR	
			126 / 6 / 3 / 3 / / /	
			Lieut. G.S. SILLIMAN, M.R.C., USA reported for duty.	J.S.
			Wounded passing through Field Ambulance during 24 hrs ending noon 2nd Dec 1917.	
			Remaining / Admitted / to C.C.S / to D.R.S / to Duty / Died / Remaining	
			OF OR / OF OR / OF OR / OF OR / OF OR / OF OR / OF OR	
	Dec.2		126 / 12 / 9 / 3 / / / 126	S.S.
			a/ADMS visits M.D.S.	

Army Form C. 2118.

WAR DIARY
or
INTELLIGENCE SUMMARY

(Erase heading not required.)

Instructions regarding War Diaries and Intelligence Summaries are contained in F.S. Regs., Part II. and the Staff Manual respectively. Title Pages will be prepared in manuscript.

Place	Date 1917	Hour	Summary of Events and Information	Remarks and references to Appendices
WOODCOTE HOUSE	Dec 3		Weekly Return of Sick and wounded arriving in No 2 Eastern from 30th Nov 1917	
			Strength Admitted To CCS To D.oS. Died Remaining	
			Off OR Off OR Off OR Off OR Off OR	
			Nil 3 — 1 — 2 — — — —	O.K.
			Maj General N. de L. Williams, CMG, DSO visited No DS. Lieut. G.C. Silliman, R.A.M.C. USA for permanent duty with 2nd No Bedford Rgt.	S.O.S.
			Invalids passing through Field Ambulance during 24 hrs Sunday noon 2nd Dec 1917	
			Remaining Admitted S.O.B. To T.B.D. To Duty Died Remaining	
			Off OR Off OR Off OR Off OR Off OR Off OR Off OR	
			Nil 2 39 2 25 — 9 — — — 1 1	S.O.S.
	Dec 4		Routine	

WAR DIARY
INTELLIGENCE SUMMARY

Army Form C. 2118.

97 (3CP) Field Ambulance

Place	Date 1917	Hour	Summary of Events and Information	Remarks and references to Appendices
WOODCOTE HOUSE	Dec 5		Wounded passing through Field Ambulance during 24 hrs ended noon 5 Dec 1917	
			Remaining: OR Nil, to 66R OR 29, to XPS OR 1 / OR 10, to Duty OR, Admitted OR 1, to Duty OR 1, Died OR 2, Remaining OR Nil 233	
			O/C ADS visited M.D.S. A.D.S. and Bearer posts. Lieut. D DAVIS, M.O.R.C. U.S.A. for permanent duty with 18th Manchester Regt.	
	Dec 6		Wounded passing through Field Ambulance during 24 hrs ended noon 6 Decr 1917	
			Remaining: OR Nil, Admitted OR 7, OR 1, OR 6, to Duty OR 1, OR, OR, Died, Remaining OR nil 335	
			Capt. G.A. HODGES, R.A.M.C. reported for duty	

Army Form C. 2118.

WAR DIARY
or
INTELLIGENCE SUMMARY

(Erase heading not required.)

Instructions regarding War Diaries and Intelligence Summaries are contained in F. S. Regs., Part II. and the Staff Manual respectively. Title Pages will be prepared in manuscript.

Place	Date 1917	Hour	Summary of Events and Information	Remarks and references to Appendices
WOODCOTE HOUSE	Dec 7		Remarks passing through Fish Ambulance during 24 hrs ended noon 7 Decr/17	
			Gunnery — to OCS — to SOS — 6 SOS — Gonorrhoea — Wounds —	
			23 22 29 8 1 9 10	
			Nil — Nil — Nil — Nil — Nil — Nil — Nil —	SOS
			Lieut J. W. FREDETTE, M.O.R.C., U.S.A. reported from leave	
	Dec 8		Number passing through Fish Ambulance during 24 hrs ended noon 8th Decr 1917.	
			Gunnery to OCS to SOS 6 SOS Gonorrhoea Wounds	
			17 22 29 9 1 9 10	
			Nil Nil Nil Nil 1 Nil — Nil —	SOS
			O/C A.Dr.S visited M.D.S	

Army Form C. 2118.

97 (C?) Field Amb[ulance]

WAR DIARY
or
INTELLIGENCE SUMMARY
(Erase heading not required.)

Place	Date	Hour	Summary of Events and Information	Remarks and references to Appendices
WOODCOTE HOUSE	Dec 9 1917		Wounded passing through Field Ambulance during 24 hrs ended noon 9 Dec 1917	
			Remaining / Admitted / Cases / Losses / to Duty / Died / Remaining	
			Off OR / Off OR / Off OR / Off OR / Off OR / Off OR / Off OR	
			nil / 1 3 / 1 3 / . . / . . / . . / nil	£38
			Routine	
	Dec 10		Wounded passing through Field Ambulance during 24 hrs ended noon 10 Dec 1917	
			Remaining / Admitted / Cases / Losses / to Duty / Died / Remaining	
			Off OR / Off OR / Off OR / Off OR / Off OR / Off OR / Off OR	
			nil / . 8 / . 8 / . 7 / . 1 / . . / nil	£28
			Lieut. N.C. ROGERS, R.A.M.C. reported from 17 Kings L'pool Regt.	

Army Form C. 2118.

WAR DIARY
or
INTELLIGENCE SUMMARY
(Erase heading not required.)

97 (?) Field Ambulance

Instructions regarding War Diaries and Intelligence Summaries are contained in F. S. Regs., Part II. and the Staff Manual respectively. Title Pages will be prepared in manuscript.

Place	Date	Hour	Summary of Events and Information	Remarks and references to Appendices
WOODCOTE HOUSE	1917 Dec 11		Received convoy from 1st Ambulance convoy to be taken over 11 Dec 1917.	
			Evening / Arrived / S.CC / Cot.S / S.Duty / Diet / Summary	
			Off / OR / Off / OR / Off / OR / Off / OR	
			Nil / 7 / / 5 / / 2 / / / Nil	
			Adams work M.D.S.	
			Capt. G.A. HODGES, R.A.M.C. for temporary duty with 2nd Bn Wilts Regt.	
	Dec 12		Received convoy from 1st Ambulance convoy to be taken over 12 Dec 1917.	
			Evening / Admitted / S.CC / Cot.S / S.Duty / Diet / Summary	
			Off / OR / Off / OR / Off / OR / Off / OR	
			1.0 / / / 3 / / 3 / / / Nil	
			Lieut. N.C. ROGERS, R.A.M.C. for temporary duty with 17 Bn. Manchester Regt.	

Army Form C. 2118.

WAR DIARY
or
INTELLIGENCE SUMMARY

(Erase heading not required.)

97 (CP) Field Ambce

Instructions regarding War Diaries and Intelligence Summaries are contained in F. S. Regs., Part II. and the Staff Manual respectively. Title Pages will be prepared in manuscript.

Place	Date	Hour	Summary of Events and Information	Remarks and references to Appendices
WOODCOTE HOUSE	Dec 13 1917		Wounded passing through Field Ambulance during 24 hrs Ended noon 13 Dec 1917 	
				Admitted / Lost / Sick / Died / Remaining	
			Remaining Off / OR — Off / OR — Off / OR — Off / OR — Off / OR	
			1/16 — 2 / 13 — . / 2 — . / 7 — . / 6 — . / . — Nil	
				31
			D.D.M.S. II Corps visited M.D.S. and A.D.S.	
	Dec 14		Wounded passing through Field Ambulance during 24 hrs Ended noon 14 Dec 1917	
			Remaining / Admitted / Sick / To Duty / Died / Remaining	
			Off / OR — Off / OR — Off / OR — Off / OR — Off / OR — Off / OR	
			1/16 — . / 2 — . / 2 — . / 8 — . / . — . / Nil	
			Routine	31

Army Form C. 2118.

WAR DIARY
or
INTELLIGENCE SUMMARY

(Erase heading not required.)

Instructions regarding War Diaries and Intelligence Summaries are contained in F. S. Regs., Part II. and the Staff Manual respectively. Title Pages will be prepared in manuscript.

97(A) Field Amb

Place	Date 1917	Hour	Summary of Events and Information											Remarks and references to Appendices
WOOLCOTS HOUSE	Dec 15		Wounds & Injury through Fire Ambulance during 24 hrs Sickness											15th Dec 1917
			Summary		Intended		L.o.C.		to duty		Died			Remarks
			off	o.r.	off	o.r.	off	o.r.	off	o.r.	off	o.r.		
			nil			15		10		4		1		nil
			Routine											S.O.S.
			Numbers passing through Field Ambulance during 24 hrs Sickness											16th Dec 1917
			Summary		Intended		w.c.c.		to duty		Died		Adj	Remarks
			off	o.r.	off	o.r.	off	o.r.	off	o.r.	off	o.r.		
Dec 16			nil		1	11	1	6		3		2		nil
			Routine											S.O.S.

Army Form C. 2118.

WAR DIARY
or
INTELLIGENCE SUMMARY
(Erase heading not required.)

97 (C.P) Field Ambce

Instructions regarding War Diaries and Intelligence Summaries are contained in F. S. Regs., Part II. and the Staff Manual respectively. Title Pages will be prepared in manuscript.

Place	Date 1917	Hour	Summary of Events and Information	Remarks and references to Appendices
WOODCOTE HOUSE	Dec 17		Wounded passing through Field Ambulance during 24 hrs ended noon 17 Dec 1917.	
			<table><tr><td colspan=2>Remaining</td><td colspan=2>Admitted</td><td colspan=2>L.C.C.S</td><td colspan=2>S.O.R.A</td><td colspan=2>L.Duty</td><td>Died</td><td>Remaining</td></tr><tr><td>off</td><td>OR</td><td>off</td><td>OR</td><td>off</td><td>OR</td><td>off</td><td>OR</td><td>off</td><td>OR</td><td></td><td></td></tr><tr><td>nil</td><td></td><td>1</td><td>16</td><td></td><td>9</td><td></td><td>5</td><td></td><td>1</td><td>2</td><td>nil</td></tr></table>	S.O.S
			Routine	
	Dec 18		Wounded passing through Field Ambulance during 24 hrs ended noon 18 Dec 1917.	
			<table><tr><td colspan=2>Remaining</td><td colspan=2>Admitted</td><td colspan=2>L.C.C.S</td><td colspan=2>S.O.R.A</td><td colspan=2>L.Duty</td><td>Died</td><td>Remaining</td></tr><tr><td>off</td><td>OR</td><td>off</td><td>OR</td><td>off</td><td>OR</td><td>off</td><td>OR</td><td>off</td><td>OR</td><td></td><td></td></tr><tr><td>nil</td><td></td><td></td><td>5</td><td></td><td>7</td><td></td><td>1</td><td></td><td></td><td></td><td>nil</td></tr></table>	
			A.D.M.S visited M.D.S	S.O.S

WAR DIARY or INTELLIGENCE SUMMARY

Army Form C. 2118.

97 (C?) Field Ambulance

Place	Date 1917	Hour	Summary of Events and Information	Remarks and references to Appendices
WOODCOTE HOUSE	Dec 19		Recruits passing through Field Ambulance during the twelve hours ending noon 19th Dec 1917.	
			Remaining / Admitted / To S.S.1 / To Duty / Remaining	
			off ors / off ors / off ors / off ors / off ors	Remanant
			nil 246 / — 8 / — — / — — / — —	nil
			Lieut. D.L. DAVIES, R.A.M.C. for temporary duty with 20th Bn. Kings Lpool Regt.	301
	Dec 20		Inmates Passing through the Ambulance during the twelve hours ending noon 20th Dec 1917.	
			Remaining / Admitted / To S.S.1 / To Duty / Remaining	
			off ors / off ors / off ors / off ors / off ors	Remanant
			nil 10 / — 9 / — — / — 1 / — —	nil S.S.
			A.D.M.S. visited M.D.S., A.D.S. and Bearer posts. Capt. H.B. JONES, R.A.M.C. reported for duty	

Army Form C. 2118.

97(CP) Field Ambulance

WAR DIARY
or
INTELLIGENCE SUMMARY
(Erase heading not required.)

Instructions regarding War Diaries and Intelligence Summaries are contained in F. S. Regs., Part II. and the Staff Manual respectively. Title Pages will be prepared in manuscript.

Place	Date 1917	Hour	Summary of Events and Information	Remarks and references to Appendices
WOODCOTE HOUSE	Dec 21		Wounded passing through Field Ambulance during 24 hrs ended noon 21st Dec 1917	Remaining
			Remaining Admitted To CCS To DRS To Duty Died	
			OR OR OR OR OR OR	
			10 10 7 · 3 · Nil	
			General HODGES, American Army visited M.D.S. A.D.M.S. visited M.D.S.	SdS
	Dec 22		Wounded passing through Field Ambulance during 24 hrs ended noon 22nd Dec 1917	Remaining
			Remaining Admitted To CCS To DRS To Duty Died	
			OR OR OR OR OR OR	
			28 11 · 17 · · Nil	
			Lieut. N.C. ROGERS, RAMC reported from 17 Bn Manchester Regt.	SdS

Army Form C. 2118.

WAR DIARY
or
INTELLIGENCE SUMMARY

(Erase heading not required.)

97(C?) Field Ambulance

Place	Date 1917	Hour	Summary of Events and Information	Remarks and references to Appendices
WOODCOTE HOUSE	Dec 23		Personnel passing through Fires Ambulance during 24 hrs ended upon 23rd Dec 1917. Running / Interviews / Sick / Total / E.Duty / Duty OR OR OR OR OR OR OR OR nil 1 11 1 3 1 1 1 nil Lieut. J.W. FREDETTE, M.O.R.C., U.S.A. for temporary duty with 2nd Bn. Bedford Regt.	SoS
	Dec 24		Personnel passing through Fires Ambulance during 24 hrs ended upon 24th Dec 1917. Running / Interviews / Sick / Total / E.Duty / Duty OR OR OR OR OR OR OR OR nil 1 13 9 4 1 nil Routine	SoS

Army Form C. 2118.

WAR DIARY
or
INTELLIGENCE SUMMARY

(Erase heading not required.)

97 (CP) Field Ambulance

Instructions regarding War Diaries and Intelligence Summaries are contained in F. S. Regs, Part II. and the Staff Manual respectively. Title Pages will be prepared in manuscript.

Place	Date 1917	Hour	Summary of Events and Information							Remarks and references to Appendices
WOODCOTE HOUSE			Wounded passing through Field Ambulance during 24 hrs Ended noon 25th Dec 1917							
			Remaining	Admitted	L.C.C.	L.O.R.D.	L.Duty	Died	Remaining	
			Off OR	Off OR	Off OR	Off OR	Off OR			
	Dec 25		Nil	. 5	. 5	. .	. .		Nil	ssd
			Routine.							
			Wounded passing through Field Ambulance during 24 hrs Ended noon 26th Dec 1917							
			Remaining	Admitted	L.C.C.	L.O.R.D.	L.Duty	Died	Remaining	
			Off OR	Off OR	Off OR	Off OR	Off OR			
	Dec 26		Nil	. 9	. 8	. 1	. .		Nil	ssd
			Routine.							

Army Form C. 2118.

WAR DIARY
or
INTELLIGENCE SUMMARY

(Erase heading not required.)

96 (CP) Field Ambce

Place	Date 1917	Hour	Summary of Events and Information	Remarks and references to Appendices
WOODCOTE HOUSE	Dec 27		Inpatients from previous though Field Ambulance during today. R&SS upon 27 Dec 1917	
			Remaining / Admitted / Local / L.of C / S.S.Dely / R&SS / Died / Remarks	
			Off OR / Off OR / Off OR / Off OR / Off OR / Off OR	
			Nil / 2 10 / 4 8 / . . / . . / . . / . . / Nil	
			Routine	
				SD
			Inpatients remaining in this Field Ambulance during this 24 hours ending noon 28 Dec 1917	
			Remaining / Admitted / Local / L.of C / S.S.Dely / R&RS / Died / Remarks	
			Off OR / Off OR / Off OR / Off OR / Off OR / Off OR	
	Dec 28		Nil 16 / . 16 / 4 8 / 9 8 / . . / . 2 / . . / Nil	

Capt. G.A. HODGES, R.A.M.C. reported from 2nd Bn Wilts Regt.
Lieut. J.W. FREDETTE, M.O.R.C. U.S.A. reported from 2nd Bn Bedfords Regt.   SD

Army Form C. 2118.

WAR DIARY
or
INTELLIGENCE SUMMARY

(Erase heading not required.)

97 (CD) Field Ambulance

Instructions regarding War Diaries and Intelligence Summaries are contained in F. S. Regs., Part II. and the Staff Manual respectively. Title Pages will be prepared in manuscript.

Place	Date 1917	Hour	Summary of Events and Information	Remarks and references to Appendices
WOODCOTE HOUSE	Dec 29		Wounded passing through Field Ambulance during 24 hrs English noon 29 Dec 1917 Remaining / Admitted / To CCS / To Field Amb / Remaining Off OR / Off OR / Off OR / Off OR / Off OR nil / . 12 / . 4 / . 5 / nil Routine	2 ST
	Dec 30		Wounded passing through Field Ambulance during 24 hrs ended noon 30 Dec 1917 Remaining / Admitted / To CCS / To Field Amb / Remaining Off OR / Off OR / Off OR / Off OR / Off OR nil . / . 3 / . 3 / . . / nil . ADMS 30 Division ADMS 90 Division } visited MDS.	Gd

Army Form C. 2118.

WAR DIARY
or
INTELLIGENCE SUMMARY

(Erase heading not required.)

97(6) Field Ambulance

Place	Date 1917	Hour	Summary of Events and Information	Remarks and references to Appendices
WOODCOTE HOUSE	Dec 31		Strength Transport, Details, Field Ambulance during the Quarter ending 31 Dec 1917 — Summary Off OR / Details Off OR / L.OOS Off OR / L.STRS Off OR / L.Oals Off OR / Died — / Nil 1 10 1 5 — 2 — 3 — Nil	
			Capt. G.H. HODGES, R.A.M.C. [?] permanent duty with 30 F.Bn. King's L'pool Regt. Lieut D.L. DAVIES, R.A.M.C. reported from 30 F.Bn. King's L'pool Regt. [signature] Lt OC 97 F.A.	
			Horses during Quarter Field Ambulance during ? ended month 1st January 1918 — Summary Riders Dr CBS COBS L.Draft Pack — Off OR OR OR OR OR OR	

Secret

War Diary of
97th Field Ambulance
for the month of
January 1918.

———//———

Volume XXVII.

Army Form C. 2118.

97th (C.P.) F.A.

WAR DIARY
or
INTELLIGENCE SUMMARY
(Erase heading not required.)

Instructions regarding War Diaries and Intelligence Summaries are contained in F. S. Regs., Part II. and the Staff Manual respectively. Title Pages will be prepared in manuscript.

Place	Date 1918	Hour	Summary of Events and Information	Remarks and references to Appendices
WOODCOTE HOUSE. I.20.c.4.3. (Sheet 28.)	Jan. 1.		1st Mounted training through Field Ambulance leaving at one o'clock Jany. 1st 1918.	
			Remainder / Attached to C.C.S. / No Duty / Remaining	
			Officers / ORanks / Officers / ORanks / Officers / ORanks / Officers / ORanks	
			S W / S W / S W / S W / S W / S W / S W / S W	
			S / / / / / / / /	
			W / 10 / / / / / 10 / nil	
			/ 10 / / / / / 10 / nil	
			Routine	ACA
	Jan. 2.		1st Mounted Brigade through Field Ambulance during 24 hrs ending noon January 2nd 1918.	
			Mounted / Attached / Sick / Remaining	
			Officers / ORanks / Officers / ORanks / Officers / ORanks / Officers / ORanks	
			S W / S W / S W / S W / S W / S W / S W / S W	
			S / 1 / / / / / 1 /	
			W / 25 / / 18 / / 7 / / Nil / Nil	
			/ 25 / / 18 / / 7 / / Nil / Nil	
			Routine	ACA

Army Form C. 2118.

WAR DIARY
or
INTELLIGENCE SUMMARY

(Erase heading not required.)

Instructions regarding War Diaries and Intelligence Summaries are contained in F. S. Regs., Part II. and the Staff Manual respectively. Title Pages will be prepared in manuscript.

Place	Date	Hour	Summary of Events and Information	Remarks and references to Appendices
WOODCOTE HOUSE	Jan 3		*[illegible handwritten entries - tabular data with numbers 2, 14, 12, 7, 6, etc., referencing Field Ambulances and units. Entry notes "Routine"]*	
	Jan 4		*[illegible handwritten entries - tabular data, "Routine"]*	

2449 Wt. W14957/M90 750,000 1/16 J.B.C. & A. Forms/C.2118/12.

Army Form C. 2118.

97/a

WAR DIARY
or
INTELLIGENCE SUMMARY

(Erase heading not required.)

Place	Date	Hour	Summary of Events and Information	Remarks and references to Appendices

Woodcote House — Jan 5 — List of Wounded passing through Field Ambulances during 24 hrs ending 5am Jan 5th 1918

Remaining	Admitted		Supported	To Duty	To C.C.S.	Died	Remaining
Off	OR	Off	OR	Off	OR	Off	OR
S	—	1	17	—	—	—	—
M	—	1	17	—	—	1	17

Routine.

aw

La Clytte N.7.c.3.5. Sheet 28 — Jan 6 — List of Wounded passing through Field Ambulances during 24 hrs ending Jan 6th 1918

Remaining	Admitted		CCS	To Duty	Remaining
Off	OR	Off	OR	Off	OR
S	—	Nil	Nil	Nil	Nil
M	—	Nil	Nil	Nil	Nil

Handed over M.D.S. Woodcote House to 62 Field Ambulance.
Moved to LA CLYTTE.
Lt. D L DAVIES RAMC and Lt. N C ROGERS RAMC granted leave 6/20. 1.18

aw

Army Form C. 2118.

WAR DIARY
or
INTELLIGENCE SUMMARY
(Erase heading not required.)

Instructions regarding War Diaries and Intelligence Summaries are contained in F. S. Regs., Part II. and the Staff Manual respectively. Title Pages will be prepared in manuscript.

Place	Date	Hour	Summary of Events and Information	Remarks and references to Appendices
WARDRECQUES E.U. rested (Ambulance Stat. 5th)	Jan 7		Sick Ambulance duty as before. Hours from 7th 1918 [table of figures]	
			Moved to WARDRECQUES. Transport by Road. Personnel by Rail. Capt. W.S. DANKS. R.A.M.C. reported from 53 C.C.S.	A.O.M.
	Jan 8		Sick cases from through the Ambulance. Hours as the card. Hours from 8th 1918 [table of figures] Routine	A.O.M.

Army Form C. 2118.

WAR DIARY
or
INTELLIGENCE SUMMARY
(Erase heading not required.)

Instructions regarding War Diaries and Intelligence Summaries are contained in F. S. Regs., Part II. and the Staff Manual respectively. Title Pages will be prepared in manuscript.

Place	Date	Hour	Summary of Events and Information	Remarks and references to Appendices
NOREDECQUES	Jan 9		Sick Wounded Strong Knopf Field Ambulance During 24 hrs Ending noon Jany 9th 1918	
			Admission — Off 2, OR 16; Remaining — Off —, OR —; To Duty — Off 2, OR 16; Evacuated — Off —, OR —; Remaining noon Jany 9th — Off —, OR —	
		S	nil	
		m	— 2 — 16 — 2 — 16 — — —	AEA
			Routine	
	Jan 10		Sick Wounded Strong Knopf Field Ambulance During 24 hrs Ending noon Jany 10th 1918	
			Admitted — Off 2, OR 14; Remaining — Off —, OR —; To Duty — Off 2, OR 14; Evacuated — Off —, OR —; Remaining noon Jany 10th — Off —, OR —	
		S	nil	
		m	— 2 — 14 — 2 — 14 — — —	
			Lieut. J. W. FREDETTE. M.O.R.C., U.S.A. left for temporary duty with 1/7 Bn. Kings L'pool Regt.	AEA

2449 Wt. W14957/M90 750,000 1/16 J.B.C. & A. Forms/C.2118/12.

Army Form C. 2118.

WAR DIARY
or
INTELLIGENCE SUMMARY
(Erase heading not required.)

Instructions regarding War Diaries and Intelligence Summaries are contained in F. S. Regs., Part II. and the Staff Manual respectively. Title Pages will be prepared in manuscript.

Place	Date	Hour	Summary of Events and Information	Remarks and references to Appendices
WARDRECQUES	Jan 11		1st Wessex Field Ambulance Strength. 11ᵗʰ 1919	
			Embarked / Detrained / Remaining near Calais	
			O.R. / O.R. / O.R. / O.R. Remaining	
			3 / 3 / nil / nil	
			3 / 3 / nil / nil	AEA
	Jan 12		Routine	
			1st Wessex Field Ambulance Strength to the Rouen of Wary 12ᵗʰ 1919	
			Embarked / Disembarked / In the Field / Remaining	
			O.R. / O.R. / O.R. / O.R.	
			7 / 7 / nil / nil	
			7 / 7 / nil / nil	AEA
			Ambulance entrained at STEENBECQUE for move to LE PARROLET	AEA

Army Form C. 2118.

975 /fa.

WAR DIARY
or
INTELLIGENCE SUMMARY
(Erase heading not required.)

Instructions regarding War Diaries and Intelligence Summaries are contained in F. S. Regs., Part II. and the Staff Manual respectively. Title Pages will be prepared in manuscript.

Place	Date	Hour	Summary of Events and Information	Remarks and references to Appendices
LE QUESNEL T.25.b.8.7 Sqt 62.D	Jan 13		Sick returned having passed through Field Ambulance during 24 hrs ended noon Jany 13th 1918 Wounded O/R Sick O/R Remaining O/R Off O/R Off O/R Off O/R S. 1 14 13 M. 1 14 1 13 Move by road to BAYONVILLERS Capt. W.S. DANKS R.A.M.C. granted leave 13/97.1.18 Capt. M.J. LOFTUS R.A.M.C. reported for duty. ACM	
BAYONVILLERS W.2.a.9.8 Sqt 62.D	Jan 14		Sick returned having passed through Field Ambulance during 24 hrs ended noon Jany 14th 1918 Wounded O/R Sick O/R Remaining O/R Off O/R Off O/R Off O/R S. 13 7 5 15 M. 13 7 5 15 Move by road to ROSIERES ACM	

Army Form C. 2118.

WAR DIARY
or
INTELLIGENCE SUMMARY
(Erase heading not required.)

Instructions regarding War Diaries and Intelligence Summaries are contained in F. S. Regs., Part II. and the Staff Manual respectively. Title Pages will be prepared in manuscript.

Place	Date	Hour	Summary of Events and Information	Remarks and references to Appendices
ROSIERES			Soft showers during hours. Lost Runners during 24 hrs below are Jany 15th 1918	
F 9 a 3 8	Jan 15		Runners Officers Off R&S O R	
Hut 66 E		5	15	
		11	15	
			Routine.	AEH
			Est. losses during hours. Lost Ambulance during 24 hrs below are Jany 16 1918	
	Jan 16		Runners Officers Offr R&S O R	
		5	15	12
		11	15	12
			Routine	AEH

Army Form C. 2118.

WAR DIARY
or
INTELLIGENCE SUMMARY

(Erase heading not required.)

97 ZA

Place	Date	Hour	Summary of Events and Information	Remarks and references to Appendices
ROSIERES	Jan 17		Cars returned having through Field Ambulance during 24 hrs ended noon Jany 17th 1918	
			Evacuated / Admitted / Sit Cas / Remaining	
			off / or / off / or / off / or / off / or	
		5	12 / 10 / 6 / 16	
		M	12 / 10 / 6 / 16	AEA
			Routine	
			Cars returned having through Field Ambulance during 24 hrs ended noon Jany 18th 1918	
			Evacuated / Admitted / Sit Cas / Remaining	
			off / or / off / or / off / or / off / or	
		5	16 / 6 / 14 / 1 / 7	
		M	16 / 6 / 14 / 1 / 7	AEA
GUERBIGNY Q.27.6.99 Sht 66E	Jan 18		Move by road to GUERBIGNY.	

Army Form C. 2118.

97

WAR DIARY
or
INTELLIGENCE SUMMARY
(Erase heading not required.)

Instructions regarding War Diaries and Intelligence Summaries are contained in F. S. Regs., Part II. and the Staff Manual respectively. Title Pages will be prepared in manuscript.

Place	Date	Hour	Summary of Events and Information	Remarks and references to Appendices
OMENCOURT. No. 24. A.2.2. 2nd 66 D	Jan 19		Ambulance leaving Kemp Less Ambulance moving ambulance now being [table: Evacuated / Remaining / off / ok — 7 / 7 — 23 / 23 — 30 / 30] at Omencourt	19th 1918 AM
	Jan 20		Sick + wounded leaving through field ambulance arriving in to band now being [table: Evacuated / Remaining / off / ok — 30 / 30 — 1 / 1 — 31 / 31] at Omencourt	20th 1918 AM
			Routine	AM.

Army Form C. 2118.

2449 Wt. W14957/M90 750,000 1/16 J.B.C. & A. Forms/C.2118/12.

Army Form C. 2118.

WAR DIARY
or
INTELLIGENCE SUMMARY

(Erase heading not required.)

Instructions regarding War Diaries and Intelligence Summaries are contained in F. S. Regs., Part II. and the Staff Manual respectively. Title Pages will be prepared in manuscript.

97

Place	Date	Hour	Summary of Events and Information	Remarks and references to Appendices
OMIECOURT	Jan. 21		Strengthenent, Ammy, Korp, Field Ambulance during 24 hr ending January 21st 1918.	
			Remained / Admitted / Evac'd / Remaining	
			Off OR / Off OR / Off OR / Off OR	
			5 31 / 1 8 / 1 6 / 1 33	
			1 31 / 1 8 / 1 6 / 1 33	
			Routine	AH
	Jan. 22		Strength returns Army Korps Field Ambulance during 24 hrs ending noon January 22nd 1918.	
			Remained / Admitted / Evac'd / Remaining	
			Off OR / Off OR / Off OR / Off OR	
			1 33 / 1 11 / 1 1 / 1 35	
			1 33 / 1 11 / 1 1 / 1 35	
			Routine. H.D.L.DAVIES R.A.M.C. reported from leave.	AH

Army Form C. 2118.

WAR DIARY
or
INTELLIGENCE SUMMARY

(Erase heading not required.)

Instructions regarding War Diaries and Intelligence Summaries are contained in F. S. Regs., Part II. and the Staff Manual respectively. Title Pages will be prepared in manuscript.

26/78

Place	Date	Hour	Summary of Events and Information	Remarks and references to Appendices
OMENCOURT			Strength Return & State Appendices Training to be carried out from Army 23/1/1916	
			Strength	Appendices	Strength	Training	Army
			off	or	off	or	off	or	off	or
	Jan 23		1	35	1	9	7	2	1	35
			1	35	1	9	7	2	1	35
			Routine								AM
			Strength Return & State Appendices Training to be carried out from Army 24/1/1916	
			Strength	Appendices	Strength	Training	Army
			off	or	off	or	off	or	off	or
	Jan 24	S	1	35	1	8	4	2	1	37
		M	1	35	1	8	4	2	1	37
			Routine								AM

Army Form C. 2118.

WAR DIARY
or
INTELLIGENCE SUMMARY

(Erase heading not required.)

Instructions regarding War Diaries and Intelligence Summaries are contained in F. S. Regs., Part II. and the Staff Manual respectively. Title Pages will be prepared in manuscript.

97/74

Place	Date	Hour	Summary of Events and Information									Remarks and references to Appendices
OMENCOURT			Sick & Wounded passing through Field Ambulance during 24 hrs ended noon Jany 25th 1918									
				Wounded		Admitted		Sick		Evacuated	Remaining	
				off	or	off	or	off	or	off	or	
	Jan 25	S		1	37	1	8	1	1	1	3	41
		N		1	37	1	8	1	1	1	3	41
			Routine									ACH
			Sick & Wounded passing through Field Ambulance during 24 hours noon Jany 26th 1918									
				Wounded		Admitted		Sick		Evacuated	Remaining	
				off	or	off	or	off	or	off	or	
	Jan 26	S		1	41	1	12	1	7	1	2	44
		N		1	41	1	12	1	7	1	2	44
			Routine									ACH

2449 Wt. W14957/M90 750,000 1/16 J.B.C. & A. Forms/C.2118/12.

Army Form C. 2118.

97th F.A.

WAR DIARY
or
INTELLIGENCE SUMMARY
(Erase heading not required.)

Instructions regarding War Diaries and Intelligence Summaries are contained in F. S. Regs., Part II. and the Staff Manual respectively. Title Pages will be prepared in manuscript.

Place	Date	Hour	Summary of Events and Information	Remarks and references to Appendices
CHAUNY. A26.a.2.6 Sheet 70D	Jan 27		The retirement journey across Field Ambulances during 24 hrs ended noon Jan 27th 1918	
			Evacuated Strether Sick Sick Injured on off on off on off on off on off Remaining	28
			5 1 44 1 17 1 15 1 12 1 28	
			2 1 44 1 17 1 15 1 12 1 28	
			Take over M.D.S. from 2/1/3 French Field Ambulance.	
			Routine.	AAH
	Jan 28		Sick and injured passing through Field Ambulances during 24 hrs ended noon Jan 28th 1918	
			Evacuated Stretcher Sick Injured on off on off on off on off on off Remaining	30
			3 1 28 1 2 1 0 1 0 1 30	
			1 1 28 1 2 1 0 1 0 1 30	
			Routine	AAH

Army Form C. 2118.

WAR DIARY
or
INTELLIGENCE SUMMARY

(Erase heading not required.)

Instructions regarding War Diaries and Intelligence Summaries are contained in F. S. Regs., Part II. and the Staff Manual respectively. Title Pages will be prepared in manuscript.

97/76

Place	Date	Hour	Summary of Events and Information	Remarks and references to Appendices
CHAUNY			Last returns having brought Field Ambulance strength to her establishment from Jany 29th 1918.	
			Reinforcements / Admitted / Sick / Duty / To Duty / Remaining	
			off / or / off / or / off / or / off / or / off / or	
	Jan 29		5 / 1 / 30 / 1 / 9 / 2 / 1 / 3 / 1 / 34	
	"		/ 1 / 30 / / 9 / / 2 / / 1 / / 34	
			Capt. H.B. Jones R.A.M.C. for permanent duty with 2 Bn. Bedfordshire Regt.	AAA
			Last returns having brought Field Ambulance strength to her establishment from Jany 30th 1918.	
			Remaining / Admitted / Sick / Duty / To Duty / Remaining	
			off / or / off / or / off / or / off / or / off / or	
	Jan 30		1 / 34 / 1 / 11 / / 2 / / 2 / 2 / 43	
	"		1 / 34 / / 11 / / / / / 2 / 43	
			Routine.	
			Enemy aircraft dropped bombs in vicinity of M.D.S.	AAA

Army Form C. 2118.

97 76

WAR DIARY
or
INTELLIGENCE SUMMARY
(Erase heading not required.)

Instructions regarding War Diaries and Intelligence Summaries are contained in F. S. Regs., Part II and the Staff Manual respectively. Title Pages will be prepared in manuscript.

Place	Date	Hour	Summary of Events and Information	Remarks and references to Appendices
CHAUNY	Jan. 31		Sick returns passing through Field Ambulances during 24 hours ended 9 a.m. 31st 1918.	
			Wounded / Sick / Admitted / Remaining	
			off / OR / off / OR / off / OR / off / OR	
		5	2 / 43 / / / 5 / / / 1 / / / 5 / 42	
		"	/ / / 1 / / 5 / / 3 / 1 / / / 1 / 42	
		"	2 / 43 / 1 / 10 / x / 4 / ✗Died 1 / 6 / 2 / 42	
			Routine.	
			Sick returns passing through Field Ambulances during 24 hours ended (unreadable)	OH
			Wounded / Sick / Admitted / Remaining	
			off / OR / off / OR / off / OR / off / OR	
		"		
		"		

A. C. Stephen Capt.
O.C. 97 FA.

A.C. Stephen Capt.
O.C. 97 FA.
Feby 1st 1918

COMMITTEE FOR THE
MEDICAL HISTORY OF THE WAR
Date -8 APR 1918

WAR DIARY or INTELLIGENCE SUMMARY

Army Form C. 2118.

Volume XXVIII
97 Fd Amb
97 F.A.

Place	Date Hour	Summary of Events and Information	Remarks and references to Appendices
CHAUNY 26.a.2.6. Sheet 70D	1918 Feb 1.	Sick & wounded passing through Field Ambulances during 24 hrs ended noon Feby 1st/18	
		Remained / Admitted / CCS / Died / Remg Off OR / Off OR / Off OR / Off OR / Off OR S — 2 42 / — 13 / — 3 / — 1 / — 51 r	
		Lt.Col. L.D. SHAW. D.S.O. R.A.M.C. leave granted to U.K. 1/15th Feb. Capt. A.C. HEPBURN. R.A.M.C. assumed temporary command of Unit.	S.D.1
	Feb 2	Sick & wounded passing through Field Ambulances during 24 hrs ended noon Feby 2nd/18	
		Remained / Admitted / CCS / Died / Remg Off OR / Off OR / Off OR / Off OR / Off OR S — 2 51 / 1 6 / — — / 1 7 / 2 50 r	S.D.1
		Routine.	

Army Form C. 2118.

WAR DIARY
or
INTELLIGENCE SUMMARY.
(Erase heading not required.)

Instructions regarding War Diaries and Intelligence Summaries are contained in F.S. Regs., Part II. and the Staff Manual respectively. Title pages will be prepared in manuscript.

Place	Date	Hour	Summary of Events and Information	Remarks and references to Appendices
CHAPNY.	Feb 3		Took Motor convoy through Town Ambulance during the hold-over Feb 1. 3f 13	
			Returned / Admitted / CCS / sent / Duty / Remg	
			off OR / off OR / off OR / off OR / off OR / off OR	
		5	2 50 / 2 / / / / / 4 / 2 118	
		"		SDS
			Inspection of M.D.S. by D.M.S. Fifth Army.	
	Feb 4		As returned during Number Field Ambulance approx to the Guardsmen Feb. 4th 13	
			Admitted / CCS / Sent / Duty / Remg	
			off OR / off OR / off OR / off OR / off OR / off OR	
		5	2 84 / 11 / 1 / / 1 10 / 1 118	
		"	Routine.	SDS

Army Form C. 2118.

97454

WAR DIARY
or
INTELLIGENCE SUMMARY.
(Erase heading not required.)

Instructions regarding War Diaries and Intelligence Summaries are contained in F. S. Regs., Part II. and the Staff Manual respectively. Title pages will be prepared in manuscript.

Place	Date	Hour	Summary of Events and Information	Remarks and references to Appendices
ALBANY	Feb 5.		Sick returns from Knox & Field Ambulance during 24 when ended now Feb 5, 18	
			Remained · admitted · died · to duty · off · or ·	
		s	off · or · off · or · off · or · off · or · off · or	
			1 · 48 · 2 · 18 · · · · · 19 · 3 · 45	
		r		
			1st Lieut J.W. FREDETTE, M.O.R.C, U.S.A. reported for temporary duty with 17 Bn. King's L'pool Regt.	SOS
	Feb 6.		Sick returns from Knox & Field Ambulance during 24 hr ended now Feb 6th 18	
			Remained · admitted · died · to duty · off · or ·	
		s	off · or · off · or · off · or · off · or · off · or	
			3 · 45 · · · 10 · · · 3 · · · · 3 · 49	
		r		
			Capt G.A. HODGES R.A.M.C. reported for duty.	SOS

Army Form C. 2118.

WAR DIARY
or
INTELLIGENCE SUMMARY.
(Erase heading not required.)

Instructions regarding War Diaries and Intelligence Summaries are contained in F. S. Regs., Part II. and the Staff Manual respectively. Title pages will be prepared in manuscript.

97-1-4

Place	Date	Hour	Summary of Events and Information	Remarks and references to Appendices
CHUNY	Feb 7		2nd intimation passing through Field Ambulance during 24 hrs ended noon Feby 7th 18	
			Wounded	Injuries (accidental)	Field Ambulance	Evacuated	
			Off / OR	Off / OR	Off / OR	Off / OR	Off / OR	
		5	3 / 49	2 / 8	1 / 2	/ 20	4 / 35	
		7						
		Routine.		
	Feb 8		2nd intimation passing through Field Ambulance during 24 hrs ended noon Feby 8th 18	
			Wounded	Injuries (accidental)	Field Ambulance	Evacuated	Sick	
			Off / OR	Off / OR	Off / OR	Off / OR	Off / OR	
		6	4 / 35	3 / 20	/ 1	2 / 6	4 / 48	
		7		1			1	
		Routine.		SOS.

WAR DIARY or INTELLIGENCE SUMMARY

Army Form C. 2118.

97/57

Place	Date	Hour	Summary of Events and Information	Remarks and references to Appendices
RIMBERCOURT D.10.a.3.3 Sheet 70E	Feb. 9		Sick & wounded passing through Field Ambulance during 24 hrs ended noon Feby 9th	
			Wounded / Gassed / Sick / D.I. / To H.C.E.R. / Died / Remng	
			Off OR / Off OR / Off OR / Off OR / Off OR / Off OR / Off OR	
			S / / 1 / +8 / 2 / 13 / / 3 / / / / / / / / 4 / / 28	
			Or / 1 / / / / / / / 1 / / / / / / / / / / 25	
			Hand over M.D.S. CHAUNY to 2/2 H.C. Field Ambulance.	
			Move by road to RIMBERCOURT.	
OMIÉCOURT N.24.a.2.2. Sheet 66D	Feb 10		Sick wounded & gassed through Field Ambulance during 24 hrs ended noon February 10th/18	
			Wounded / Gassed / Sick / D.I. / To C.C.S. / Died / Remng	
			Off OR / Off OR / Off OR / Off OR / Off OR / Off OR / Off OR	
			S / / / / / / / 28 / / 12 / / / / / / / / / / / 10	
			Or /	
			Move by road to OMIÉCOURT.	
			Capt. W.S.DANKS. R.A.M.C. reported from leave.	
			Lieut. J.W.FREDETTE M.O.R.C. U.S.A. detailed for course of instruction at XVIII Corps R.A.M.C. School	

Army Form C. 2118.

97--

WAR DIARY
or
INTELLIGENCE SUMMARY.

(Erase heading not required.)

Instructions regarding War Diaries and Intelligence Summaries are contained in F. S. Regs., Part II. and the Staff Manual respectively. Title pages will be prepared in manuscript.

Place	Date	Hour	Summary of Events and Information	Remarks and references to Appendices
OMIECOURT	Feb. 11		Sick returned during known — ccs — First Ambulance — during 24 hrs (under) now total 1/ off 11	
			Brought forward	
			off OR — off OR — off OR — off OR — off OR — off OR	
			S — 40 — 6 — 7 — 39	
			— — — — — — — — — — — — 28	
			Routine	
	Feb. 12		Sick returned from Wagon First Ambulance during 24 hours — now total 11 12 13	
			Boys — M. Cologne — off OR — off OR — off OR — off OR — off OR — off OR	
			S — 39 — 3 — — 7 — — 35	
			Capt. W.S. DANKS, RAMC assumes temporary command of Unit vice Capt. A. CHEPBURN, RAMC.	SDs.

Army Form C. 2118.

974

WAR DIARY
or
INTELLIGENCE SUMMARY.
(Erase heading not required.)

Instructions regarding War Diaries and Intelligence Summaries are contained in F. S. Regs., Part II. and the Staff Manual respectively. Title pages will be prepared in manuscript.

Place	Date	Hour	Summary of Events and Information									Remarks and references to Appendices
OMIECOURT	Feb. 13		Sick returned through Field Ambulance. Returns 20 inclusive morning Feb 13th									
				Reinf		BdE		CCS		Buty		Regt OR
				OR	OFF	OR	OFF	OR	OFF	OR	OFF	OR
				5		35		9		3		44
			Routine									828
	Feb.14		Sick returned through Field Ambulance during 24 hr ended noon Feby 14/18									
				Reinf		BdE		CCS		Buty		Regt OR
				OR	OFF	OR	OFF	OR	OFF	OR	OFF	OR
				5		44		4		1		5		39
			Routine									808

Army Form C. 2118.

Army Form C. 2118.

95

WAR DIARY
or
INTELLIGENCE SUMMARY.

(Erase heading not required.)

Instructions regarding War Diaries and Intelligence Summaries are contained in F. S. Regs., Part II. and the Staff Manual respectively. Title pages will be prepared in manuscript.

Summary of Events and Information

Place	Date	Hour	Summary of Events and Information	Remarks and references to Appendices
OMIECOURT	Feb 15		6th Divisional Train. Motor Ambulances having to be used mostly by 8/9	
			Troops	Wagons	Riders				
			Off	OR	Off	OR	Off	OR	Off	OR	Off	OR	Bicy		
			5	39		7		14		2		2		49	
			Routine												
			List returned showing Front & Dust Ambulance convoy authorised from Feb 16.18												
			Horses	Mules	Cars	3rd Line	Lorries		
			Off	OR	Off	OR	Off	OR	Off	OR	Off	OR		
	Feb 16		5	49		6		4				9		42	
			Routine												

Army Form C. 2118.

97th Fld [Amb]

WAR DIARY
or
INTELLIGENCE SUMMARY

(Erase heading not required.)

Instructions regarding War Diaries and Intelligence Summaries are contained in F. S. Regs., Part II. and the Staff Manual respectively. Title Pages will be prepared in manuscript.

Place	Date	Hour	Summary of Events and Information	Remarks and references to Appendices
OMIECOURT	Feb 17		Sick & Wounded passed through Field Ambulance during 24 hrs (ended) noon Feb 17/18	
			Adm'd / Rmnd / Evacd / Disch / Rmng	
			Offr TR / Offr OR / Offr OR / Offr OR / Offr OR	
			S 42 9 4 7 40	
			R	
			Lieut Col L.D. SHAW D.S.O. R.A.M.C. reported from leave and resumed command of 97 (SP) Field Ambulance.	
			Capt G.A. HODGES R.A.M.C. granted leave to PARIS.	S.D.
			2/Lieut J.W. FREDETTE M.O.R.C. U.S.A. reported from XVIII Corps R.A.M.C. School	
	Feb 18		Sick & Wounded passing through Field Ambulance during 24 hrs (ended) noon Feb 18/19	
			Adm'd / Rmnd / Evacd / Disch / Rmng	
			Offr TR / Offr OR / Offr OR / Offr OR / Offr OR	
			S 40 9 6 4 39	
			R	
			Routine	S.D.

2449 Wt. W14957/M90 750,000 1/16 J.B.C. & A. Forms/C.2118/12.

WAR DIARY
or
INTELLIGENCE SUMMARY

Army Form C. 2118.

Place	Date	Hour	Summary of Events and Information	Remarks and references to Appendices
ONENCOURT	Feb 19		Auth Strength Instand/Warrant Rank Outcomes During the Week non Feb 19.18	
			Officers / Other Ranks — off / ot / off / ot / off / ot / off / ot / off / ot	Rept off/ot
			S 39 / 4 / 2 / / / / / / 4 / 37	
			M	
			Capt. A. HEPBURN, R.A.M.C. granted leave to U.K. 19.2.18 – 5.3.18.	
				↓ 28
			Casualties among troops to whom Fd. Ambulance was in technical rem Feb 20th	
			Killed / Wounded / Sick / S.P. / S.O. / I/O P.N. / Duty / Remg.	
			off/ot / off/ot / off/ot / / / / off/ot / off/ot	NA / off / ot
	Feb 20		S / / / 10 / 1 / / / / 4 / 37	
			Lieut. D.L. DAVIES, R.A.M.C. with 1 Bearer Sub-Division report to O.C. 96 Field Ambulance for duty in Line.	SAS

Army Form C. 2118.

97½

WAR DIARY
or
INTELLIGENCE SUMMARY
(Erase heading not required.)

Place	Date	Hour	Summary of Events and Information	Remarks and references to Appendices
OMIÉCOURT	Feb 21		6th Manchester passing through Field Ambulance during 24 hours but now Feb 21/18	Reinf off OR
		S	off OR 41	off OR 6	DFD off OR 1	DFD off OR 35	DFD off OR 9	110 FA off OR 2	off OR —
		M							Jan
			Capt. W.S. DANKS, R.A.M.C. and Advance party proceed to DURY to take over Ambulance site.	SDS
DURY K30.c.9.7 Sheet 66D	Feb 22		6th Manchester passing through Field Ambulance during 24 hours from Feb 22 /18	Reinf off OR 35
		S	off OR —	off OR 8	DFD off OR —	DFD off OR 2	DFD off OR —	110 FA off OR 1	off OR —
		M							
			Drove by road to DURY and take over Ambulance site from 110 Field Amb. Hand over Hospital at OMIÉCOURT to 60 Field Ambulance.	SDS

Army Form C. 2118.

WAR DIARY
or
INTELLIGENCE SUMMARY
(Erase heading not required.)

Instructions regarding War Diaries and Intelligence Summaries are contained in F. S. Regs., Part II. and the Staff Manual respectively. Title Pages will be prepared in manuscript.

Place	Date	Hour	Summary of Events and Information	Remarks and references to Appendices
DURY	Feb 23		Sick Ambulance Census Noon Feb 23	
			Sick Injuries Injuries Sick Ambulance Census noon Feb 23	
			Rank OR OR OR OR OR OR	
			S 5 off in 5 off in 2 off in 110 in off in 1	7
			H off in off in off in off in off in off in	
			Routine Hospital improvements	S2S
	Feb 24		Sick Ambulance Census noon Feb 24th	
			Admitted Injuries Injuries Sick Ambulance Census noon Feb 24th	
			Rank OR OR OR OR OR OR	
			S 7 off in 2 off in 9 off in off in off in 1	15
			H off in off in off in off in off in off in	
			Routine Hospital improvements	SDS

Army Form C. 2118.

WAR DIARY
or
INTELLIGENCE SUMMARY

(Erase heading not required.)

Instructions regarding War Diaries and Intelligence Summaries are contained in F. S. Regs., Part II. and the Staff Manual respectively. Title Pages will be prepared in manuscript.

97559

Place	Date	Hour	Summary of Events and Information	Remarks and references to Appendices

			Sick evacuated passing through Field Ambulance during 24hrs Ended Febr 25/18	
				Regt	CCS	SICK	off	OR	off	OR	off	OR	off	OR	Duty	off	OR
			S	1	15			7		1						1	20
			x														

DURY | Feb 25 | | Routine Hospital improvements | |

			Sick evacuated among through Field Ambulance during 24hrs Ended Feb 26/18	
				Regt	CCS	SICK	off	OR	off	OR	off	OR	off	OR	Duty	off	OR
			S	1	20		22		1		1	8		1		4	31
			x				1										

| Feb 26 | | Routine Hospital improvements. | |

Army Form C. 2118.

WAR DIARY
or
INTELLIGENCE SUMMARY
(Erase heading not required.)

Instructions regarding War Diaries and Intelligence Summaries are contained in F. S. Regs., Part II. and the Staff Manual respectively. Title Pages will be prepared in manuscript.

Place	Date	Hour	Summary of Events and Information	Remarks and references to Appendices
DOM	Feb. 27		Sick evacuated through field ambulance during 24 hours ended May 27/18 Sick Offr — Offr OR — OR 13 Sick evacuated through field ambulance during 24 hours ended Feb 27/18 OR on Off — OR 1 Off — OR 3 Off — OR 34	
			Capt. G.A. HODGES, R.A.M.C. for temporary duty with 19 Bn. X 2pool Rgt.	S.D.8
	Feb. 28		Sick evacuated through field ambulance during 24 hours ending Feb 28/18 Off — OR — Off — OR 1 Off — OR 1 no evac. Off — OR 11 Off — OR 6 Off — OR 43	
			Lieut E.B. RINGROSE, R.A.M.C. leave granted to U.K. 28.2.18 – 14.3.18	S.D.8 Signed W.[?] F.A. O.C. 97 [?]

Secret

War Diary
of
97th Field Ambulance.
for the month of
March 1918

Volume XXIX

Army Form C. 2118.

WAR DIARY
or
INTELLIGENCE SUMMARY
(Erase heading not required.)

97th (1/6?) Field Ambulance

Instructions regarding War Diaries and Intelligence Summaries are contained in F. S. Regs., Part II. and the Staff Manual respectively. Title Pages will be prepared in manuscript.

Place	Date	Hour	Summary of Events and Information	Remarks and references to Appendices
DURY K.30.c.9.7 Sheet 66D	Mar 1		Sick and Wounded passing through Field Ambulance during 24 hours ending noon 1st March 1918.	
			<table> Remained Adm. From 98 F Amb. D.R.S. To G.C.S. To 30 Div. Sak. Coy 110 F Amb. To XVIIIth Corps Duty Capt. R. Stm Henry Remain Off OR Off OR Off OR Off OR Off OR Off OR Off OR Off OR Off OR Sick - 43 2 20 8 - 9 - 2 1 - 4 - - - 49 Wounded Totals - 43 2 20 - 9 2 1 - 4 - - - 49 </table> Routine	SDS
	Mar 2		Sick and Wounded passing through Field Ambulance during 24 hours ending Noon 2nd March 1918.	
			Remained Admitted From F Amb D.R.S. To G.C.S. To 30 Div Sals Coy 110 F Amb Duty To XVIIIth Corps Capt R. Stm Remain Off OR Off OR Off OR Off OR Off OR Off OR Off OR Off OR Off OR Sick - 49 1 16 - 5 - 10 - - 1 8 - - 1 42 Wounded Totals - 49 1 16 - 5 - 10 - - 1 8 - - 1 42 Routine Relief of Bearers in line Capt M.J.Loftus. Reme. i/c.	SDS

Army Form C. 2118.

WAR DIARY
or
INTELLIGENCE SUMMARY

(Erase heading not required.)

Instructions regarding War Diaries and Intelligence Summaries are contained in F. S. Regs., Part II. and the Staff Manual respectively. Title Pages will be prepared in manuscript.

Place	Date	Hour	Summary of Events and Information	Remarks and references to Appendices
DURY	Mar 3		Noon 3rd March 1918	
			Routine	
	Mar 4		Noon 4th March 1918	
			Relief of bearer in line Lieut. D.L. DAVIES. R.A.M.C. reported to Adv. Dr. S.S.	

2449 Wt. W14957/M90 750,000 1/16 J.B.C. & A. Forms/C.2118/12.

WAR DIARY or INTELLIGENCE SUMMARY

Army Form C. 2118.

97th (2/2) Field Ambulance

Place	Date	Hour	Summary of Events and Information	Remarks and references to Appendices
DURY	Mar 5		Sick and Wounded passing through Field Ambulance during 24 hours ending noon 5th March 1918.	

Sick and Wounded passing through Field Ambulance during 24 hours ending noon 5th March 1918.

	Remaining		Admitted from 98 Fd Amb		to DRS		to CCS		To 30 Div Sani. Cory		110 Fd Amb		To 6 Div Sani Coy		To XVIII Corps Off R. Stn		Remaining	
	Off	OR	Off	OR	Off	OR	Off	OR	Off	OR	Off	OR	Off	OR	Off	OR	Off	OR
Sick	-	39	-	23	-	7	-	1	-	3	-	5					-	46
Wounded																		
Totals	-	39	-	23	-	7	-	1	-	3	-	5					-	46

Routine.

| Mar 6 | | Sick and Wounded passing through Field Ambulance during 24 hours ending noon 6th March 1918. | |

	Remaining		Admitted from 98 Fd Amb		to DRS		to CCS		To 30 Div Sani. Cory		110 Fd Amb		To 6 Div Sani Coy		To XVIII Corps Off R. Stn		Remaining	
	Off	OR	Off	OR	Off	OR	Off	OR	Off	OR	Off	OR	Off	OR	Off	OR	Off	OR
Sick	-	46	2	30	-	17	-	10	1	3	-	6					1	40
Wounded																		
Totals	-	46	2	30	-	17	-	10	1	3	-	6					1	40

Routine. Lieut. J.W.FREDETTE M.O.R.C. U.S.A. for temporary duty with 17th Bn Manchester Regt. S.o.S.

Army Form C. 2118.

WAR DIARY
or
INTELLIGENCE SUMMARY
(Erase heading not required.)

Army Form C. 2118. / 3rd (C.R.) Field Ambulance

Place	Date	Hour	Summary of Events and Information	Remarks and references to Appendices
DURY Post 9			Sick report, wounded, transfer of 3rd (C.R.) Field Ambulance during 24 hours ending noon 7th March 1918.	
				O.R.s	O.R.s	O.R.s	O.R.s	O.R.s		
			Remained	Off	O.R.	Admitted	Off	O.R.	Discharged to Duty	Off	O.R.	Transferred	Off	O.R.	Died	Off	O.R.	Remained	Off	O.R.	
			Sick	1	40	-	1	35	-	8	2	9	-	3	-	-	-	53	
			Wounded																
			Totals	1	40	-	1	35	-	8	2	9	-	3	-	-	-	53	
			Routine															SOS
			Sick and Wounded during 24 hours ending noon 8th March 1918.	
				O.R.s	O.R.s	O.R.s	O.R.s	O.R.s		
			Remained	Off	O.R.	Admitted	Off	O.R.	Discharged	Off	O.R.	Transferred	Off	O.R.	Died	Off	O.R.	Remained	Off	O.R.	
	Mar 8		Sick	-	53	-	46	-	X	1	-	12	-	10	-	5	-	9	-	63	
			Wounded															-	1	
			Totals	-	53	-	46	-	1	1	-	12	-	10	-	5	-	9	-	64	
			Routine															SOS

WAR DIARY or INTELLIGENCE SUMMARY

Army Form C.2118.

9th (C.F.) Field Ambulance

Place	Date	Hour	Summary of Events and Information	Remarks and references to Appendices
Duryher	Mar. 9.		Sick and Wounded passing through Field Ambulance during 24 hours ending 9th March 1918.	

	Remaining		Admitted from R.F.amb.		To D.R.S.		To C.C.S.		To 30 Div. Sani. Coy.		To 110 F.amb. Duty		To XVIII Corps Off. R. St.		Remaining	
	Off	OR	Off	OR	Off	OR	Off	OR	Off	OR	Off	OR	Off	OR	Off	OR
Sick	-	63	1	29	-	16	-	11	-	-	-	10	-	-	1	147
Wounded	-	1	-	-	-	-	-	-	-	-	-	-	-	-	-	1
Totals	-	64	1	29	-	16	-	11	-	-	-	10	-	-	1	148

Capt. D. CAMPBELL R.A.M.C. reported for duty.
Routine. Capt. A.C. HEPBURN. R.A.M.C. reported from leave. SDS

| Mar. 10. | | | Sick and Wounded passing through Field Ambulance during 24 hours ending from 10th March 1918. | |

	Remaining		Admitted from R.F.amb.		To D.R.S.		To C.C.S.		To 30 Div. Sani. Coy.		To 110 F.amb. Duty		To XVIII Corps Off. R. St.		Remaining	
	Off	OR	Off	OR	Off	OR	Off	OR	Off	OR	Off	OR	Off	OR	Off	OR
Sick	1	47	1	39	-	15	-	3	-	-	9	-	-	-	2	56
Wounded	-	1	-	-	-	1	-	-	-	-	-	-	-	-	-	-
Totals	1	48	1	39	-	16	-	3	-	-	9	-	-	-	2	56

Lieut. J.W. FREDETTE M.O.R.C. U.S.A. reported from 17th Bn. Hancocks Regt. SDS

WAR DIARY
or
INTELLIGENCE SUMMARY

(Erase heading not required.)

Army Form C. 2118.

Place	Date	Hour	Summary of Events and Information	Remarks and references to Appendices
DURY	Mar 11		Sick and Wounded passing through Field Ambulance	Off (C of E) Lieut D L Davies
			from 11th March 1918.	
			Remaining Admitted to CCS to Units to Duty to 110 Field Amb to Sel Sec C Remaining	
			Off OR Off OR Off OR Off OR Off OR Off OR Off OR Off OR	
		Sick	2 26 17 12 16 2 35	
		Wounded		
		Totals	2 66 1 19 . 12 . 18 5 6 2 1 35	
			Lieut. D L DAVIES. home for temporary duty at 61 C.C.S.	S.d.S
			Sick and Wounded passing through Field Ambulance	
			during 24 hours ending from 12th March 1918.	
			Remaining Admitted to CCS to Units to Duty to S.I.W. to Sel Sec C Remaining	
			Off OR Off OR Off OR Off OR Off OR Off OR Off OR Off OR	
		Sick	1 35 48 26 9 1 8 4 1 1 1 36	
		Wounded	1 1	
		Totals	1 35 2 24 9 1 8 4 1 1 1 37	
	Mar 12			
			Capt. D. CAMPBELL RAMC. for temporary duty with 18th R.L. Regt.	S.d.S

Army Form C. 2118.

WAR DIARY
or
INTELLIGENCE SUMMARY
(Erase heading not required.)

94th (CD) Field Ambulance

Place	Date	Hour	Summary of Events and Information	Remarks and references to Appendices
DURY	Mar 13		Sick and Wounded passing through Field Ambulance during 24 hours.	
			Remained from 98 F Amb / Admitted from / To RPS / To CCS / To 30 Fld Amb 110 Fld Amb / To XVIIIth Corps M.R. Stn / Remained	
			Off OR / Off OR / Off OR / Off OR / Off OR / Off OR / Off OR	
			Sick 1 36 / - 16 / - 6 / - 4 / - 1 / - 5 / 1 30	
			Wounded - 1 / - - / - - / - 1 / - - / - - / - -	
			Totals 1 37 / - 16 / - 6 / - 5 / - 1 / - 5 / 1 36	S.O.S.
			Relief of Bearers in line Capt. R.C. HEPBURN, R.A.M.C. i/c	
	Mar 14		Sick and Wounded passing through Field Ambulance during 24 hours and clearing from 1st March 1918.	
			Remained from 98 F Amb / Admitted from / To RPS / To CCS / To 30 Fld Amb 110 Fld Amb / To XVIIIth Corps Off. R. Stn / Remained	
			Off OR / Off OR / Off OR / Off OR / Off OR / Off OR / Off OR	
			Sick - 36 / - 23 / - 8 / - 3 / - - / - 3 / - 45	
			Wounded - - / - - / - - / - - / - - / - - / - -	
			Totals - 36 / - 23 / - 8 / - 3 / - - / - 3 / - 45	S.O.S.
			Relief of Bearers Capt. M.J. LOFTUS, R.A.M.C. reported to H.Q. Ao	

Army Form C. 2118.

WAR DIARY
or
INTELLIGENCE SUMMARY
(Erase heading not required.)

Instructions regarding War Diaries and Intelligence Summaries are contained in F. S. Regs., Part II. and the Staff Manual respectively. Title Pages will be prepared in manuscript.

Place	Date	Hour	Summary of Events and Information	Remarks and references to Appendices
DURY	Mar 15		Sick and Wounded Evacuated through Field Ambulance from 15th March 1918. Officers	Other Ranks Sick / Wounded / GSW / SW / Acc / OK / GSW / OK / SW / Acc / OK / GSW / Remained 45 . . . . . 21 . . 9 . 8 . 1 . 3 . . 45 Attached Total . 45 . . . . 21 . . 9 . 8 . 1 . 3 . . 45 Routine. S.O.S.	
	Mar 16		Sick and Wounded Evacuated from 16th March 1918. Officers	Other Ranks Sick / Wounded / GSW / SW / Acc / OK / GSW / OK / SW / Acc / OK / GSW / Remained 45 . . . . . 17 . . 12 . 10 . 2 . 1 . . 37 Attached Totals . 45 . . . . 17 . . 12 . 10 . 2 . 1 . . 37 Lieut. E. B. RINGROSE RAMC reported from leave. S.O.S.	

Army. Form C. 2118.

WAR DIARY
or
INTELLIGENCE SUMMARY
(Erase heading not required.)

97th (C.D.) Field Ambulance

Place	Date	Hour	Summary of Events and Information	Remarks and references to Appendices

DURY — Mar 17

Sick and Wounded passing through Field Ambulance during 24 hours ending from 17th March 1918.

	Remaining from 98 F Amb		From DRS		To CCS		To 30 Div Sdw Coy		To 110 F Amb		To Duty		To XVIII Corps R.S.'s		Remaining	
	Off	OR	Off	OR	Off	OR	Off	OR	Off	OR	Off	OR	Off	OR	Off	OR
Sick		37	1	20			9					3		2		43
Wounded																
Totals		37	1	20			9					3		2		43

Capt. M.J. LOFTUS. R.A.M.C. for temporary duty with 148 Bde. R.F.A.

S.O.S.

Mar 18

Sick and Wounded passing through Field Ambulance during 24 hours ending from 18th March 1918.

	Remaining from 98 F Amb		From DRS		To CCS		To 30 Div Sdw Coy		To 110 F Amb		To Duty		To XVIII Corps Off R.S.'s		Remaining	
	Off	OR	Off	OR	Off	OR	Off	OR	Off	OR	Off	OR	Off	OR	Off	OR
Sick		43		17			10		4					1		45
Wounded																
Totals		43		17			10		4					1		45

Capt. G.P. HODGES. R.A.M.C. reported from 19th K.L. Regt. Lieut D.L.DAVIES R.A.M.C. reported from 61 CCS. Lieut J.W.FREDETTE M.O.R.C. U.S.A. for temporary duty at 61 CCS.

Army Form C. 2118.

WAR DIARY
or
INTELLIGENCE SUMMARY

(Erase heading not required.)

Instructions regarding War Diaries and Intelligence Summaries are contained in F.S. Regs., Part II. and the Staff Manual respectively. Title Pages will be prepared in manuscript.

Place	Date	Hour	Summary of Events and Information	Remarks and references to Appendices
DURY	Mar. 19		Soft and wounded passing through Field Ambulance during 24 hours ending noon 19th March 1918.	
			[Table: Sick and wounded Officers/O.R. numbers] Scot 45 · 16 · 11 · 9 · 3 · 2 — 36 / Admitted 45 · 16 · 11 · 9 · 3 · 2 — 36	
			Capt. G.A. HODGES R.A.M.C. for temporary duty at 4th Army School of Artillery.	
			Lieut. D.L. DAVIES R.A.M.C. struck off strength to England on termination of Contract.	S.O.S.
	Mar. 20		Sick and wounded passing through Field Ambulance during 24 hours ending noon 20th March 1918.	
			[Table] Scot 36 · 21 · 5 · 7 · 3 · 2 — 40 / Admitted 36 · 21 · 5 · 7 · 3 · 2 — 40	S.O.S.
			Routine	

Army Form C. 2118.

WAR DIARY
or
INTELLIGENCE SUMMARY

(Erase heading not required.)

97th (C.B.) Field Ambulance

Place	Date	Hour	Summary of Events and Information	Remarks and references to Appendices
DURY	Mar. 21		Sick and Wounded passing through Field Ambulance during 24 hours ending Noon 21st March 1918.	

	Rem'd		Admit'd		98th F. Amb.		D.R.S.		C.C.S.		Sick Conv.		110 F. Amb.		Duty		To XVIII Corps R. Sta.		Remain'd	
	Off	OR	Off	OR	Off	OR	Off	OR	Off	OR	Off	OR	Off	OR	Off	OR	Off	OR	Off	OR
Sick		40	1	32				8	1	16	DIED					1		1		43
Wounded	1			9		1	1			6		2								2
Totals	1	41	1	41		1	1	9	1	22		2				1		1		45

Extra Bearers in line.
Casualties in Unit :- Capt. R.C. HEPBURN R.A.M.C. reported missing believed P.O.W.
Killed O.R. 2. Wounded O.R. 3. Missing believed P.O.W.
O.R.b 23.
S.D.S.

| | | | | Sick and Wounded passing through Field Ambulance during 24 hours ending Noon 22nd March 1918. | |

	Rem'd		Admitt'd		98th F. Amb		D.R.S.		C.C.S.		Sick Conv		110 F. Amb		Duty		To XVIII Corps Rec. Sta.		Remain'd	
	Off	OR	Off	OR	Off	OR	Off	OR	Off	OR	Off	OR	Off	OR	Off	OR	Officers	OR	Off	OR
Sick	43		3	15				25		3	12									17	4
Wounded	2		6	27				6		6	21									1	
Totals	45		9	42				31		9	33									18	5

| ESMERY HALLON | Mar. 22 | | Move by road to ESMERY HALLON. | S.D.S. |

Capt. M.J. LOFTUS. R.A.M.C. reported from 148th Bde. R.F.A.

WAR DIARY
or
INTELLIGENCE SUMMARY
(Erase heading not required.)

Army Form C. 2118.

No 1 C.F. Field Ambulance

Place	Date	Hour	Summary of Events and Information	Remarks and references to Appendices
ROIGLISE	Mar 23		Scott cont. Wounded passing through Field Ambulance during 24 hours ending noon 23rd March 1918.	
			 Scott	Kms 1st Cdn 1st Cdn OR OR 2nd Cdn OR OR 3rd Cdn OR OR 4 OR OR 5th OR Rmng 4 — 1 — 13 — — — — — — — — 1 1 Wounded 1 — 2 — 73 — — — — — — — 1 7 — — 1 1 Total 5 — 3 — 86 — — — — — — — 2 2 67 — — 1 1 7 — 3 84	
			Move by road to ROIGLISE. Lieut. J.N. FREDETTE M.O.R.C. U.S.A. reported from 61 C.C.S. Capt. G.P. HODGES R.A.M.C. reported from Fifth Army School of Artillery.	S.O.S.
	Mar 24		Scott and wounded passing through Field Ambulance during 24 hrs ending noon 24th March 1918.	
			 Ranks 1st Cdn OR OR 2nd OR OR 3rd OR OR 4 OR OR 5 OR Rmng Scott — — — — — — — — — — — — 4 — — — 1 1 Wounded — — — — — — — — — — — — 4 — — — 1 1 Total — — — — — — — — — — — — 8 — — — 1 1	S.O.S.
			Bearer clearing wounded from forward area.	

Army Form C. 2118.

WAR DIARY
or
INTELLIGENCE SUMMARY

(Erase heading not required.)

99th (C.D.) Field Ambulance

Instructions regarding War Diaries and Intelligence Summaries are contained in F. S. Regs., Part II. and the Staff Manual respectively. Title Pages will be prepared in manuscript.

Place	Date	Hour	Summary of Events and Information	Remarks and references to Appendices
HANGEST.	Mar 25		Sick and Wounded passing through 99th Field Ambulance during 24 hours ending Noon 25th March 1918.	
			<table><tr><td colspan="2">Remd Admd</td><td colspan="2">From 98 F.Amb</td><td colspan="2">To CCS</td><td colspan="2">To 30 Divn Sch. Cnp.</td><td colspan="2">To 110 F.Amb</td><td colspan="2">To Duty</td><td colspan="2">To XVIIIth Corps Offrs R.Stn.</td><td colspan="2">Remaing</td></tr><tr><td>Off</td><td>OR</td><td>Off</td><td>OR</td><td>Off</td><td>OR</td><td>Off</td><td>OR</td><td>Off</td><td>OR</td><td>Off</td><td>OR</td><td>Off</td><td>OR</td><td>Off</td><td>OR</td></tr><tr><td colspan="16">Sick</td></tr><tr><td colspan="16">Wounded — NIL —</td></tr><tr><td colspan="16">Totals</td></tr></table>	SDS
			Move by road to HANGEST.	
	Mar 26		Sick and Wounded passing through 99th Field Ambulance during 24 hours ending Noon 26th March 1918.	
			<table><tr><td colspan="2">Remains</td><td colspan="2">Adm from 98 F.Amb</td><td colspan="2">To CCS</td><td colspan="2">To 30 Divn Sch. Cnp.</td><td colspan="2">To 110 F.Amb</td><td colspan="2">To Duty</td><td colspan="2">To XVIIIth Corps Offrs R.Stn.</td><td colspan="2">Remaing</td></tr><tr><td>Off</td><td>OR</td><td>Off</td><td>OR</td><td>Off</td><td>OR</td><td>Off</td><td>OR</td><td>Off</td><td>OR</td><td>Off</td><td>OR</td><td>Off</td><td>OR</td><td>Off</td><td>OR</td></tr><tr><td colspan="16">Sick</td></tr><tr><td colspan="16">Wounded — NIL —</td></tr><tr><td colspan="16">Totals</td></tr></table>	SDS
			Evacuating wounded from line. Established A.D.S. at HANGEST. Transport moved off by road to SAENS.	

Army Form C. 2118.

WAR DIARY
or
INTELLIGENCE SUMMARY
(Erase heading not required.)

Instructions regarding War Diaries and Intelligence Summaries are contained in F.S. Regs., Part II. and the Staff Manual respectively. Title Pages will be prepared in manuscript.

2/9th (S.R.) Field Ambulance

Place	Date	Hour	Summary of Events and Information	Remarks and references to Appendices
MOREUIL	Mar. 27		Sick and Wounded passing through Field Ambulance during 24 hours ending noon 27th March 1918. Sick — Off. OR 0 / Wounded — Off. OR 29 / Sit. & Sev. in Hosp. Off. OR 3 55 / Died — Off. OR . . / Remaining — Off. OR . . Stretcher — B — 3 55 Walking — . 3 84 Evacuating wounded from line. Establishing A.D. Stations (2). Transport moved by road to LONGPRÉ.	SOS
ROUVREL	Mar. 28		Sick and Wounded passing through Field Ambulance during 24 hours ending noon 28th March 1918. Sick — Off. OR . . / Wounded — Off. OR 24 / Sit. & Sev. in Hosp. Off. OR 16 304 / Died — Off. OR . . / Remaining — Off. OR . . . . 16 328 Evacuating wounded from line. Transport moved by road to ABBEVILLE.	SOS

2449 Wt. W14957/M90 750,000 1/16 J.B.C. & A. Forms/C.2118/12.

Army Form C. 2118.

WAR DIARY
or
INTELLIGENCE SUMMARY
(Erase heading not required.)

97th Field Ambulance.

Instructions regarding War Diaries and Intelligence Summaries are contained in F.S. Regs., Part II. and the Staff Manual respectively. Title Pages will be prepared in manuscript.

Place	Date	Hour	Summary of Events and Information	Remarks and references to Appendices
GOYEN-COURT	Mar. 29		Sick and Wounded passing through Field Ambulance during 24 hours ending noon 29th March 1918.	
			<table> <tr><td></td><td colspan="2">Remained</td><td colspan="2">Admitted</td><td colspan="2">To 7 Hosp</td><td colspan="2">To C.C.S.</td><td colspan="2">To 30 Sml Sak. Conf.</td><td colspan="2">To 110 F.Amb</td><td colspan="2">To XVIIICorps Duly Offrs R.Stn</td><td colspan="2">Rmg</td></tr><tr><td></td><td>Off</td><td>OR</td><td>Off</td><td>OR</td><td>Off</td><td>OR</td><td>Off</td><td>OR</td><td>Off</td><td>OR</td><td>Off</td><td>OR</td><td>Off</td><td>OR</td><td>Off</td><td>OR</td></tr><tr><td>Sick</td><td></td><td>8</td><td></td><td></td><td></td><td></td><td></td><td></td><td></td><td></td><td></td><td></td><td></td><td></td><td></td><td>-</td></tr><tr><td>Wounded</td><td></td><td></td><td>13</td><td>212</td><td></td><td></td><td></td><td>8</td><td></td><td></td><td></td><td></td><td></td><td></td><td></td><td>-</td></tr><tr><td>Totals</td><td></td><td></td><td>13</td><td>220</td><td></td><td></td><td></td><td></td><td></td><td></td><td></td><td></td><td></td><td></td><td>13</td><td>212</td></tr> </table>	
			Evacuating wounded from line. 1st Lieut. W.B. MANCHESTER M.O.R.C. U.S.A. reported for duty.	S.O.S.
			Transport at ABBEVILLE.	
			Sick and Wounded passing through Field Ambulance during 24 hours ending noon 30th March 1918.	
			<table><tr><td></td><td colspan="2">Remd</td><td colspan="2">Admitted</td><td colspan="2">To 7 Hosp</td><td colspan="2">To C.C.S.</td><td colspan="2">To 30 Sml Sak Conf.</td><td colspan="2">To 110 F.Amb</td><td colspan="2">To XVIII Corps Duly Offrs R.St</td><td colspan="2">Rmg</td></tr><tr><td></td><td>Off</td><td>OR</td><td>Off</td><td>OR</td><td>Off</td><td>OR</td><td>Off</td><td>OR</td><td>Off</td><td>OR</td><td>Off</td><td>OR</td><td>Off</td><td>OR</td><td>Off</td><td>OR</td></tr><tr><td>Sick</td><td colspan="16">NIL</td></tr><tr><td>Wounded</td><td colspan="16"></td></tr><tr><td>Totals</td><td colspan="16"></td></tr></table>	
SALEUX	Mar 30		Personnel move by road to SALEUX.	S.O.S.
			Transport at ABBEVILLE.	

WAR DIARY
or
INTELLIGENCE SUMMARY

Army Form C. 2118.

Place	Date	Hour	Summary of Events and Information	Remarks and references to Appendices
SALEUX	Mar 31		from 31st March 1916.	
			Sick 9	
			Wounded 6	
			Total 15	
			Evacuating wounded. Personnel now by road to Raileux Station entrained for St VALERY. 3 a.m. night 31 Mar./1 April. Transport move by road from ABBEVILLE to OFFEUX. Sick and Wounded passing through Field Ambulances SOS during 24 hours ending	
			Sick	
			Wounded	
			Total	

16/2902.

97th Field Ambulance

Army Form C. 2118.

Volume XXX

97th (CP) Field Ambulance and W.R.Stn.

Vol 30

WAR DIARY
or
INTELLIGENCE SUMMARY
(Erase heading not required.)

Place	Date 1918	Hour	Summary of Events and Information	Remarks and references to Appendices
OFFEUX Sheet:- ABBEVILLE 14 1/100,000	1 Apr.		Sick and Wounded passing through Field Ambulance and W.R.Stn. during 24 hrs. ending noon 1st April 1918. Remained / Admitted / To C.C.S. / To Duty / Remaining OFF. O.R. / OFF. O.R. / OFF. O.R. / OFF. O.R. / OFF. O.R. Sick Wounded Totals Personnel move by road from ST. VALERY to OFFEUX.	S.D.S.
	2 Apr.		Sick and Wounded passing through Field Ambulance and D.R.Stn. during 24 hrs. ending noon 2nd April 1918. Remained / Admitted / To C.C.S. / To Duty / Remaining OFF. O.R. / OFF. O.R. / OFF. O.R. / OFF. O.R. / OFF. O.R. Sick Wounded Totals Major W. R. Thompson R.A.M.C. reported for duty.	S.D.S.

Army Form C. 2118.

WAR DIARY
or
INTELLIGENCE SUMMARY

(Erase heading not required.)

99th (C.P.) Field Ambulance ENSF

Instructions regarding War Diaries and Intelligence Summaries are contained in F. S. Regs., Part II. and the Staff Manual respectively. Title Pages will be prepared in manuscript.

Place	Date 1918	Hour	Summary of Events and Information	Remarks and references to Appendices
OFFEUX	3 Apl		Sick and Wounded passing through F.A. Australian and ENSF. during 24 hrs ending noon 3rd April 1918	
			Received / Admitted / To C.C.S. / Remained (columns: Off / OR / Off / OR / Off / OR / Off / OR)	
			Sick: - / 7 / 1 / 7 / - / - / 1 / 7	
			Wounded: 1 / - / - / - / - / - / 1 / -	
			Total: 1 / 7 / 1 / 7 / - / - / 1 / 7	
			Capt. M.J. LOFTUS Rame for permanent duty with 18th Bn. King's L'pool Regt.	
			Capt. D. CAMPBELL RAMC reported from 18th Bn. K.L. Regt.	23S
			Sick and Wounded passing through F.A. Australian and ENSF. during 24 hrs ending noon 4th April 1918	
			Received / Admitted / To C.C.S. / Remained	
			Sick: 1 / 7 / 2 / 9 / 1 / 5 / 2 / 10	
			Wounded: - / - / - / 2 / - / 1 / - / 1	
			Total: 1 / 7 / 2 / 11 / 1 / 6 / 2 / 11	
	4 Apl		Routine	SDS

Army Form C. 2118.

97th (C.P.) Field Ambulance

WAR DIARY
or
INTELLIGENCE SUMMARY
(Erase heading not required.)

Place	Date 1918	Hour	Summary of Events and Information	Remarks and references to Appendices
OFFEUX	5 Apr.		Sick and Wounded passing through Field Ambulance & R.A.P. during 24 hrs. ending noon 5th April 1918.	
			Remaining / Admitted from Off.F.A. / To C.C.P. / To Corps Conval. Depot / To Corps Skin Depot / To Duty / Remaining	
			Sick: 2 / 10 / 1 / - / - / 2 / - / - / - / 3 / - / 8	
			Wounded: - / 1 / 2 / 3 / - / - / - / - / - / - / - / 1	
			Total: 2 / 11 / 3 / 3 / - / - / - / - / - / 3 / - / 9	
			Unit entrained at FRESSENVILLE.	SDS
			Sick and Wounded passing through Field Ambulance & R.A.P. during 24 hrs. ending noon 6th April 1918.	
			Remaining / Admitted from Off.F.A. / To C.C.P. / To Corps Conval. Depot / To Corps Skin Depot / To Duty / Remaining	
			Sick: - / 8 / 1 / - / - / - / - / - / - / - / - / 9	
			Wounded: - / 1 / 1 / - / - / - / - / - / - / - / - / 1	
			Total: - / 9 / - / - / - / - / - / - / - / - / - / 10	
ELVERDINGHE B.15.a.5.7. Sheet 28.	6 Apr.		Unit detrained at ROUSBRUGGE and marched to ELVERDINGHE.	SDS

Army Form C. 2118.

WAR DIARY
or
INTELLIGENCE SUMMARY
(Erase heading not required.)

97th (C.P.) Field Ambulance.

Place	Date 1918	Hour	Summary of Events and Information	Remarks and references to Appendices
CANADA FARM	P.18.a.2.7 Sht. 28.	7AM	Sick and Wounded passing through 97th Field Ambulance & D.R.Sta. during 24 hrs. ending noon 7th April 1918. **Remaining / Admitted from 97 F.A. to C.C.S. / To Corps General Depot / To Corps Skin Depot / On Duty / Remaining** OFF OR / OFF OR / OFF OR / OFF OR / OFF OR / OFF OR Sick: - 9 / 1 - / - 3 / - - / - - / - 12 Wounded: 1 1 / - - / - - / - - / - - / 1 1 Totals: 1 10 / 1 - / - 3 / - - / - - / 1 13 Move to CANADA FARM and take over M.A.S. from 2nd Field Ambulance	S.D.S.
		8AM	Sick and Wounded passing through 97th Field Ambulance & D.R.Sta. during 24 hrs. ending noon 8th April 1918. **Remaining / Admitted from 97 F.A. to C.C.S. / To Corps General Depot / To Corps Skin Depot / On Duty / Remaining** OFF OR / OFF OR / OFF OR / OFF OR / OFF OR / OFF OR Sick: 1 12 / 2 52 / - 3 / - 8 / 2 77 Wounded: - 1 / - 2 / - - / - - / - 1 Totals: 1 13 / 2 54 / - 3 / - 8 / 2 78 Routine - Improvements	S.D.S.

Army Form C. 2118.

WAR DIARY
or
INTELLIGENCE SUMMARY

(Erase heading not required.)

9th (C.P.) Field Amb. C.E.

Instructions regarding War Diaries and Intelligence Summaries are contained in F. S. Regs., Part II. and the Staff Manual respectively. Title Pages will be prepared in manuscript.

Place	Date 1918	Hour	Summary of Events and Information	Remarks and references to Appendices
CANADA FARM	9 A/18		Sick and Wounded Evacuated through Field Ambulance & F.D.S. during 24 hrs nothing of unusual effect 1918. **Admitted** from 9th F.A. F.C.E.S. Corps Rest Stn Gen. Hosp. 2 Batt. Remained Off OR Off OR Off OR Off OR Off OR Off OR Off OR Sick 2 22 — — 3 — 1 — — — — — 2 83 Wounded — — — — — — — — — — — — — — Total 2 28 — — 3 — 1 — — — — — 2 88 Lieut. J.W. FREDETTE. M.O.R.C. U.S.A. for permanent duty at Base Hospital No. 27 A.E.F. Capt. D. CAMPBELL, RAMC and 7 squads of Bearers proceed to 98th C.F.A. for duty in line.	S.O.S.
	10 A/18		Sick and Wounded followed thru 9th C.F.A. Field Ambulance & A.D.S. during 24 hrs as follows: **Admitted** from 9th C.F.A. C.R.S Corps Rest Stn Gen Hosp Batt. Off Ret Remained Off OR Off OR Off OR Off OR Off OR Off OR Off OR Sick 2 63 1 18 1 11 — — 1 — 4 2 2 79 Wounded — — — — — — — — — — — — — — Total 2 81 1 18 1 11 — — 1 — 4 2 2 87 Routine - Improvements	S.O.S.

Army Form C. 2118.

WAR DIARY
or
INTELLIGENCE SUMMARY

(Erase heading not required.)

9th (C.P.) Field Ambulance

Instructions regarding War Diaries and Intelligence Summaries are contained in F.S. Regs., Part II. and the Staff Manual respectively. Title Pages will be prepared in manuscript.

Place	Date 1918	Hour	Summary of Events and Information	Remarks and references to Appendices
CANADA FARM	11 Apr.		Sick and Wounded passing through Field Ambulance & D.R.Sn. during 24 hrs. ending noon 11th April 1918.	
			<table><tr><td rowspan="2"></td><td colspan="2">Remaining</td><td colspan="2">Admitted</td><td colspan="2">From 9th F.A.</td><td colspan="2">3rd C.C.S.</td><td colspan="2">3rd Cdn. Conval. Depot</td><td colspan="2">3rd Cdn. Div. Baths Dept.</td><td colspan="2">To Duty</td><td colspan="2">Remaining</td></tr><tr><td>OFF</td><td>O.R</td><td>OFF</td><td>O.R</td><td>OFF</td><td>O.R</td><td>OFF</td><td>O.R</td><td>OFF</td><td>O.R</td><td>OFF</td><td>O.R</td><td>OFF</td><td>O.R</td><td>OFF</td><td>O.R</td></tr><tr><td>Sick</td><td>2</td><td>79</td><td>2</td><td>17</td><td></td><td>10</td><td></td><td></td><td></td><td></td><td></td><td></td><td></td><td>1</td><td>4</td><td>87</td></tr><tr><td>Wounded</td><td>2</td><td>8</td><td></td><td></td><td></td><td></td><td></td><td></td><td></td><td></td><td></td><td></td><td></td><td>1</td><td></td><td>3</td></tr><tr><td>Totals</td><td>4</td><td>87</td><td>2</td><td>17</td><td></td><td>10</td><td></td><td></td><td></td><td></td><td></td><td></td><td></td><td>1</td><td>4</td><td>88</td></tr></table>	S.O.S.
			Routine - Improvements	
	12 Apr.		Sick and Wounded passing through Field Ambulance & D.R.Sn. during 24 hrs. ending noon 12th April 1918.	
			<table><tr><td rowspan="2"></td><td colspan="2">Remaining</td><td colspan="2">Admitted</td><td colspan="2">From 9th F.A.</td><td colspan="2">3rd C.C.S.</td><td colspan="2">3rd Cdn. Corps Conval. Depot</td><td colspan="2">3rd Cdn. Div. Baths Report</td><td colspan="2">To Duty</td><td colspan="2">Remaining</td></tr><tr><td>OFF</td><td>O.R</td><td>OFF</td><td>O.R</td><td>OFF</td><td>O.R</td><td>OFF</td><td>O.R</td><td>OFF</td><td>O.R</td><td>OFF</td><td>O.R</td><td>OFF</td><td>O.R</td><td>OFF</td><td>O.R</td></tr><tr><td>Sick</td><td>4</td><td>87</td><td>1</td><td>24</td><td></td><td>2</td><td>6</td><td></td><td></td><td></td><td></td><td></td><td></td><td>1</td><td>3</td><td>99</td></tr><tr><td>Wounded</td><td></td><td>1</td><td></td><td></td><td></td><td></td><td></td><td></td><td></td><td></td><td></td><td></td><td></td><td>1</td><td></td><td>2</td></tr><tr><td>Totals</td><td>4</td><td>88</td><td>1</td><td>24</td><td></td><td>2</td><td>6</td><td></td><td></td><td></td><td></td><td></td><td></td><td>1</td><td>3</td><td>101</td></tr></table>	S.O.S.
			Routine - Improvements	

Army Form. C. 2118.

WAR DIARY
or
INTELLIGENCE SUMMARY

(Erase heading not required.)

97th (C.D.) Field Amb.

Place	Date 1918	Hour	Summary of Events and Information	Remarks and references to Appendices
CANADA FARM.	13 Apl.		Sick and wounded passing through Field Ambulance B.E.F. during 24 hrs ending 9 noon 13th April 1918. **Received / Admitted / from Offr / A / 2 CCS / 2 CCS / Conv Depot / Gen Hospt / 3 CCS / 2 Bart / Remaining** Offr: 2 / — / 2 / — / — / — / — / — / — / — OR: 99 / 25 / 25 / 1 / — / 10 / 23 / 4 / 3 / 97 Totals: 3 / 101 / 2 / 25 / 1 / — / 10 / 23 / 4 / 3 / 99 Routine - Improvements.	SOS
	14 Apl.		Sick and wounded passing through Field Ambulance B.E.F. during 24 hrs ending 9 noon 14th April 1918. **Received / Admitted / from Offr / A / 2 CCS / 2 CCS / Staging / 3 CCS / 2 Bart / Remaining** Offr: 1 / — / — / — / — / — / 1 / — / — / — OR: 97 / 25 / 25 / 6 / 10 / 22 / 27 / 17 / 10 / 65 Totals: 5 / 97 / 6 / 25 / 10 / 22 / 27 / 18 / 10 / 65 Routine - Improvements.	SOS

Army Form C. 2118.

WAR DIARY
or
INTELLIGENCE SUMMARY

(Erase heading not required.)

97ᵗʰ (C.P.) Field Amb.

Place	Date 1918	Hour	Summary of Events and Information	Remarks and references to Appendices
CANADA FARM	15 Apr.		Sick and Wounded passing through Field Ambulance & D.R.Stn. during 24 hrs. ending noon 15ᵗʰ April 1918.	

	Remained Admitted		From 98 F.A.	To C.C.S. Con Report.	To Corps Skin Report.	To Corps Report.	To Duty	Remaining
	OFF.	O.R.	OFF.	O.R.	OFF.	O.R.	OFF.	O.R.	OFF.	O.R.	OFF.	O.R.	OFF.	O.R.	OFF.	O.R.
Sick	10	65		13		3		6		1		5	6	57
Wounded			1	3		1								3
Totals	10	65	1	16		5		6		1		5	6	60

Routine - Improvements.   S.D.S.

| | | | Sick and Wounded passing through Field Ambulance & D.R.Stn. during 24 hrs. ending noon 16ᵗʰ April 1918. | |

	Remaining	Admitted	From 98 F.A.	To C.C.S. Con Report.	To Corps Skin Report.	To Corps Report.	To Duty	Remaining
	OFF.	O.R.	OFF.	O.R.	OFF.	O.R.	OFF.	O.R.	OFF.	O.R.	OFF.	O.R.	OFF.	O.R.	OFF.	O.R.
Sick	6	57		21		14		3		2		1		1	6	59
Wounded		3			1				1						3
Totals	6	60		21	1	14		3		3		1		1	6	62

| 16 Apr. | | Capt. D. CAMPBELL R.A.M.C. and bearers return to Hd. Qrs. from 98 F.A. | |

Routine - Improvements.   S.D.S.

Army Form C. 2118.

WAR DIARY
or
INTELLIGENCE SUMMARY
(Erase heading not required.)

Instructions regarding War Diaries and Intelligence Summaries are contained in F.S. Regs., Part II. and the Staff Manual respectively. Title Pages will be prepared in manuscript.

Place	Date 1918	Hour	Summary of Events and Information	Remarks and references to Appendices
CANADA FARM.	17 Apr		Sick and Wounded returned taken away from unit during 24 hrs ending noon 17th April 1918	9th (C.P.) Field Amb A.I.F.
			Remained / Returned	
			Off / N.C.O. / O.R. / O.R. / S.B. / S/S / Off / N.C.O. / O.R. / O.R. / S.B. / S/S / Off / N.C.O. / O.R. / O.R. / S.B. / S/S	
			Sick _ / 3 / 60 / 5 / 29 / _ / _ / X / _ / _ / _ / _ / _ / 12 / _ / _ / _ / _ / 1 / 2 / 1 / 6 / 57 / 3	
			Wounded 3 / 3 / 62 / 8 / 29 / _ / _ / _ / 3 / _ / _ / _ / _ / 11 / _ / _ / _ / _ / 1 / 2 / 1 / 6 / 59	
			Routine – Improvements	S.O.S.
	18 Apr		Sick and Wounded evacuated through Field Amb Australia A.I.F. during 24 hrs ending noon 18th April 1918	
			Remained / Evacuated	
			Off / N.C.O. / O.R. / O.R. / S.B. / S/S / Off / N.C.O. / O.R. / O.R. / S.B. / S/S / Off / N.C.O. / O.R. / O.R. / S.B. / S/S	
			Sick _ / 6 / 57 / 2 / 23 / _ / _ / _ / _ / _ / _ / _ / 6 / 52 / _ / _ / _ / _ / 1 / 2 / 21 / _ / _	
			Wounded 6 / 37 / 3 / 26 / _ / _ / _ / _ / _ / _ / _ / 3 / _ / _ / _ / _ / 1 / 2 / 23 / _ / _ / 6 / 55	
			Routine – Improvements	S.O.S.

Army Form C. 2118.

WAR DIARY
or
INTELLIGENCE SUMMARY
(Erase heading not required.)

9th (C.P.) Field Ambulance

Place	Date 1918	Hour	Summary of Events and Information	Remarks and references to Appendices
CANADA FARM	19 Ap.		Sick and Wounded admitted passing through Field Ambulance & D.R.S. during 24 hrs. ending noon 19th April 1918. Remaining / Admitted from 9th F.A. / To C.C.S. / To Corps Conv. Depot / To Corps Shower Depot / To Duty / Remaining OFF. O.R. / OFF. O.R. / OFF. O.R. / OFF. O.R. / OFF. O.R. / OFF. O.R. / OFF. O.R. Sick: 1 7 / 1 / 2 / 1 3 Wounded: 1 8 / 3 / 2 / 1 3 Open as Divisional Rest Station Sick and Wounded passing through Field Ambulance & D.R.S. during 24 hrs. ending noon 20th April 1918. Remaining / Admitted from 9th F.A. Col. / To C.C.S. / To Corps Conv. Depot / To Corps Shower Depot / To Duty / D.R.S. / Remaining Sick: 1 3 / 1 8 / 1 / 1 / 1 8 / 1 8 Wounded: 1 3 / 1 / 1 / 1 2 / 1 8 Routine - Improvements	S.S. S.S.
	20 Ap.			

WAR DIARY or INTELLIGENCE SUMMARY

Army Form C. 2118.

97th (C.P.) Field Amb: Ct

Place	Date	Hour	Summary of Events and Information	Remarks and references to Appendices
CANADA FARM.	21 Apl		Sick and Wounded passing through Field Ambulance & D.R.Sta. during 24 hrs. ending noon 21st April 1918.	
			<table><tr><td></td><td colspan="2">Remaining</td><td colspan="2">Admitted from 96th F.A.</td><td colspan="2">To C.C.S.</td><td colspan="2">To Corps Conv. Depot</td><td colspan="2">To Corps Skin Depot</td><td colspan="2">To Duty</td><td colspan="2">Remaining</td></tr><tr><td></td><td>OFF</td><td>OR</td><td>OFF</td><td>OR</td><td>OFF</td><td>OR</td><td>OFF</td><td>OR</td><td>OFF</td><td>OR</td><td>OFF</td><td>OR</td><td>OFF</td><td>OR</td></tr><tr><td>Sick</td><td>1</td><td>8</td><td>-</td><td>10</td><td>-</td><td>4</td><td>-</td><td>1</td><td></td><td></td><td></td><td></td><td>1</td><td>13</td></tr><tr><td>Wounded</td><td>-</td><td>2</td><td>-</td><td>-</td><td>-</td><td>-</td><td>-</td><td>-</td><td></td><td></td><td></td><td></td><td></td><td></td></tr><tr><td>Totals</td><td>1</td><td>8</td><td>-</td><td>10</td><td>-</td><td>4</td><td>-</td><td>1</td><td></td><td></td><td></td><td></td><td>1</td><td>13</td></tr></table>	S.D.S.
			Routine - Improvements	
	22 Apl		Sick and Wounded passing through Field Ambulance & D.R.Sta. during 24 hrs. ending noon 22nd April 1918.	
			<table><tr><td></td><td colspan="2">Remaining</td><td colspan="2">Admitted from 98th F.H.</td><td colspan="2">To C.C.S.</td><td colspan="2">To Corps Conv. Depot</td><td colspan="2">To Corps Skin Depot</td><td colspan="2">To Duty</td><td colspan="2">Remaining</td></tr><tr><td></td><td>OFF</td><td>OR</td><td>OFF</td><td>OR</td><td>OFF</td><td>OR</td><td>OFF</td><td>OR</td><td>OFF</td><td>OR</td><td>OFF</td><td>OR</td><td>OFF</td><td>OR</td></tr><tr><td>Sick</td><td>1</td><td>13</td><td>-</td><td>6</td><td>-</td><td>2</td><td>-</td><td>2</td><td></td><td></td><td></td><td></td><td>1</td><td>15</td></tr><tr><td>Wounded</td><td>-</td><td>-</td><td>-</td><td>-</td><td>-</td><td>-</td><td>-</td><td>-</td><td></td><td></td><td></td><td></td><td></td><td></td></tr><tr><td>Totals</td><td>1</td><td>13</td><td>-</td><td>6</td><td>-</td><td>2</td><td>-</td><td>2</td><td></td><td></td><td></td><td></td><td>1</td><td>15</td></tr></table>	S.D.S.
			Routine - Improvements	

Army Form C. 2118.

WAR DIARY
or
INTELLIGENCE SUMMARY

(Erase heading not required.)

Army (C.P.) Field Amb. C.A.

Place	Date 1918	Hour	Summary of Events and Information	Remarks and references to Appendices
CANADA FARM	23 Apl		Sick and Wounded taken through of Field Ambulance D.A.D.S during 24 hrs ending Green 23rd April 1918	
			Remaining Returned Sick Deft to CCS to Corps Sick Depot to Body Remaining	
			OFF OR / OFF OR / OFF OR / OFF OR / OFF OR / OFF OR / OFF OR	
			Sick 10 / 3 / 16 / 11 / 2 / / 21	
			Wounded - / - / - / - / - / / -	
			Totals 13 / 3 / 16 / 11 / 2 / / 21	
			Routine Improvements.	S.D.S.
			Sick and Wounded taken through of Field Ambulance D.A.D.S during 24 hrs ending noon 24th April 1918	
			Remaining Returned Sick Deft to CCS to Corps Sick Depot to Body Remaining	
			OFF OR / OFF OR / OFF OR / OFF OR / OFF OR / OFF OR / OFF OR	
			Sick 2 / 21 / 2 / 23 / 6 / 1 / 2	
			Wounded - / - / - / - / - / - / -	
			Totals 2 / 21 / 2 / 23 / 6 / 1 / 2	
Point Du Jour G.30.a.8.8. Sheet 27.	24 Apl		Unit moved by road to LEDERZEELE AREA.	S.D.S.

Army Form C. 2118.

WAR DIARY
or
INTELLIGENCE SUMMARY
(Erase heading not required.)

Instructions regarding War Diaries and Intelligence Summaries are contained in F. S. Regs., Part II. and the Staff Manual respectively. Title Pages will be prepared in manuscript.

9th (C.P.) Field Ambulance, U.S.A.

Place	Date 1918	Hour	Summary of Events and Information	Remarks and references to Appendices
POINT DU JOUR	25 Apl.		Sick and Wounded passing through Field Ambulance during 24 hrs ending noon 25th April 1918.	D.F.R.
			Reinforcing / Automatic / From 9th F.A. / to C.C.S. / to Corps Central Depot / to Corps Min. Depot / Remaining	
			OFF / OR / OFF / OR / OFF / OR / OFF / OR / OFF / OR / OFF / OR / OFF / OR	
			Sick 2 / / / / / / / / / / / / / 1 / 2 / 1	
			Wounded / / / / / / / / / / / / / /	
			Totals 2 / / / / / / / / / / / / 1 / 2 / 1	
			Routine - Improvements	S.o.S.
	26 Apl.		Sick and Wounded passing through Field Ambulance during 24 hrs ending noon 26th April 1918.	D.F.R.
			Reinforcing / Automatic / From 9th F.A. / to C.C.S. / to Corps Central Depot / to Corps Sick Depot / Remaining	
			OFF / OR / OFF / OR / OFF / OR / OFF / OR / OFF / OR / OFF / OR / OFF / OR	
			Sick 1 / / / / / / / / / / / / / / 1	
			Wounded / / / / / / / / / / / / / /	
			Totals 1 / / / / / / / / / / / / / 1	
			Capt. G.A. HODGES R.A.M.C. 1st Temporary duty with 4th Tank Bde.	S.o.S.
			1st Lieut. W.B. MANCHESTER M.O.R.C. U.S.A. 1st Permanent duty with 18 Bde. R.G.A.	

Army Form C. 2118.

WAR DIARY
or
INTELLIGENCE SUMMARY

(Erase heading not required.)

9th (P) Field Ambulance

Instructions regarding War Diaries and Intelligence Summaries are contained in F. S. Regs., Part II. and the Staff Manual respectively. Title Pages will be prepared in manuscript.

Place	Date 1918	Hour	Summary of Events and Information	Remarks and references to Appendices
Point DuJuk	27 April		Sick and wounded evacuated through Field Ambulance to F.A.Dn. during 24 hrs. ending 27th April 1918.	
			Admitted from R.A.P. to C.C.S. / To Corps Conval Depot / To Corps Sick Depot / To Duty / Remaining	
			Off / OR / Off / OR / Off / OR / Off / OR / Off / OR	
			Sick: 1 / Wounded: 1 / Total:	S.D.
			Routine	
	28 April		Sick and wounded passing through Field Ambulance to F.A.Dn. during 24 hrs. ending noon 28th April 1918.	
			Admitted from 9th F.A. to C.C.S. / To Corps Conval Depot / To Corps Sick Depot / To Duty / Remaining	
			Off / OR / Off / OR / Off / OR / Off / OR / Off / OR	
			Sick: 1 / Wounded: 1 / Total:	S.D.
			Routine	

Army Form C. 2118.

WAR DIARY
or
INTELLIGENCE SUMMARY

(Erase heading not required.)

Ops (CD) Field Amb ᴸᵗ

Place	Date	Hour	Summary of Events and Information	Remarks and references to Appendices
POINT DU JOUR	29 Apr		Sick and wounded passing through Field Ambulance & D.R.Stn. during 24 hrs ending 3ᵃᵐ April 1918. Remaining Admitted from O.F.A. to C.C.S. To CORPS. CONVAL. DEPOT To CORPS. SKIN DEPOT To Duty Remaining OFF OR OFF OR OFF OR OFF OR OFF OR OFF OR OFF OR Sick 1 1 Wounded Totals Routine	S D S
	30 Apr		Sick and Wounded passing through Field Ambulance & D.R.Stn. during 24 hrs ending from 30 April 1918. Remaining Admitted from O.F.A. to C.C.S. To CORPS. CONVAL. DEPOT To CORPS. SKIN DEPOT To Duty Remaining OFF OR OFF OR OFF OR OFF OR OFF OR OFF OR OFF OR Sick 1 1 Wounded Totals Routine	S D S H Ostram G J Shaw OF 97 ˢᴬ

med/283

No. 94 F.A.

COMMITTEE FOR
MEDICAL HISTORY
Date 9 JUL 1918

97 Field Ambulance
Army Form C. 2118.
Volume XXXI
May 1918.

No 31

WAR DIARY
or
INTELLIGENCE SUMMARY.
(Erase heading not required.)

Place	Date 1918	Hour	Summary of Events and Information	Remarks and references to Appendices
Point DuJour G.30.a.8.8 Sheet 27.	1 May		No patients treated in Hospital. Field Ambulance, training and Routine.	Signed [sig]
	2 May		do. do.	S.S.
	3 May		do. do.	S.S.
	4 May		do. do.	S.S.

Army Form C. 2118.

WAR DIARY
or
INTELLIGENCE SUMMARY.
(Erase heading not required.)

Place	Date 1918	Hour	Summary of Events and Information	Remarks and references to Appendices
POINT DU JOUR	5 May		No patients treated in Hospital. Field Ambulance training & Routine. Capt. D. CAMPBELL, M.C. R.A.M.C. proceeded for permanent duty with 16 Bn. Manchester Regt.	S.S.
	6 May		No patients treated in Hospital. Field Ambulance, training & Routine.	S.S.
	7 May		do	S.S.
	8 May		do	S.S.
			Capt. G.P. HODGES. R.A.M.C. detailed for permanent duty with No. 4 Tank Bde.	S.S.

Army Form C. 2118.

WAR DIARY
or
INTELLIGENCE SUMMARY.
(Erase heading not required.)

Instructions regarding War Diaries and Intelligence Summaries are contained in F. S. Regs., Part II. and the Staff Manual respectively. Title pages will be prepared in manuscript.

Place	Date	Hour	Summary of Events and Information	Remarks and references to Appendices
Point Du Jour	1918 9 May		Capt. F. Goss, R.A.M.C. (SR) reported for duty. Capt. F. Goss, R.A.M.C. (SR) proceeded for permanent duty with 17th Kings Liverpool Regt.	S.O.S.
	10 May		No patients treated in Hospital of Field Ambulance. Training and routine	S.O.S.
	11 May		do	S.O.S.
	12 May		do	S.O.S.

Army Form C. 2118.

WAR DIARY
or
INTELLIGENCE SUMMARY.
(Erase heading not required.)

Instructions regarding War Diaries and Intelligence Summaries are contained in F. S. Regs., Part II. and the Staff Manual respectively. Title pages will be prepared in manuscript.

Place	Date 1918	Hour	Summary of Events and Information	Remarks and references to Appendices
Point Du Jour	13th May		No patients treated in Hospital. Field Ambulance, training & Routine.	S.O.S.
	14th May		do	S.O.S.
	15th May		Ambulance move by road from Point Dujour to AUDRUICQ and entrain	S.O.S.
	16th May		Ambulance detrained at WOINCOURT and marched to MESNIL VAL. Major W.R. Thompson R.A.M.C. proceeded to 35th American Division for temporary duty as Liaison Officer.	S.O.S.

Army Form C. 2118.

WAR DIARY
or
INTELLIGENCE SUMMARY.

(Erase heading not required.)

Instructions regarding War Diaries and Intelligence Summaries are contained in F. S. Regs, Part II. and the Staff Manual respectively. Title pages will be prepared in manuscript.

Place	Date	Hour	Summary of Events and Information	Remarks and references to Appendices
MESNIL VAL G.E. 0.50 Sheet 14 ABBEVILLE	17/May		97 Field Ambulance attached to 35th American Division for training of American Medical personnel. Speciding Hospital for reception of sick.	S.S.
	18/May		Collection of sick from 35th American Division Major N.L. GIST, M.C., U.S.A. } attached temporarily for instruction. 1st Lieut. W.M. HOEL, M.C., U.S.A. }	S.S.
	19/May		Sick passing through Field Ambulance during 24 hrs ending noon 19 May 1918	

	Received	Admitted		To C.C.S		Remaining	
		OFF.	O.R.	OFF.	O.R.	OFF.	O.R.
	Nil		5		3		2

Routine.   S.S.

WAR DIARY or INTELLIGENCE SUMMARY.

Army Form C. 2118.

Place	Date 1918	Hour	Summary of Events and Information	Remarks and references to Appendices
MESNIL YNZ	20 May		Sick passing through Field Ambulance during 24 hours ending noon 20 May 1918 Remained O.R. | Admitted To C.C.S. O.R. | To duty O.R. | Remaining O.R. 2 | 9 | 7 | — | 4 Routine.	S.O.S.
	21 May		Sick passing through Field Ambulance during 24 hours ending noon 21 May 1918 Remained O.R. | Admitted O.R. | To C.C.S. O.R. | To duty O.R. | Remaining O.R. 4 | 8 | — | — | 12 Routine.	S.O.S.
	22 May		Sick passing through Field Ambulance during 24 hours ending noon 22 May 1918 Remained O.R. | Admitted O.R. | To C.C.S. O.R. | To duty O.R. | Remaining O.R. 12 | 38 | 14 | 1 | 35 Routine.	S.O.S.

Army Form C. 2118.

WAR DIARY
or
INTELLIGENCE SUMMARY.
(Erase heading not required.)

Instructions regarding War Diaries and Intelligence Summaries are contained in F. S. Regs., Part II. and the Staff Manual respectively. Title pages will be prepared in manuscript.

Place	Date 1918	Hour	Summary of Events and Information					Remarks and references to Appendices
MESNIL VAL	23 May		Sick passing through Field Ambulance during 24 hours ending noon 23 May 1918					S.O.S.
			Remained O.R.	Admitted OFF	O.R.	To CCS OFF	O.R.	Remaining O.R.	
			35	1	6	1	7	34	
			Routine.						
	24 May		Sick passing through Field Ambulance during 24 hours ending noon 24 May 1918					S.O.S.
			Remained O.R.	Admitted O.R.	To CCS O.R.			Remaining O.R.	
			34	10	1			43	
			Routine.						
	25 May		Sick passing through Field Ambulance during 24 hours ending noon 25 May 1918					S.O.S.
			Remained O.R.	Admitted O.R.	To CCS O.R.	To duty O.R.		Remaining O.R.	
			43	19	4	1		57	
			Routine.						

Army Form C. 2118.

WAR DIARY
or
INTELLIGENCE SUMMARY.
(Erase heading not required.)

Instructions regarding War Diaries and Intelligence Summaries are contained in F. S. Regs., Part II. and the Staff Manual respectively. Title pages will be prepared in manuscript.

Place	Date 1918	Hour	Summary of Events and Information	Remarks and references to Appendices
MERNIL VPL	26 May		Sick passing through Field Ambulance during 24 hours ending noon 26 May 1918.	
			Remained / Admitted to CCS / To duty / Remaining	
			OR / OR / OR / OR / OR	
			57 / 9 / 5 / 3 / 58	
			Routine	S.S.
	27 May		Sick passing through Field Ambulance during 24 hours ending noon 27 May 1918.	
			Remained / Admitted to CCS / To duty / Remaining	
			OR / OR / OR / OR / OR	
			58 / 2 / 5 / 1 / 54	
			Small detachment u/c of Major N.S. Davis RAMC proceeded for duty (Gunnery) to OISEMONT to establish Aid Post for 33rd American Division whilst detraining	S.S.
	28 May		Sick passing through Field Ambulance during 24 hours ending noon 28 May 1918.	
			Remained / Admitted to CCS / To duty / Remaining	
			OR / OR / OR / OR	
			54 / 4 / 1 / 57	
			Capt. L. APP. T. Davis, M.C. RAMC attached for temporary duty. One section of Ambulance u/c Major N.S. Davis RAMC proceeded to BIENCOURT. Ref. 16. 1. I 30.71 to establish hospital for sick of the 33rd American Division	S.S.

(A8041) D. D. & L. London, E.C. W. W2771/M 51 750,000 5/17 Sch. 83 Forms/C2118/24

Army Form C. 2118.

WAR DIARY
or
INTELLIGENCE SUMMARY.

(Erase heading not required.)

Instructions regarding War Diaries and Intelligence Summaries are contained in F. S. Regs., Part II. and the Staff Manual respectively. Title pages will be prepared in manuscript.

Place	Date 1918	Hour	Summary of Events and Information	Remarks and references to Appendices
MESNIL VAL	29 May		Sick passing through Field Ambulance during 24 hrs ending noon 29 May 1918	
			Received Admitted to CCS To duty Remaining	
			O.R. O.R. O.R. O.R.	
			57 18 7 1 67	
			Routine	SoS
	30 May		Sick passing through Field Ambulance during 24 hrs ending noon 30 May 1918	
			Received Admitted to CCS Remaining	
			O.R. O.R. O.R.	
			67 4 71	
			Routine	SoS
	31 May		Sick passing through Field Ambulance during 24 hrs ending noon 31 May 1918	
			Received Admitted to CCS To 98 F.A. Totally Remaining	
			O.R. OFF. O.R. O.R. O.R. OFF. O.R.	
			71 1 9 4 20 1 55	
			Routine	

D. J. Law
S/L 47th Field Amb
O.C. 47th Field Amb

140/3070.

97. F.O.

June 1918

COMMITTEE FOR THE
MEDICAL HISTORY OF THE WAR
Date 7 AUG 1918

Army Form C. 2118.

Volume XXXII
97 (2½) Field Ambulance

WAR DIARY
or
INTELLIGENCE SUMMARY.
(Erase heading not required.)

Instructions regarding War Diaries and Intelligence Summaries are contained in F. S. Regs., Part II. and the Staff Manual respectively. Title pages will be prepared in manuscript.

Place	Date	Hour	Summary of Events and Information	Remarks and references to Appendices
DESVRES			Sick during hours Field Ambulance during 24 hours ending noon 1st June 1918	
C.C.O.50.			Remained / Admitted / To 98 FA / To duty / Remaining	
Le?? 11			OFF OR / OFF OR / OFF OR / OFF OR / OFF OR	
BERNEVILLE	1st June		1 55 / 4 4 / 4 4 / - 11	
			Major W.L. GIST, M.C., R.G.) attached temporarily for instruction, transferred to 98th Field Ambulance	W.A. Thompson Major R.A.M.C. (T)
			Capt W.D. NOEL, M.C., N.G.)	O.C. 97th (2½) Field Ambulance
			Capt W.E. TILLET, M.P., M.G. attached temporarily for instruction	
	2nd June		Sick passing through Field Ambulance during 24 hours ending noon 2nd June 1918	
			Remained / Admitted / To CCS / To duty / Remaining	
			OFF OR / OFF OR / OFF OR / OFF OR / OFF OR	
			1 11 / 13 / 1 4 / 3 / - 17	W.A.T.
			Ambulance moved by road from NESMYER to BIENCOURT and take over BIENCOURT HOSPITAL subgrounds as hospital for half of 33rd American Division.	
BIENCOURT	3rd June		Sick passing through Field Ambulance during 24 hours ending noon 3rd June 1918	
L.T.30.a.			Remained / Admitted / To CCS / To duty / Remaining	
Sheet 11			OFF OR / OFF OR / OFF OR / OFF OR / OFF OR	
DIEPPE			17 / 7 / - / 1 / 23	W.A.T.
			Routine and Hospital improvements	

Army Form C. 2118.

WAR DIARY
or
INTELLIGENCE SUMMARY.

97 (S.R) Field Ambulance

(Erase heading not required.)

Place	Date 1918	Hour	Summary of Events and Information	Remarks and references to Appendices
BIENCOURT	4 Jun		SICK passing through Field Ambulance during 24 hours ending noon 4th June 1918.	
			Evacuated / Remaining O.R. / Off. O.R. / Off. O.R. 93 / 1 1 / 1 31	W.T.S.
			Various hospital appointments	
	5 Jun		SICK passing through the 97 S.R Field Ambulance during 24 hours ending noon 5th June 1918.	
			Received / Evacuated / To Duty / Remaining O.R. / Off. O.R. / Off. O.R. / Off. O.R. 1 / 31 / 95 / 6 / 1 / 1 / 49	W.T.S.
			Routine Hospital arrangements	
	6 Jun		SICK passing through Field Ambulance during 24 hours ending noon 6th June 1918.	
			Received / Evacuated / To Duty / Remaining O.R. / Off. O.R. / Off. O.R. / Off. O.R. 49 / 1 / 14 / 12 / 2 / 1 / 49	W.T.S.

1st Lieut. J.W. STIERS, R.A.C. U.S.A attached for temporary duty.

Army Form C. 2118.

WAR DIARY
or
INTELLIGENCE SUMMARY.
(Erase heading not required.)

Army Form C. 2118.

Instructions regarding War Diaries and Intelligence Summaries are contained in F. S. Regs., Part II. and the Staff Manual respectively. Title pages will be prepared in manuscript.

97 (2/1) Field Ambulance.

Place	Date	Hour	Summary of Events and Information	Remarks and references to Appendices
BIENCOURT	1918 7 June		Sick passing through Field Ambulance during 24 hours ending noon 7th June 1918.	
			Received — Admitted — To C.C.S. — To Duty — Remaining OFF: 1 / OR: 49 — OFF: 2 / OR: 15 — OFF: 2 / OR: 4 — OFF: 1 / OR: 1 — OFF: — / OR: 59	W.T.J.
			Capt. Louis N. Yerkes, M.R.C., U.S.A. reported for temporary duty	
			Sick passing through Field Ambulance during 24 hours ending noon 8th June 1918. Received — Admitted — To C.C.S. — To Duty — Remaining OFF: — / OR: — — OFF: — / OR: 17 — OFF: — / OR: 11 — OFF: — / OR: — — OFF: 1 / OR: 63	W.T.J.
			Major W.B. Thompson reported for duty from 355th American Division	
	8/6/18		Sick passing through Field Ambulance during 24 hours ending 6 p.m. 8th June 1918. Received — Admitted — To C.C.S. — To Duty — Remaining OFF: 1 / OR: 63 — OFF: 1 / OR: 49 — OFF: — / OR: 13 — OFF: 3 / OR: — — OFF: 2 / OR: 96	W.T.J.
			Capt Louis N. Yerkes M.O. case transferred to 96 Field Ambulance for temporary duty. Major L. Of. J. Davis, M.C. Name attached for temporary duty return to 96 Field Ambulance	

Army Form C. 2118.

WAR DIARY
or
INTELLIGENCE SUMMARY.

(Erase heading not required.)

97 (SH) Field Ambulance

Instructions regarding War Diaries and Intelligence Summaries are contained in F. S. Regs., Part II. and the Staff Manual respectively. Title pages will be prepared in manuscript.

Place	Date	Hour	Summary of Events and Information	Remarks and references to Appendices
BIENCOURT	9/15		Sick Parading through Field Ambulance during 24 hours ending 6 p.m. 10th June 1915	
			Remained	Admitted	On R.		
			OR	OR	OFF.	OR	
			2	90	10	1	11	63	
			Routine Hospital Improvements	
	10 June		Sick Parading through Field Ambulance during 24 hours ending 6 p.m. 11th June 1915	
			Remained	Admitted	On R.		
			OFF	OR	OR	OFF	OR	
			1	95	11	5	1	97	W.A.S.
			Routine Hospital Improvements	
	11 June		Sick Parading through Field Ambulance during 24 hours ending 6 p.m. 12th June 1915	
			Remaining	Admitted	On Duty	Remaining		
			OFF	OR	OR	OFF	OR	
			1	97	1	5	1	89	W.A.S.
			Routine Hospital Improvements	

Army Form C. 2118.

WAR DIARY
or
INTELLIGENCE SUMMARY.   97 (2) Field Ambulance

(Erase heading not required.)

Instructions regarding War Diaries and Intelligence Summaries are contained in F. S. Regs., Part II. and the Staff Manual respectively. Title pages will be prepared in manuscript.

Place	Date	Hour	Summary of Events and Information	Remarks and references to Appendices
BEAUCOURT	13 June 1915		Sick passing through Field Ambulance during 24 hours ending 6 p.m. 13th June 1915. 	Remained	Admitted	To Duty	Remaining
OFF	O.R.	OFF	O.R.	OFF	O.R.	OFF	O.R.
1	39	2	52	2	5	1	86	 Routine Hospital Improvements	W.N.T.
	14 June		Sick passing through Field Ambulance during 24 hours ending 6 p.m. 14th June 1915. 	Remaining	Admitted	To Duty	Remaining
OFF	O.R.	OFF	O.R.	OFF	O.R.	OFF	O.R.
1	86	4	3	3	1	82	 Routine Hospital Improvements	W.N.T.
	15 June		Sick passing through Field Ambulance during 24 hours ending 6 p.m. 15th June 1915. 	Remained	Admitted	To C.C.S.	To Duty	Remaining
OFF	O.R.	OFF	O.R.	OFF	O.R.	OFF	O.R.	OFF	O.R.
1	82		11		4		5	1	84 | Routine Hospital Improvements	W.N.T.

Army Form C. 2118.

WAR DIARY
or
INTELLIGENCE SUMMARY.

(Erase heading not required.)

97 (2nd) Field Ambulance

Place	Date 1918	Hour	Summary of Events and Information	Remarks and references to Appendices
BIENVILLERS	16 June		Sick leaving through Field Ambulance during 24 hours ending 6 p.m. 16th June 1918. Received / Admitted / To C.C.S. / To Duty / Remaining. OFF: 1 / 3 / 2 / - / - . OR: 24 / - / - / 10 / 75. W.A.T. Routine Hospital Employment.	
	17 June		Sick passing through Field Ambulance during 24 hours ending 6 p.m. 17th June 1918. Remained / Admitted / To C.C.S. / To Duty / Remaining. OFF: 1 / 1 / 2 / 1 / -. OR: 75 / 7 / - / 3 / 78. W.A.T. R.32 L.D. Benn D.S.O., R.A.M.C. evacuated sick to No.16 (Ville) General Hospital	
	18 June		Sick passing through Field Ambulance during 24 hours ending 6 p.m. 18th June 1918. Remained / Admitted / To C.C.S. / To Duty / Remaining. OFF: - / - / - / - / -. OR: 78 / 27 / 3 / 2 / 100. W.A.T. Major W.A. Thompson R.A.M.C. assumed temporary command of 97 Field Ambulance	

Army Form C. 2118.

WAR DIARY
or
INTELLIGENCE SUMMARY.
(Erase heading not required.)

97 (SP) Field Ambulance

Instructions regarding War Diaries and Intelligence Summaries are contained in F. S. Regs., Part II. and the Staff Manual respectively. Title pages will be prepared in manuscript.

Place	Date 1915	Hour	Summary of Events and Information	Remarks and references to Appendices
BIENVILLERS	19 June		Sick passing through Field Ambulance during 24 hours ending 6 p.m. 19th June 1915	
			Remained / Admitted / To C.C.S. / To Duty / Remaining	
			OFF O.R. / OFF O.R. / OFF O.R. / OFF O.R. / OFF O.R.	
			— 100 / 1 52 / — 4 / — 3 / 1 145	W.W.I.
			Routine Hospital Improvements	
	20 June		Sick passing through Field Ambulance during 24 hours ending 6 p.m. 20th June 1915	
			Remained / Admitted / To C.C.S. / To Duty / Remaining	
			OFF O.R. / OFF O.R. / OFF O.R. / OFF O.R. / OFF O.R.	
			1 145 / — 9 / — — / — 12 / 1 142	W.W.I.
			Routine Hospital Improvements	
	21 June		Sick passing through Field Ambulance during 24 hours ending 6 p.m. 21st June 1915	
			Remained / Admitted / Transferred to 65FA from 65FA / To C.C.S. / To Duty / Remaining	
			OFF O.R. / OFF O.R. / OFF O.R. / OFF O.R. / OFF O.R. / OFF O.R.	
			1 142 / — 3 / — 6 / — 14 / — 6 / 1 143	W.W.I.
			Routine Hospital Improvements	

Army Form C. 2118.

WAR DIARY
or
INTELLIGENCE SUMMARY.   97 (C?) Field Ambulance

(Erase heading not required.)

Instructions regarding War Diaries and Intelligence Summaries are contained in F.S. Regs., Part II. and the Staff Manual respectively. Title pages will be prepared in manuscript.

Place	Date 1918	Hour	Summary of Events and Information	Remarks and references to Appendices
BIENCOURT			Sick passing through Field Ambulance during 24 hours ending 6 p.m. 22nd June 1918	
			Received / Admitted / Trans. from 64 F.A. / To C.C.S. / To Duty / Remaining	
			OFF / OR // OFF / OR // OFF / OR // OFF / OR // OFF / OR // OFF / OR	
	22 June		1 / 143 // 2 / 37 // – / 27 // 9 / 1 / 7 // 3 // 2 / 206	A.A.A.
			1st Lieut F.N. DIERS. M.R.C., U.S.A. Attached for temporary duty return to 33rd American Division. 1st Lieut W. STILLET, M.R.C., U.S.A.	
			Sick passing through Field Ambulance during 24 hours ending 6 p.m. 23rd June 1918	
			Received / Admitted / To C.C.S. / To Duty / Remaining	
			OFF / OR // OFF / OR // OFF / OR // OFF / OR // OFF / OR	
	23 June		2 / 206 // – / 4 // – / 17 // 4 // 2 / 179	A.A.A.
			Routine Hospital Improvements.	
			Sick passing through Field Ambulance during 24 hours ending 6 p.m. 24th June 1918	
			Received / Admitted / To C.C.S. / To Duty / Remaining	
			OFF / OR // OFF / OR // OFF / OR // OFF / OR // OFF / OR	
	24 June		2 / 179 // – / 8 // – / 1 // – / 22 // 2 / 164	A.A.A.
			Routine Hospital Improvements.	

Army Form C. 2118.

WAR DIARY
or
INTELLIGENCE SUMMARY.

97 (CP) Field Ambulance

(Erase heading not required.)

Instructions regarding War Diaries and Intelligence Summaries are contained in F.S. Regs., Part II. and the Staff Manual respectively. Title pages will be prepared in manuscript.

Place	Date 1918	Hour	Summary of Events and Information	Remarks and references to Appendices
BIENCOURT	25 June		SICK passing through Field Ambulance during 24 hours ending 6 pm 25 June 1918. Remained: Off —, OR 2, Admitted: Off —, OR 104, To CCS: Off —, OR 9, To 65 F.A: Off —, OR 59, On Duty: Off —, OR 32, Remaining: Off 2, OR 82, Nil. Clearing out hospital of patients and Red Cross Stores, preparing to move.	W.W.A.
	26 June		SICK passing through Field Ambulance during 24 hours ending 6pm 26 June 1918. Remained —, Admitted —, Nil —, Remaining — Nil. Unit moved by road from BIENCOURT to FOREST L'ABBAYE	W.W.A.
FOREST L'ABBAYE 1.4 90.50	27 June		SICK passing through Field Ambulance during 24 hours ending 6pm 27 June 1918. Remained —, Admitted —, OR 2, Nil —, Remaining — Nil. Unit resting at FOREST L'ABBAYE	W.W.A.
Sheet 14 LABBEVILLE				

Army Form C. 2118.

WAR DIARY
or
INTELLIGENCE SUMMARY. 97 (SP) Field Ambulance

(Erase heading not required.)

Place	Date	Hour	Summary of Events and Information	Remarks and references to Appendices
HELVELINGHEM G.20.C.8.6. Sheet 27A.	28/June		SICK passing through Field Ambulance during 24 hours ending 6am 28th June 1918. Remained Admitted Returned NIL NIL NIL K.T.A.T.	
			Unit moved by rail and entrain at Rubrouck type (Sheet 6 ABBEVILLE) and detrained at AUDRUICQ (Sheet 27A) and marched to HELVELINGHEM.	
	29/June		SICK passing through Field Ambulance during 18 hours ending noon 29th June 1918. Remained Admitted Returned O.K. 6 NIL K.T.A.T.	
			Capt. T. G.D.? M.E.A. R.A.M.C. reported for duty and is to take on the appt. of S.M.O. Field Ambulance.	
	30/June		SICK passing through Field Ambulance during 24 hours ending noon 30 June 1918. Remained Admitted Returned O.K. O.K. O.K. 6 33 39 C.A.M.E. (Capt) Field Ambulance	
			Major N.S.DARKS R.A.M.C. O/C of our Later proceed to EPERLECQUES, Sheet 27A. K.33. & other Hospital Headquarters remain at HELVELINGHEM.	N.N.Thompson Major R.A.M.C. O.C.97th (Capt) Field Ambulance

140/3131

COMMITTEE FOR THE
MEDICAL HISTORY OF THE WAR
Date -5 SEP

97ᵗʰ F.a.

Jul Oct 1918

Volume XXXIII

Army Form C. 2118.

July 1918.

97th Field Ambulance

WAR DIARY
or
INTELLIGENCE SUMMARY.
(Erase heading not required.)

Instructions regarding War Diaries and Intelligence Summaries are contained in F. S. Regs., Part II. and the Staff Manual respectively. Title pages will be prepared in manuscript.

Place	Date 1918	Hour	Summary of Events and Information	Remarks and references to Appendices
HELVELINGHEM G.30.b.8.6 Sheet 97A	1st July		Sick passing through 97th Field Ambulance during 24 hours ending noon 1st July 1918. Received / Admitted / To C.C.S. / Remaining O.R. / O.R. / O.R. / O.R. 39 / 29 / 6 / 62 Routine	SD/
	2nd July		Sick passing through Field Ambulance during 24 hours ending noon 2nd July 1918. Received / Admitted / To C.C.S. / To Duty / Remaining O.R. / OFF / O.R. / OFF / O.R. / OFF / O.R. / O.R. 62 / 1 / 24 / 1 / 3 / 3 / 80 2nd Lieut. C.E. BRADLEY. M.O.R.C. U.S.A. reported for duty.	S.D.
	3rd July		Sick passing through Field Ambulance during 24 hours ending noon 3rd July 1918. Received / Admitted / To C.C.S. / To Duty / Remaining O.R. / OFF / O.R. / OFF / O.R. / O.R. / O.R. 80 / 1 / 26 / 1 / 2 / 21 / 83 Capt. M.W. LITTLEWOOD. R.A.M.C. } reported for duty. " G.H. KEARNEY. R.A.M.C. }	S.D.

Army Form C. 2118.

WAR DIARY
or
INTELLIGENCE SUMMARY.
(Erase heading not required.)

97th Field Ambulance

Place	Date	Hour	Summary of Events and Information	Remarks and references to Appendices
HELVELINGHEM	1918			
	4th July		Sick passing through Field Ambulance during 24 hours ending noon 4th July 1918	
			Remained Admitted To CCS To Duty Remaining O.R. OFF. O.R. OFF. O.R. O.R. O.R. 83 1 26 1 1 21 87	
			Routine	
	5th July		Sick passing through Field Ambulance during 24 hours ending noon 5th July 1918	
			Remained Admitted To CCS To Duty Remaining O.R. O.R. O.R. O.R. O.R. 87 30 12 14 91	
			Capt. G.R. SHIEL R.A.M.C. posted to 148 Bde R.F.A. for permanent duty	
	6th July		Sick passing through Field Ambulance during 24 hours ending noon 6th July 1918	
			Remained Admitted To CCS To Duty Remaining O.R. OFF. O.R. OFF. O.R. O.R. O.R. 91 1 26 1 6 8 103	
			Lt.Col. L.D. SHAW D.S.O. R.A.M.C. resumes command of 97 F.Amb. on return from No.16 (N.Za.) Gen. Hospital	

Army Form C. 2118.

WAR DIARY
or
INTELLIGENCE SUMMARY.
(Erase heading not required.)

97th Field Ambulance

Instructions regarding War Diaries and Intelligence Summaries are contained in F. S. Regs., Part II. and the Staff Manual respectively. Title pages will be prepared in manuscript.

Place	Date 1918	Hour	Summary of Events and Information	Remarks and references to Appendices
HELVELINGHEM	7th July		Sick passing through Field Ambulance during 24 hours ending noon 7th July 1918	
			Remained / Admitted / to CCS / to Duty / Remaining — OR / OR / OR / OR / OR — 103 / 23 / 43 / 46 / 37	
			At Lieut. M.J. McMahon R.A.M.C. reported for duty.	SOS
	8th July		Sick passing through 97th Field Ambulance during 24 hours ending noon 8th July 1918	
			Remained — OR 37 / Admitted — OFF 2, OR 28 / to CCS — OFF 2, OR 38 / to Duty — OR 25 / Remaining — OR 2	SOS
			"Field Ambulance moved by road from HELVELINGHEM to ST MOMELIN Lieut. E.B. RINGROSE R.A.M.C. Evacuated sick to No 36 CCS.	
ST MOMELIN Sect 5a HAZEBROUCK	9th July		Sick passing through 97th Field Ambulance during 24 hours ending noon 9th July 1918	
			Remained — OR 2 / Admitted — OFF 2, OR 44 / to CCS — OFF 2, OR 36 / to Duty — OR — / Remaining — OR 10	SOS
			Field Ambulance moved by road from ST MOMELIN to MAISON BLANCHE. Pte. CE BRADLEY R.A.M.C. proceeded to 98 Field Ambulance for temporary duty.	

Army Form C. 2118.

WAR DIARY
or
INTELLIGENCE SUMMARY.
(Erase heading not required.)

97th Field Ambulance

Place	Date 1918	Hour	Summary of Events and Information				Remarks and references to Appendices
NIMSON BLANCHE O.26.c.3. Sheet 27	10th July		Sick passing through Field Ambulance during 24 hours ending noon 10th July 1918				
			Removed	Admitted	To Duty	Remaining	
			O.R.	O.R.	O.R.	O.R.	
			10	1	9	2	NIL
			Capt. N.W. Littlewood R.A.M.C. Bearer proceed to Le Corbeux. Q.M. a 27 Sheet 27 appointed to 89th Inf. Bde.				SOS
	11th July		Sick passing through Field Ambulance during 24 hours ending noon 11th July 1918				
			NIL				SOS
			1st Lieut N.J. McMAHON M.O.R.C. U.S.A. for temporary duty with 2/17th London Regt.				
	12th July		Sick passing through Field Ambulance during 24 hours ending noon 12th July 1918				
			NIL				SOS
			Routine.				

Army Form C. 2118.

WAR DIARY
or
INTELLIGENCE SUMMARY.
(Erase heading not required.)

97th Field Ambulance

Instructions regarding War Diaries and Intelligence Summaries are contained in F. S. Regs., Part II. and the Staff Manual respectively. Title pages will be prepared in manuscript.

Place	Date 1918	Hour	Summary of Events and Information	Remarks and references to Appendices
MAISON BLANCHE	13 July		Sick passing through Field Ambulance during 24 hours ending noon 13th July 1918	
			Routine	
			Nil	
	14 July		Sick passing through Field Ambulance during 24 hours ending noon 14th July 1918	
			Nil	
			Reconnoitring roads for evacuation from line, and site for main Dressing Station	SoS
			Sick passing through Field Ambulance during 24 hours ending noon 15th July 1918	
	15 July		Nil	
			Lieut E. B. Ringrose, R.A.M.C. reported from 36 C.C.S	SoS

Army Form C. 2118.

WAR DIARY
or
INTELLIGENCE SUMMARY.
(Erase heading not required.)

97th Field Ambulance

Place	Date	Hour	Summary of Events and Information	Remarks and references to Appendices
MAISON BLANCHE	16 July		Sick parade through Field Ambulance during 24 hours ending noon 16th July 1918	SoS
			NIL	
			Establishing routes for evacuation from line, and site for Main Dressing Station	
			Sick passing through Field Ambulance during 24 hours ending noon 17th July 1918	SoS
	17 July		NIL	
			Small party proceeds to STEENVOORDE to prepare M.D.S. site J.36.d.4.0 Sheet 27.	
			Sick passing through Field Ambulance during 24 hours ending noon 18th July 1918	SoS
	18 July		NIL	
			Routine — collection of Sick &c.	SoS

Instructions regarding War Diaries and Intelligence Summaries are contained in F. S. Regs., Part II. and the Staff Manual respectively. Title pages will be prepared in manuscript.

Army Form C. 2118.

WAR DIARY
or
INTELLIGENCE SUMMARY.
(Erase heading not required.)

97th Field Ambulance

Place	Date 1918	Hour	Summary of Events and Information	Remarks and references to Appendices
MAISON BLANCHE	19 July		Sick passing through Field Ambulance during 24 hours ending noon 19th July 1918	
			NIL	
			Routine work on M.D.S. site, and collection of sick re.	SOS
			Sick passing through Field Ambulance during 24 hours ending noon 20th July 1918	
	20 July		NIL	
			Head Quarters of Field Ambulance move from MAISON BLANCHE to STEENVOORDE	SOS
			Sick passing through Field Ambulance during 24 hours ending noon 21st July 1918	
			NIL	
STEENVOORDE F.6.a.4.6. Sheet 27	21 July		Routine work on M.D.S. site, and collection of sick re.	SOS

Army Form C. 2118.

WAR DIARY
or
INTELLIGENCE SUMMARY.
(Erase heading not required.)

97th Field Ambulance

Place	Date	Hour	Summary of Events and Information	Remarks and references to Appendices
STEENVOORDE	22/7/18		Sick passing through Field Ambulance during the two weeks ending noon 22nd July 1918	501
			Routine work on A.D.S. site, and collection of sick &c.	
	23 July		NIL	
			Sick passing through Field Ambulance during 24 hours ending noon 23rd July 1918	23
			Major W.A. THOMPSON R.A.M.C. proceeded to report to A.D.M.S. 50th British Division for duty. Struck off strength of 97 F. Amb.	
			Sick passing through Field Ambulance during 24 hours ending noon 24th July 1918	22
	24 July		NIL	
			Routine work on A.D.S. site, and collection of sick &c.	20

Army Form C. 2118.

WAR DIARY
or
INTELLIGENCE SUMMARY.
(Erase heading not required.)

97th Field Ambulance

Instructions regarding War Diaries and Intelligence Summaries are contained in F. S. Regs., Part II. and the Staff Manual respectively. Title pages will be prepared in manuscript.

Place	Date 1918	Hour	Summary of Events and Information	Remarks and references to Appendices
STEENVOORDE	25 July		Sick passing through Field Ambulance during 24 hours ending noon 25th July 1918	SoS
			Nil	
			Routine work on M.D.S. site, and collection of Sick &c.	SoS
	26 July		Sick passing through Field Ambulance during 24 hours ending noon 26th July 1918	SoS
			Nil	
			Routine work on M.D.S. site, and collection of Sick &c.	SoS
	27 July		Sick passing through Field Ambulance during 24 hours ending noon 27th July 1918.	SoS
			Nil	
			Routine work on M.D.S. site, and collection of Sick &c.	

Army Form C. 2118.

WAR DIARY
or
INTELLIGENCE SUMMARY.
(Erase heading not required.)

97th Field Ambulance

Place	Date 1918	Hour	Summary of Events and Information	Remarks and references to Appendices
STEENVOORDE	28 July		Sick leaving through Field Ambulance during 24 hours ending noon 28th July 1918	
			NIL	
			1st Lieut N.J. Mc MAHON M.O.R.C., U.S.A. reported from 2/17th London Regt	SOS
	29 July		Sick passing through Field Ambulance during 24 hours ending noon 29th July 1918	
			NIL	
			Routine collection of sick &c.	SOS
	30 July		Sick passing through Field Ambulance during 24 hours ending noon 30th July 1918	
			NIL	
			Routine collection of sick &c.	SOS

Army Form C. 2118.

WAR DIARY
or
INTELLIGENCE SUMMARY.

(Erase heading not required.)

97th Field Ambulance

Place	Date 1918	Hour	Summary of Events and Information	Remarks and references to Appendices
STEENVOORDE	31st July		Sick passing through Field Ambulance during 24 hours ending noon 31st July 1918	
			NIL	SS
			Routine. Collection of Sick &c.	E Schrand Lt Col O C 97 FA

40/3200.

COMMITTEE FOR THE
MEDICAL HISTORY OF THE WAR
Date 5 OCT 1918

97. F.A.

Aug 1918.

24

Volume XXXIV

August 1918.

Army Form C. 2118.

WAR DIARY
or
INTELLIGENCE SUMMARY.
(Erase heading not required.)

No. Field Ambulance

Place	Date	Hour	Summary of Events and Information	Remarks and references to Appendices
STEENVOORDE P&46 Sheet 27	1/8/18		Sick passing through Field Ambulance during 24 hours ending noon 1st August 1918	NIL
	2/8/18		Routine; collection of sick etc	NIL
			Sick passing through Field Ambulance during 24 hours ending noon 2 August 1918	S.J. Dean Lt OC 24 F.A.
			CASUALTIES Pass M.A.HINDLE RAMC 87292 Pte J HEWITT RAMC 92033 Pte D.J. FORBES RAMC were KILLED IN ACTION Routine etc	19/-
	3/8/18		Sick passing through Field Ambulance during 24 hours ending noon 3rd August 1918	NIL
			Routine etc	SOS

Army Form C. 2118.

WAR DIARY
or
INTELLIGENCE SUMMARY.
(Erase heading not required.)

97 (o) Field Ambulance

Instructions regarding War Diaries and Intelligence Summaries are contained in F. S. Regs., Part II. and the Staff Manual respectively. Title pages will be prepared in manuscript.

Place	Date	Hour	Summary of Events and Information	Remarks and references to Appendices
STEENVOORDE	4/8/18		Sick passing through Field Ambulance during 24 hours ending noon 4th August 1918	
			Routine	
			NIL	SS
	5/8/18		Sick passing through Field Ambulance during 24 hours ending noon 5 August 1918	
			Capt. C.A. KEARNEY RAMC. proceeded on 14 days leave to PARIS.	
			Routine	
			NIL	SS
	6/8/18		Sick passing through Field Ambulance during 24 hours ending noon 6th August 1918	
			NIL	
			Lt. A.J. MINNION MORC detailed for duty as M.O.i/c 118 Bn R Inniskilling Regs vice off p/o G.W. KRICK MRC returned to Routine	SS

Army Form C. 2118.

WAR DIARY
or
INTELLIGENCE SUMMARY.

(Erase heading not required.)

Instructions regarding War Diaries and Intelligence Summaries are contained in F. S. Regs., Part II. and the Staff Manual respectively. Title pages will be prepared in manuscript.

Place	Date	Hour	Summary of Events and Information	Remarks and references to Appendices
STEENVOORDE	7/8/18		Sick passing through Field Ambulance during 24 hours ending noon 7 August 1918	
			NIL	
			Capt. H.L. SHANNON M.O.R.C. reports for duty. Capt. M.W. LITTLEWOOD R.A.M.C. appointed Acting Major while Commanding Section of Field Ambulance Note (not of Appointment). Commences 2nd No 202 dt 25/8/18	SD
	8/8/18		Sick passing through Field Ambulance during 24 hours ending noon 8 August 1918	
			NIL	
			Routine	SD

WAR DIARY
or
INTELLIGENCE SUMMARY.

Army Form C. 2118.

Place	Date	Hour	Summary of Events and Information	Remarks and references to Appendices
STEEN VOORDE	7/5/18		Sick leaving through 76th Ambulance. Artillery period ending noon of August 6th.	
			I find J.W. SHERRICK M.O.R.C. reported to duty. Major N.S. DAVIS, R.A.M.C. 2nd out division proceeded to Le Treport (Rest) G.S.L 52 and took over the Advanced Dressing Station there from 102 Field Ambulance. Major M.W. LITTLEWOOD R.A.M.C. 76 2 Bearer Sub-division proceeded to relieve Bearers of 107 Field in the line. Main Collecting Post established at WESTOUTRE (Sheet 28) M.9.c.5.3	S.

Army Form C. 2118.

WAR DIARY
INTELLIGENCE SUMMARY.
(Erase heading not required.)

97/107 Field Ambulance

Place	Date	Hour	Summary of Events and Information	Remarks and references to Appendices
GODEWAERSVELDE Q.6.a central Sheet 27	10/8/18		Sick passing through Field Ambulance during 24 hours ending noon 10 August 1918.	
			Head Quarters moved by road to GODEWAERSVELDE Sheet 27 Q.6.a central Remainder of personnel through this a.m. at LE BREBANT	SDS
	11/8/18		Sick passing through Field Ambulance during 24 hours ending noon 11 August 1918.	
			Bearers in the line. Evacuation of wounded.	SDS
	12/8/18		Sick passing through Field Ambulance during 24 hours ending noon 12 August 1918.	
			Bearers in the line. Evacuation of wounded.	SDS

Army Form C. 2118.

WAR DIARY
or
INTELLIGENCE SUMMARY.

(Erase heading not required.)

97/4 Field Ambulance

Instructions regarding War Diaries and Intelligence Summaries are contained in F. S. Regs., Part II. and the Staff Manual respectively. Title pages will be prepared in manuscript.

Place	Date	Hour	Summary of Events and Information	Remarks and references to Appendices
GODEWAERSVELDE	12/8/18		Sick passing through Field Ambulance during 24 hours ending noon 13th August 1918	
			Capt G H KEARNEY RAMC rejoins from French Lines. Capt H L SHANNON MOTC granted leave to Paris. Evacuation of wounded	S 1
	14/8/18		Sick passing through Field Ambulance during 24 hours ending noon 14th August 1918 Bearers in the line Evacuation of wounded	S 2
	15/8/18		Sick passing through Field Ambulance during 24 hours ending noon 15th August 1918 Bearers in the line Evacuation of wounded	S 3

Army Form C. 2118.

WAR DIARY
INTELLIGENCE SUMMARY.
(Erase heading not required.)

97 1st/1st Field Ambulance

Place	Date	Hour	Summary of Events and Information	Remarks and references to Appendices
GODEWAERSVELDE	16/8/18		Sick having through Coll Amb Linn during 24 hours ending 12n 16 August 19	
	17/8/18		Bearers up the line relieved night 16/17 Augst by bearers 96 Field Ambulance and Section 98 Field Ambulance. Evacuation of wounded	SOS
			Sick passing through Coll Amb in during 24 hours ending 12n 17 Aug 18	SOS
			Evacuation of wounded	
	18/8/18		Sick passing through Coll Amb in during 24 hours ending 12n 18 August 18	SOS
			Evacuation of wounded &c	SOS

Army Form C. 2118.

WAR DIARY
or
INTELLIGENCE SUMMARY.

(Erase heading not required.)

Instructions regarding War Diaries and Intelligence Summaries are contained in F. S. Regs., Part II. and the Staff Manual respectively. Title pages will be prepared in manuscript.

Place	Date	Hour	Summary of Events and Information	Remarks and references to Appendices
STEENWERSTEDE	19/8/18		Sick passing through Field Ambulance during 24 hours ending noon 19th August 1918	
			Nil	
			Capt G.H. KEARNEY R.A.M.C. evacuated for temporary duty with 38 Field A.F.A. (slightly wounded)	D.L.
	20/8/18		Sick passing through Field Ambulance during 24 hours ending noon 20th August 1918	
			NIL	
			Evacuation of wounded. Owing to the line reinforced by Reserve Rauro.	D.L.

Army Form C. 2118.

WAR DIARY
or
INTELLIGENCE SUMMARY.
(Erase heading not required.)

Instructions regarding War Diaries and Intelligence Summaries are contained in F. S. Regs., Part II. and the Staff Manual respectively. Title pages will be prepared in manuscript.

Place	Date	Hour	Summary of Events and Information	Remarks and references to Appendices
EDE INNERS - VELDT	29/8/18		Note: having shipped J.C.'s Ambulance during period ending Mon 21 August 1918	appx 1
			NIL.	
			Officers shown by 3" Brit'd Armours wore inocs evacuated without the slightest hitch. 6/3/15 Pte CRACE I. Crops (Pett: Elect) Capt H.L. SHANNON reported from French leave	3

WAR DIARY
or
INTELLIGENCE SUMMARY.

(Erase heading not required.)

Army Form C. 2118.

Instructions regarding War Diaries and Intelligence Summaries are contained in F. S. Regs., Part II. and the Staff Manual respectively. Title pages will be prepared in manuscript.

97/1 Field Ambulance

Place	Date	Hour	Summary of Events and Information	Remarks and references to Appendices
GODEWAERSVELDE	22/8/18		Sick passing through Field Ambulance during 24 hours ending noon 22 August 1918	
			Evacuation of wounded. Established new Aid Posts – Relay Posts etc	
	23/8/18		Sick passing through Field Ambulance during 24 hours ending noon 23rd August 1918	SS
			LT J.W. SHERRICK MORC detailed for duty with about 12 American Stretcher Bearers in the line relieved by Reserve Bearers. Normal operations.	SS
	24/8/18		Sick passing through Field Ambulance during 24 hours ending noon 24 August 1918	SS
			Evacuation of wounded	

Army Form C. 2118.

WAR DIARY
of
INTELLIGENCE SUMMARY.
(Erase heading not required.)

97/2/ Field Ambulance

Place	Date	Hour	Summary of Events and Information	Remarks and references to Appendices
GODEWAERSVELDE	25/8/18		Sick passing through Field Ambulances during 24 hours ending noon 25th August 1918	
			Evacuation of wounded	Nil
				SOS
	26/8/18		Sick passing through Field Ambulance during 24 hours ending noon 26 August 1918	
			Evacuation of wounded	Nil
				SOS
	27/8/18		Sick passing through Field Ambulance during 24 hours ending noon 27 August 1918	
			Evacuation of wounded	Nil
				SOS

Army Form C. 2118.

WAR DIARY
or
INTELLIGENCE SUMMARY.
(Erase heading not required.)

97(a) Field Ambulance

Instructions regarding War Diaries and Intelligence Summaries are contained in F. S. Regs., Part II. and the Staff Manual respectively. Title pages will be prepared in manuscript.

Place	Date	Hour	Summary of Events and Information	Remarks and references to Appendices
	28/8/19		Sick passing through field Ambulance during 24 hours ending 12 noon 28 August 1919	
			Evacuation of wounded	N.il
				SD1
	29/8/18		Sick passing through field Ambulance during 24 hours ending noon 29 August 18	
			1st F.G.W.RICK. MORO details for duty. Nil. Days that armoured cars off strength of 97 F.A. Evacuation of wounded	Nil
				SD1
	30/8/19		Sick passing through field Ambulance during 24 hours ending noon 30 August 18	
			Major W.S. DAVIES R.A.M.C. proceeded from LE BREBBIS and opened a new Advanced Dressing Station at S.36.75 Sheet 28	nil
				SD1

Army Form C. 2118.

WAR DIARY
or
INTELLIGENCE SUMMARY.
(Erase heading not required.)

Place	Date	Hour	Summary of Events and Information	Remarks and references to Appendices
LE BREBANT Sheet 28 G.31.A.5.2.	3/11/18		Sick passing through Field Ambulance during forenoon during hours 9th March 1918	
			Nil	
			Head Quarters moved by road to LE BREBANT. No advanced Dressing Station established at 1729 a 7.4 (Sheet 28) Evacuation of wounded	O.C. 9.M.D. F.A.

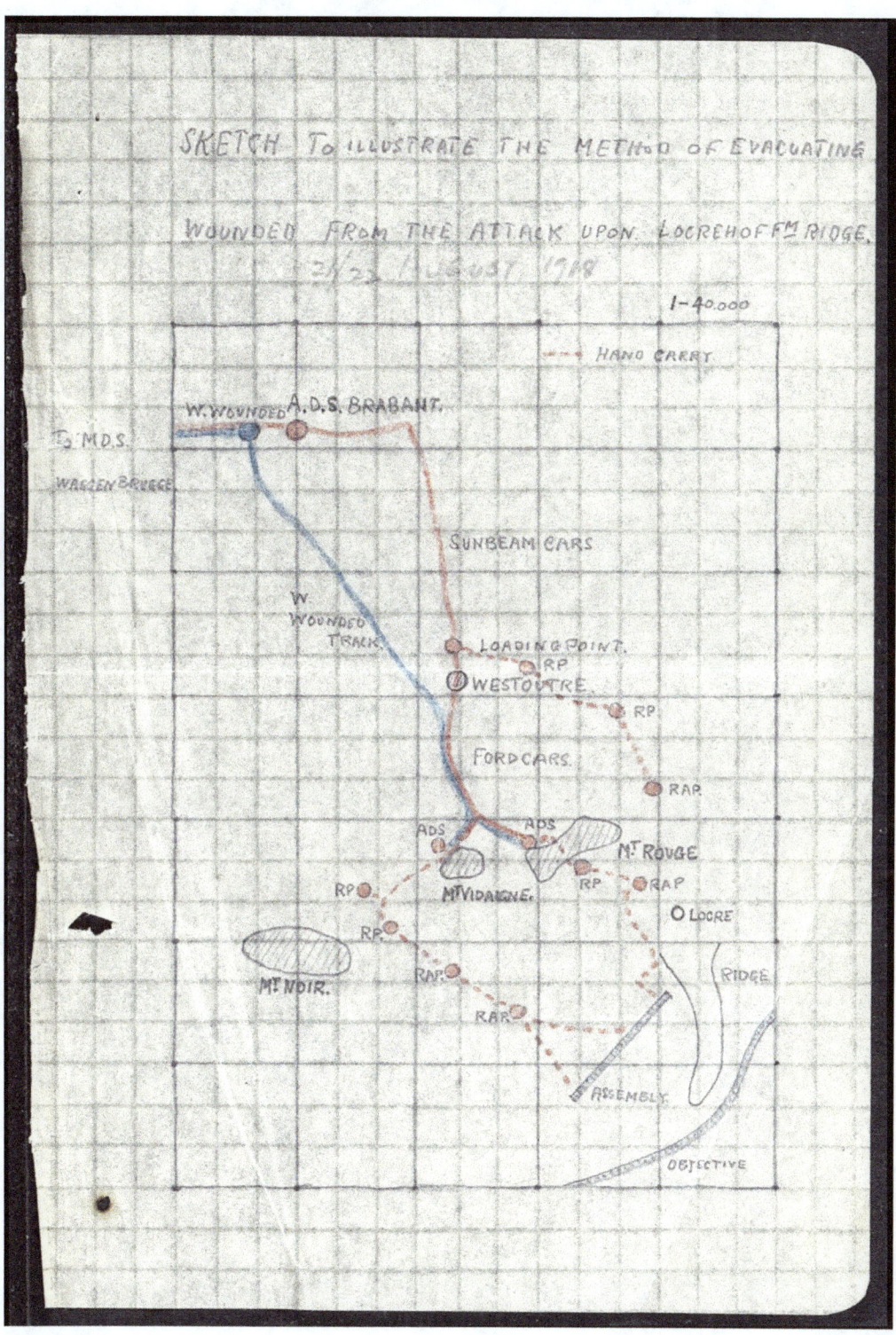

140/3259

97. F. Amb.

COMMITTEE FOR THE
MEDICAL HISTORY OF THE WAR
Date 9 NOV 1933

WAR DIARY
or
INTELLIGENCE SUMMARY.
(Erase heading not required.)

Army Form C. 2118.

Vol. 35
Volume XXXV
97 Field Ambulance

Place	Date	Hour	Summary of Events and Information	Remarks and references to Appendices
LE BIZET Sheet 28 G.31.d.5.2	1/9/18		Sick passing through Field Ambulance during 24 hours ending Noon 1st September 1918.	Nil
			Nil	
			Actions - Evacuation of wounded through A.D.S at S3 6.7.5	Mort Wks Renx W.D.97 Pt.1
			Sick passing through Field Ambulance during 24 hours ending Noon 2nd September 1918.	Nil
LOCRE M29.a.7.5 Sheet 28	2/9/18		Head Quarters moved by road to LOCRE Sheet 28 M.29 a.7.5. Lt C.E. BRADLEY M.O.R.C reported from temp. duty with 91 Sanitation Capt H.L. SHANNON M.O.R.C detailed for temp. duty with 98 Field Amb. Le Wounded evacuated through M.29 a.7.5 LOCRE. (Temp A.D.S at S3 6.7.5 close)	Nil

Army Form C. 2118.

WAR DIARY
or
INTELLIGENCE SUMMARY.
(Erase heading not required.)

97th Field Ambulance

Instructions regarding War Diaries and Intelligence Summaries are contained in F. S. Regs., Part II and the Staff Manual respectively. Title pages will be prepared in manuscript.

Place	Date	Hour	Summary of Events and Information	Remarks and references to Appendices
LOCRE	3/9/18		Men passing through Field Ambulance forward walking from Kilombe 3/9/18	
			NIL	
do	4/9/18		Evacuation of wounded through new MDS established at LOCRE	nil
			Men passing through Field Ambulance period ending dawn of 4th September 1918	nil
			NIL	
do	5/9/18		Routine Movements at this Unit. 6 members of personnel evacuated sick to rest station	nil
			Men passing through Field Ambulance — NIL	

C & D Sub Ambulances took over NL MDT & Ambulance Barge (Nieppe) & HAASDOORNE Sheet 28 S 3.b.2.2. Relieving the 3rd Canadian Divisional Station.

Army Form C. 2118.

WAR DIARY or INTELLIGENCE SUMMARY.
(Erase heading not required.)

97th Field Ambulance

Place	Date	Hour	Summary of Events and Information	Remarks and references to Appendices
HAGEDOORNE Sheet 28 B.3.a.3.9.	6/9/18		Sick passing through Field Ambulance, period ending noon September 6th 1918	
			Remained / Admitted / To C.C.S / To 96 F.A / To Duty / Remaining — OFF 20 / OR 20	Nil
			Capt H.L. SHANNON M.R.C. U.S.A. reported from 96th Field Ambulance. Capt G.H. NEARNEY R.A.M.C. reported from R.F.A. 38 Inf Bns. ROUTINE — Improvements at the Main Dressing Station	
	7/9/18		Sick passing through Field Ambulance, period ending noon September 7th 1918	
			Remained / Admitted / To C.C.S / To 96 F.A / To Duty / Remaining — OR 20 / OFF 2 OR 72 / OR 4 / OR 2 OR 78	Nil
			ROUTINE — Improvements at the Main Dressing Station	
	8/9/18		Sick passing through Field Ambulance, period ending noon September 8th 1918	
			Remained / Admitted / To C.C.S / To 96 F.A / To Duty / Remaining — OR / OFF 3 OR 47 / OR 1 / OR 2 OR 45	Nil
			Routine etc.	

Army Form C. 2118.

WAR DIARY
of 97 R Field Ambulance
INTELLIGENCE SUMMARY.
(Erase heading not required.)

Instructions regarding War Diaries and Intelligence Summaries are contained in F. S. Regs., Part II. and the Staff Manual respectively. Title pages will be prepared in manuscript.

Place	Date	Hour	Summary of Events and Information	Remarks and references to Appendices
HAGEDOORNE	9/9/18		Sick & wounded passing through Field Ambulance period ending Noon 9th September 1918	Nil

	REMAINED		Admitted		e. To C.C.S		96 To F.A		DUTY		Remaining	
	OFF	OR	OFF	OR	OFF	OR	OFF	OR	OFF	OR	OFF	OR
SICK	1	-	2	105	1	15	2	105				
WOUNDED			1	16				1				
			3	121	1	15	2	106				

Routine etc.

| - Do - | 10/9/18 | | Sick & wounded passing through Field Ambulance period ending Noon 10 September 1918 | Nil |

	Remained		Admitted		To C.C.S		To F.A		Duty		Remaining	
	OFF	OR	OFF	OR	OFF	OR	OFF	OR	OFF	OR	OFF	OR
SICK				58	3	26	2	96		20		55
WOUNDED				29		3						3
				87		29						58

Routine etc.
Improvements at the main dressing station

Army Form C. 2118.

WAR DIARY
INTELLIGENCE SUMMARY.
(Erase heading not required.)

97th Field Ambulance

Place	Date	Hour	Summary of Events and Information	Remarks and references to Appendices
HAGEDOORNE	11/9/18		Sick and wounded passing through Field Ambulance period ending noon 11th September 1918	

	Remaining		Admitted		CCS		30 2 M.R.		50 Lab		Remaining	
	Off	OR	Off	OR	Off	OR	Off	OR	Off	OR	Off	OR
SICK			5	78		3		75		2		
WOUNDED				30		28						
			5	108		31						77

Routine etc.   Nil

| | | | Sick and wounded passing through Field Ambulance period ending noon 12th September 1918 | |

	Remaining		Admitted		2 OCS		2 96 2 Camb		2 Lab		Remaining	
	Off	OR	Off	OR	Off	OR	Off	OR	Off	OR	Off	OR
SICK			2	40		1		2	39			
WOUNDED			1	5		4	1	1				
			3	45		5		3	40			

-do-	12/9/18			
			Major M.W. LITTLEWOOD RAMC ℅ leaves his duties on proceeds to report to OC 98 Field Ambulance for duty in the line	
		6 PM	Field Ambulance moved by road to WESTOUTRE Sheet 28 M9c 4.8 Mid and established a new main dressing station	

Army Form C. 2118.

WAR DIARY
or
INTELLIGENCE SUMMARY.
(Erase heading not required.)

97th Field Ambulance.

Instructions regarding War Diaries and Intelligence Summaries are contained in F. S. Regs., Part II. and the Staff Manual respectively. Title pages will be prepared in manuscript.

Place	Date	Hour	Summary of Events and Information	Remarks and references to Appendices
WESTOUTRE M9.c.4.8 Sheet 28	13/9/1918		Sick + wounded passing through Field Ambulance period ending 13th September 1918	
		12 NOON	<table>Remained / Admitted / to CCS / to 2.9f.29 / to 2nd duty / Remaining off/OR off/OR off/OR off/OR off/OR off/OR SICK: /1/74 / /3 / /1/74 / / / / WOUNDED: / / /5 / / /2 / / / / /1/79 / /3 / /1/76 / / / /</table>	
			Routine - Construction of M & D S	Nil
–do–	14/9/18		Sick + wounded passing through Field Ambulance period ending 12 NOON 14th September 1918	
			<table>Remained / Admitted / to CCS / to 2.96.9 and / to duty / Remaining off/OR off/OR off/OR off/OR off/OR off/OR SICK: /1/69 / /14 / / /1/69 / / / WOUNDED: /1/14 / /13 / / /1 / / / /1/83 / /13 / / /1/70 / / /</table>	
			Lt. Col. L. D. Shaw DSO RAMC proceeded on leave to United Kingdom. Major W.S. Danks RAMC assumes temporary command of 97th Field Ambulance in the absence of Lt. Col. Shaw.	
			Routine unchanged.	
			Capt C.R. Reckitt RAMC reported for duty	Nil

Army Form C. 2118.

WAR DIARY
of
INTELLIGENCE SUMMARY.
(Erase heading not required.)

97 R Field Ambulance

Instructions regarding War Diaries and Intelligence Summaries are contained in F. S. Regs., Part II. and the Staff Manual respectively. Title pages will be prepared in manuscript.

Place	Date	Hour	Summary of Events and Information	Remarks and references to Appendices
WESTOUTRE	15/9/18		Sick & wounded passing through Field Ambulance during period ending noon 15th September 1918	Nil

	Remained		Admitted		3rd C.C.S.		2o 98th		98th 2 and		2o July		Remained	
	Off.	OR	Off.	OR	Off.	OR	Off.	OR	Off.	OR	Off.	OR	Off.	OR
SICK			3	89	2	36	1	86		DIED 1				
WOUNDED			2	38			1	2		1				
			5	127	2	39	2	88						

Routine etc.

| | | | Sick & wounded passing through Field Ambulance during period ending noon 16th September 1918 | Nil |

| 16/9/18 | | | | | | | | | | | | | | |

	Remained		Admitted		2o CCS		2o 98 F. Amb.		2o July		Remained	
	Off.	OR	Off.	OR	Off.	OR	Off.	OR	Off.	OR	Off.	OR
SICK			2	56	1	8	1	56				
WOUNDED			2	64		8	1					

Routine etc. MAJOR M.W. LITTLEWOOD RAMC reports from 98th Field Ambulance

Sick & wounded passing through Field Ambulance during period ending noon 17th September 1918

| 17/9/18 | | | | | | | | | | | | | | |

	Remained		Admitted		2o CCS		2o 96 F Amb		2o duty		Remained	
	Off.	OR	Off.	OR	Off.	OR	Off.	OR	Off.	OR	Off.	OR
SICK			1	82	1	4	1	78				3
WOUNDED			2	35	2	27		5				3
			3	117	2	31	1	83				

Capt G.H. KEARNEY RAMC detailed for temporary duty with 1/5 R Sussex Militia Transport.

Nil

Army Form C. 2118.

WAR DIARY
of
INTELLIGENCE SUMMARY.
(Erase heading not required.)

8.   97th Field Ambulance

Place	Date	Hour	Summary of Events and Information	Remarks and references to Appendices
WESTOUTRE	18/9/18		Sick & wounded passing through Field Ambulance during period ending noon 18th September 1918	
			<table><tr><td></td><td colspan="2">Remaining</td><td colspan="2">admitted</td><td colspan="2">To C.C.S.</td><td colspan="2">To 96 F. Amb.</td><td colspan="2">To duty</td><td colspan="2">Remaining</td></tr><tr><td></td><td>Off</td><td>OR</td><td>Off</td><td>OR</td><td>Off</td><td>OR</td><td>Off</td><td>OR</td><td>Off</td><td>OR</td><td>Off</td><td>OR</td></tr><tr><td>SICK</td><td></td><td>90</td><td>4</td><td>7</td><td></td><td>5</td><td></td><td>4</td><td></td><td>1</td><td></td><td>1</td></tr><tr><td>WOUNDED</td><td></td><td>7</td><td></td><td></td><td></td><td>5</td><td></td><td></td><td></td><td>1</td><td></td><td>1</td></tr><tr><td></td><td>4</td><td>97</td><td>4</td><td>7</td><td></td><td>10</td><td></td><td>4</td><td></td><td>1</td><td></td><td>1</td></tr></table>	Nil
- do -	19/9/18		Routine &c	
			Sick & wounded passing through Field Ambulance during period ending noon 19 September 1918	
			<table><tr><td></td><td colspan="2">Remaining</td><td colspan="2">admitted</td><td colspan="2">To C.C.S.</td><td colspan="2">To 96 F. Amb.</td><td colspan="2">To duty</td><td colspan="2">Remaining</td></tr><tr><td></td><td>Off</td><td>OR</td><td>Off</td><td>OR</td><td>Off</td><td>OR</td><td>Off</td><td>OR</td><td>Off</td><td>OR</td><td>Off</td><td>OR</td></tr><tr><td>SICK</td><td>1</td><td>84</td><td>1</td><td>7</td><td></td><td>2</td><td></td><td>1</td><td></td><td></td><td>1</td><td>82</td></tr><tr><td>WOUNDED</td><td></td><td>7</td><td></td><td></td><td></td><td>6</td><td></td><td></td><td></td><td></td><td></td><td>1</td></tr><tr><td></td><td>1</td><td>91</td><td>1</td><td>7</td><td></td><td>8</td><td></td><td>1</td><td></td><td></td><td>1</td><td>83</td></tr></table>	Nil
- do -	20/9/18		Routine &c	
			Sick & wounded passing through Field Ambulance during period ending noon 20th September 1918	
			<table><tr><td></td><td colspan="2">Remaining</td><td colspan="2">admitted</td><td colspan="2">To C.C.S.</td><td colspan="2">To 96 F. Amb.</td><td colspan="2">To duty</td><td colspan="2">Remaining</td></tr><tr><td></td><td>Off</td><td>OR</td><td>Off</td><td>OR</td><td>Off</td><td>OR</td><td>Off</td><td>OR</td><td>Off</td><td>OR</td><td>Off</td><td>OR</td></tr><tr><td>SICK</td><td>1</td><td>79</td><td>2</td><td>18</td><td>1</td><td>15</td><td></td><td>1</td><td></td><td>1</td><td>1</td><td>78</td></tr><tr><td>WOUNDED</td><td></td><td></td><td></td><td></td><td></td><td></td><td></td><td></td><td></td><td></td><td></td><td>1</td></tr><tr><td></td><td>1</td><td>79</td><td>2</td><td>18</td><td>1</td><td>15</td><td></td><td>1</td><td></td><td>1</td><td>1</td><td>79</td></tr></table>	Nil

1st Lieut. C.E. BRADLEY M.O.R.C. proceeded for temporary duty with 98th Field Ambulance — Routine etc

Army Form C. 2118.

WAR DIARY
or
INTELLIGENCE SUMMARY.
(Erase heading not required.)

97th Field Ambulance

Place	Date	Hour	Summary of Events and Information	Remarks and references to Appendices
WESTOUTRE	21/9/18	Noon	Sick Wounded passing through Field Ambulance for period ending Noon 21st September 1918	nil

	Remaining		Admitted		2 CCS		3 CCS		3 Rest		3 Dty		Remaining	
	Off	OR	Off	OR	Off	OR	Off	OR	Off	OR	Off	OR	Off	OR
SICK	1	64	2	16		1		13					1	64
WOUNDED		1	2	80				14		2				65

Routine – improvements to site

| - do - | 22/9/18 | | Sick Wounded passing through Field Ambulance for period ending noon 22nd September 1918 | nil |

	Remaining		Admitted		2 Cd		3c Amb		3 Duty		Remaining	
	Off	OR	Off	OR	Off	OR	Off	OR	Off	OR	Off	OR
SICK	1	63	1	2				2	1	63		
WOUNDED		65		2									

Routine etc

| - do - | 23/9/18 | | Sick Wounded passing through Field Ambulance for period ending noon 23rd September 1918 | nil |

	Remaining		Admitted		3c CCS		3c gd 3 Amb		2c duty		Remaining	
	Off	OR	Off	OR	Off	OR	Off	OR	Off	OR	Off	OR
SICK	2	75		20	1	19		2		74	1	
WOUNDED		95	3			20			3	74	1	

Routine etc –

final

Army Form C. 2118.

WAR DIARY
or
INTELLIGENCE SUMMARY.
(Erase heading not required.)

97th Field Ambulance

Place	Date	Hour	Summary of Events and Information	Remarks and references to Appendices
WESTOUTRE	24/9/18		Sick wounded passing through Field Ambulance during period ending Noon 24th September 1918	

			admitted To CCS To 2/1 To 3rd To duty Remaining
			         Off OR Off OR Off OR Off OR Off OR Off OR
			 SICK 2 49 — 4 — — — 45 2 —
			 WOUNDED 2 20 2 19 — 2 — 1 — —
			         4 69 2 23 — 2 — 46 2 —
				Nil

			Major H. HARDING RAMC reported to be attached for instructional purposes. Routine.	
-do-	25/9/18		Sick wounded passing through Field Ambulance during period ending Noon 25th September 1918	

			Remaining admitted To CCS To 2/1 To 3rd To duty Remaining
			         Off OR Off OR Off OR Off OR Off OR Off OR Off OR
			 SICK 3 68 3 — — 1 — 2 — — — 66 — —
			 WOUNDED 3 20 3 — — 1 — 12 — 1 — 3 1 2
			         6 88 6 — — 2 — 14 — 3 — 69 1 2	

			Routine etc.-	
-do-	26/9/18		Sick wounded passing through Field Ambulance during period ending noon 26 September 1918	Nil

			Remaining admitted To CCS To 2/1 To 3rd To duty Remaining
			         Off OR Off OR Off OR Off OR Off OR Off OR Off OR
			 SICK 4 74 4 — — 4 — — — — — 4 — 70 — —
			 WOUNDED 3 24 3 — — 3 — 15 — — — — — 8 1 2
			         7 98 7 — — 7 — 19 — — — 4 — 78 1 2	

			Capt. H.L. SHANNON MORE detailed for temporary duty with 2nd Reception Camp	

Army Form C. 2118.

WAR DIARY
of
INTELLIGENCE SUMMARY.
(Erase heading not required.)

97th Field Ambulance

Instructions regarding War Diaries and Intelligence Summaries are contained in F. S. Regs., Part II. and the Staff Manual respectively. Title pages will be prepared in manuscript.

Place	Date	Hour	Summary of Events and Information	Remarks and references to Appendices
WESTOUTRE	21/9/18		Sick wounded passing through Field Ambulance period ending 21st September 1918	
				Remaining admitted To C.C.S. To 90 Field Amb. To duty Died Remaining	
				Off OR Off OR Off OR Off OR Off OR Off OR	
			SICK 3 46 1 2 26 20	
			WOUNDED 3 5 2 3 2 1	
			6 51 3 3 2 28 1 20	
			Capt G.H. KEARNEY R.A.M.C. reported from 7/6 Br.R. Mountain Field Amb.	✓
- do -	28/9/18		Sick wounded passing through Field Ambulance period ending 28th September 1918	
				Remaining admitted To C.C.S. To 98th F.Amb. To duty Remaining	
				Off OR Off OR Off OR Off OR Off OR Off OR	
			SICK 20 2 66 9 2 36 5 36	
			WOUNDED 1 22 1 16 1 5	
			20 3 88 1 25 2 37 5 41	
			Routine etc.	✓

Army Form C. 2118.

WAR DIARY
or
INTELLIGENCE SUMMARY.
(Erase heading not required.)

97th Field Ambulance

Instructions regarding War Diaries and Intelligence Summaries are contained in F. S. Regs., Part II. and the Staff Manual respectively. Title pages will be prepared in manuscript.

Place	Date	Hour	Summary of Events and Information	Remarks and references to Appendices
LOCRE. Sheet 28. M.29.a.7.5	29/9/16		Sick admissions passing through Field Ambulance. Periods ending noon 29th September 1916.	

	Remained	Admitted	To CCS	To 96 Bd	To duty	Remaining
	Off	OR	Off	OR	Off	OR	Off	OR	Off	OR	Off	OR
SICK	–	36	1	63	1	22	–	34	–	9	–	34
WOUNDED	5	–	7	162	7	152	1	–	–	5	–	9
	5	41	8	225	8	174	1	34	–	14	–	43

Field Ambulance moved by road to LOCRE M.29.a.7.5. Sheet 28 and established a new main dressing station – Continue –

| –do– | 30/9/16 | | Sick admissions passing through Field Ambulance periods ending noon 30 September 1916 | Nil |

	Remained	Admitted	To CCS	To M.D. Front	To duty	Remaining
	Off	OR	Off	OR	Off	OR	Off	OR	Off	OR	Off	OR
SICK	–	34	2	63	–	20	2	26	–	–	–	56
WOUNDED	9	–	3	73	3	62	–	3	DIED 1	5/1	11	–
	43	–	5	141	3	82	2	29	5/1		67	

Capt. G.H. KEARNEY RAMC granted leave to United Kingdom from 30. 9. 15. to 14. 10. 16.

Nil

Roderick C.E.
[signature] Lt Col
RAMC
97 F.Amb

Volume XXXVI
October 1918. Army Form C. 2118.
97 (CP) Field Ambulance

WAR DIARY
or
INTELLIGENCE SUMMARY
(Erase heading not required.)

Place	Date 1918	Hour	Summary of Events and Information	Remarks and references to Appendices
NEUVE EGLISE T. 10 central	1 Oct		Sick and Wounded passed through F. Amb. during 24 hrs ending noon 1 Oct 1918	
				To CCS	To 96 F.A.	Sick		
				Remaining	Admitted	OFF OR	OFF OR	OFF OR	To duty OFF OR	Remaining OFF OR	
			SICK OFF 1 OR 54	2 70	2 14	— 59	— 5	OFF 1 OR 51	51 7	
			WOUNDED 1 87	2 130	2 70	4 63	1 5	— 58	58	
			Field Ambulance moved by road to NEUVE EGLISE and established Main Dressing Station.	SDS ⟩ 97 FA
	2 Oct		Sick and Wounded passed through F. Amb. during 24 hrs ending noon 2 Oct 1918	
				To CCS	To 96 F.A.	Died	To duty	Remaining	
				Remaining	Admitted	OFF OR	OFF OR	OFF OR	OFF OR	OFF OR	
			SICK OFF 1 OR 58	1 105	1 14	1 39	— —	2 24	100 5	
			WOUNDED — 46	2 151	2 44	1 40	— 1	— 6	— 105	
			Central — Evacuation information	SDS
Spanbroek Farm N.30.a.3.3	3 Oct		Sick and Wounded passed through F. Amb. during 24 hrs ending noon 3 Oct 1918	
				To CCS	To 96 F.A	Died	To duty	Remaining	
				Remaining	Admitted	OFF OR	OFF OR	OFF OR	OFF OR	OFF OR	
			SICK OFF 1 OR 100	3 38	1 14	2 —	— —	1 2	OFF 2 OR 135	
			WOUNDED 2 105	4 55	4 45	— 12	— 1	— 7	— 9 145	
			Ambulance moved by road to HALLCUT Farm and established Main Dressing Station. Capt J.H.L. SHANNON R.A.M.C. USA proceeded to ENGLAND in return to AMERICA for instruction in X-Rays. Lieut CE BARRLEY R.A.M.C. USA reported from tempory duty at 30 Field Bakery.	97 FA 9 (k) FA and was detailed for temporarily duty at 8 Br. Fld Bakery

Army Form C. 2118.

WAR DIARY
or
INTELLIGENCE SUMMARY.

(Erase heading not required.)

97th (OP) Field Ambulance

Instructions regarding War Diaries and Intelligence Summaries are contained in F. S. Regs., Part II. and the Staff Manual respectively. Title pages will be prepared in manuscript.

Place	Date	Hour	Summary of Events and Information	Remarks and references to Appendices
AIRCRAFT FARM	1918			
	4 Oct		Sick and Wounded passed through 7.O. n.t during 24 hrs ending noon 4th Oct 1918.	
			<table>Remained / Admitted / to C.C.S. / to 96 F.A. / to duty / Remaining OFF OR / OFF OR / OFF OR / OFF OR / OFF OR / OFF OR SICK: 136 / 1 41 / 1 28 / 142 / / 7 WOUNDED: 9 / 2 23 / 2 22 / 10 / / 7 145 / 3 64 / 3 50 / 152 / / 7</table>	Sgd
			Routine – Evacuation of Sick and Wounded &c.	
	5 Oct		Sick and Wounded passed through 7.Amb during 24 hrs ending noon 5th Oct 1918.	
			<table>Remained / Admitted / to C.C.S. / to 96 F.A. / Died / to duty / Remaining OFF OR / OFF OR / OFF OR / OFF OR / OFF OR / OFF OR / OFF OR SICK: / 2 47 / 7 / 2 40 / / / 2 WOUNDED: / 1 26 / 40 / 1 3 / / / 1 3 93 / 47 / 3 43 / / /</table>	Sgd
			Routine – Evacuation of Sick and Wounded &c.	
	6 Oct		Sick and Wounded passed through 7.Amb during 24 hrs ending noon 6th Oct 1918.	
			<table>Remained / Admitted / to C.C.S. / to N.R.S. / Died / to duty / Remaining OFF OR / OFF OR / OFF OR / OFF OR / OFF OR / OFF OR / OFF OR SICK: / 1 64 / 3 / 1 61 / / / 3 WOUNDED: / 14 / 11 / / / / 3 1 78 / 14 / 1 61 / / /</table>	Sgd
			Lieut L. SEIDLER R.A.M.C. U.S.A. reported for temporary duty.	

Army Form C. 2118.

WAR DIARY
or
INTELLIGENCE SUMMARY.

(Erase heading not required)

97th Coy Field Ambulance

Place	Date	Hour	Summary of Events and Information	Remarks and references to Appendices
AIRCRAFT FARM	7 Oct		SICK and WOUNDED passed through 97 Coy during 24 hrs ending Noon 7th Oct 1918.	

	Remained		Admitted		96 F.A.		96 F.A.		
	OFF	OR	OFF	OR	OFF	OR	OFF	OR	
SICK		35		7		48			Remaining
WOUNDED	1	13		13					
	1	68	1	20		48			

Lieut L SEIDLER, M.O.R.C. U.S.A. proceeded to duty at 66 Base Hospital A.E.F.

| | 6 Oct | | SICK and WOUNDED passed through 97 Amb during 24 hrs ending Noon 8th Oct 1918. | |

	Remained		Admitted		To C.C.S.		To 96 F.A.		
	OFF	OR	OFF	OR	OFF	OR	OFF	OR	Remaining
SICK		31		18		18		31	
WOUNDED		17		13		13		3	
		48		31		31		34	

Major W.S. DAVIES R.A.M.C. 9th Col. Leave to UK from 8th Oct to 5th Nov 1918.
Major N. LITTLEWOOD R.A.M.C. assumed command of 97 F Amb during absence on leave of Lieut. Col. L.D. SHAW A.S.O., R.A.M.C.

SICK and WOUNDED passed through 97 Amb during 24 hrs ending Noon 9th Oct 1918.

	Remained		Admitted		To C.C.S.				Remaining
	OFF	OR	OFF	OR	OFF	OR	OFF	OR	
SICK		48		8		12		44	
WOUNDED	2	19		2		5		16	
	2	67		10		17		60	

| | 9 Oct | | | |

Routine Evacuation of Sick and Wounded Cases.
Cols: 2 R. REDGITT R.A.M.C. evacuated Oct 5 to CCS

WAR DIARY or INTELLIGENCE SUMMARY

Army Form C. 2118.

97 (CD) Field Ambulance

Place	Date	Hour	Summary of Events and Information	Remarks and references to Appendices
WYTSCHAETE N 30 a.17 Sheet 28	19/10	10 AM	Sick and WOUNDED passed through F. Amb. during 24 hr. ending noon 19th Oct 1918.	

Sick and WOUNDED passed through F. Amb. during 24 hr. ending noon 19th Oct 1918.

	Remained	Admitted		To CCS		To 98 FA		To 98 FA Sick		To 98 FA Remaining	
		OFF	OR	OFF	OR	OFF	OR	OFF	OR	OFF	OR
SICK		1	49		14				1		35
WOUNDED		4	31	4	26		3				
		5	80	4	40		1		1		38

Ambulance moved to road 16 N 30 a.17 and established Main Dressing Station.

SDS

| | 11 Oct | | Sick and WOUNDED passed through F. Amb. during 24 hr. ending noon 11 Oct 1918. | |

	Remaining	Admitted		To CCS		To 98 FA				Remaining	
		OFF	OR	OFF	OR	OFF	OR			OFF	OR
SICK			64		14		50				
WOUNDED			17		15		2				
			81		29		52				

Capt. T.B. Cavey RAMC Lance Corporal for temporary duty.

SDS

| | 12 Oct | | Sick and WOUNDED passed through F. Amb. during 24 hr. ending noon 12th Oct 1918. | |

	Remained	Admitted		To CCS		To 99 FA				Remaining	
		OFF	OR	OFF	OR	OFF	OR			OFF	OR
SICK		1	49	1	46		48				
WOUNDED		5	46	5	21						
		6	95	6	67		48				

Evacuation of Sick and Wounded RC

SDS

Army Form C. 2118.

WAR DIARY
or
INTELLIGENCE SUMMARY.
(Erase heading not required.)

97 (CP) Field Ambulance

Instructions regarding War Diaries and Intelligence Summaries are contained in F. S. Regs., Part II. and the Staff Manual respectively. Title pages will be prepared in manuscript.

Place	Date	Hour	Summary of Events and Information	Remarks and references to Appendices
N 30 c Slat 26	1918		SICK and WOUNDED passed through F. Amb. during 24 hrs ending noon 13th Oct 1918	
		1504	<table>SICK / WOUNDED — Remained / Admitted / To CCS / To 96 FA / Died / Remaining Off Or Off Or Off Or Off Or Off Or Off Or SICK: — 5 83 — 1 — — 4 69 — — WOUNDED: — — 5 53 — 42 — 14 — 10 — 1</table> Total 5 136 1 56 4 79 1	SOS
			Capt D.R. PIKE RAMC reported to temporary duty. Capt F.B. CAMPBELL MC RAMC proceeded to 96 Fd Amb for duty Lt Colonel C.F. BRADLEY MOIC h36 reported from 6 hr 96 Water Borderers.	
			SICK and WOUNDED passed through F. Amb. during 24 hrs. ending noon 14th Oct 1918	
	14 Oct		<table>Remained / Admitted / To CCS / To 96 FA / Died / Remaining Off Or Off Or Off Or Off Or Off Or Off Or SICK: — — 3 61 1 31 2 30 — — 1 — WOUNDED: — — 4 70 2 29 2 30 — — 1 —</table>	SOS
			Routine – Evacuation of Sick and wounded to Cabling Walking wounded collecting post	
			SICK and WOUNDED passed through 24 hr. during 24 hr. ending noon 15th Oct 1918.	
		1600	<table>Remained / Admitted / To CCS / To 96 FA / Died / Remaining Off Or Off Or Off Or Off Or Off Or Off Or SICK: 7 104 7 158 7 104 — 30 — — — — WOUNDED: 7 265 7 262 — 158 2 — — — 1 —</table> Total 54 53	SOS
			P.O.W. WOUNDED Evacuation of Sick and wounded thro' 96 MDS and Walking Wounded collecting post Capt G.H. GARNET REMO reported from leave Major H. HARDING RAMC proceeded to 95 Field Amb or duty as Commanding Officer	

Army Form C. 2118.

WAR DIARY
or
INTELLIGENCE SUMMARY.
(Erase heading not required.)

97(2/1) Field Ambulance

Instructions regarding War Diaries and Intelligence Summaries are contained in F.S. Regs., Part II. and the Staff Manual respectively. Title pages will be prepared in manuscript.

Place	Date 1918	Hour	Summary of Events and Information														Remarks and references to Appendices

16 Oct

D.30.a.1.7 Sheet 28 — Sick and Wounded passed through 7 Oct. during 24 hrs. ending noon 16 Oct 1918

	Remained		Admitted		To CCS		To 98 FA		Died		Remaining	
	OFF	OR	OFF	OR	OFF	OR	OFF	OR	OFF	OR	OFF	OR
SICK			3	64		44						13
WOUNDED				21		20		7		1		
			3	85	3	64		7		1		13

P.O.W. WOUNDED — 5

Lt Col L D Shaw DSO RAMC reported from leave but assumed command of 97 Fd Amb.
Capt D R Pike RAMC proceeded to 98 Fd Amb for duty.

SDC

17 Oct

Hollebeke P.7.c central — Sick and Wounded passed through 24 hrs during 24 hrs ending noon 17 Oct 1918

	Remained		Admitted		To CCS		To 98 FA		To duty		Remaining	
	OFF	OR	OFF	OR	OFF	OR	OFF	OR	OFF	OR	OFF	OR
SICK		13	3	76	3	50		39				
WOUNDED			3	17	3	14		2		1		
		13	6	93	6	64		41		1		

Ambulance moved by road to 6 Hollebeke and established Main Dressing Station.
SDC

18 Oct

Hollebeke — Sick and Wounded passed through 24 hrs during 24 hrs ending noon 18 Oct 1918

	Remained		Admitted		To CCS		To 98 FA				Remaining	
	OFF	OR	OFF	OR	OFF	OR	OFF	OR			OFF	OR
SICK			2	38	2	11		27				
WOUNDED				2		2						
			2	40	2	13		27				

Ambulance moved by road out of open from Dressing Station at Konce
14 Field CE Bagley RAMC M.R.O. proceeding to 6th [?] Station Borders for temp duty
SDC

Army Form C. 2118.

WAR DIARY
or
INTELLIGENCE SUMMARY.
(Erase heading not required)

97(2/1) Field Ambulance

Instructions regarding War Diaries and Intelligence Summaries are contained in F. S. Regs., Part II. and the Staff Manual respectively. Title pages will be prepared in manuscript.

Place	Date 1918	Hour	Summary of Events and Information	Remarks and references to Appendices
RONCQ	19/10		Sick and Wounded passed through F. Amb during 24 hrs ending noon 19th Oct 1918.	
				Remained
			Admitted / To CCS	OFF / OR
			OFF OR / OFF OR	
			SICK 1 5 / 1 5	
			WOUNDED 2 7 / 2 7	
			3 12 / 3 12	
			Routine – Evacuation of Sick and Wounded to.	SDC
	20 Oct		Sick and Wounded passed through F. Amb. during 24 hrs ending noon 20th Oct 1918.	
				Remaining
			Admitted / To CCS	OFF / OR
			OFF OR / OFF OR	
			SICK 8 103 / 8 88	15
			WOUNDED 12 / 12	15
			8 115 / 8 100	
			Routine – evacuation of Sick and Wounded to.	SSS
	21 Oct		Sick and WOUNDED passed through F. Amb. during 24 hrs ending noon 21st Oct 1918.	
				Died Totals / Remaining
			Admitted / To CCS	OFF OR / OFF OR
			OFF OR / OFF OR	14
			SICK 15 / 3 92 / 1	
			WOUNDED 3 31 / 3 30 / 1	14
			3 6 123 / 6 122 / 1	
STERRENHOEK S.14.a.5.6 Sheet 29	21 Oct		Ambulance moved by road to STERRENHOEK	SDC

WAR DIARY
or
INTELLIGENCE SUMMARY.

(Erase heading not required.)

97 (2D) Field Ambulance

Army Form C. 2118.

Instructions regarding War Diaries and Intelligence Summaries are contained in F. S. Regs., Part II. and the Staff Manual respectively. Title pages will be prepared in manuscript.

Place	Date 1918	Hour	Summary of Events and Information	Remarks and references to Appendices
COYGHEM U.19.c.4.7 Sheet 94	22 Oct		Sick and Wounded passed through 7 Amb. during 24 Hrs ending noon 22nd Oct 1918.	
			SICK — Remained Off 14 OR — / Admitted To 98 F.A. Off — OR — / Remaining Off 14 OR —	
			WOUNDED — / — / Nil / — / 14 / —	
			Reuse Dry Road to COYGHEM and established Advanced Dressing Station	S.S.
	23 Oct		Sick and Wounded passed through 7 Amb. during 24 hrs ending noon 23rd Oct 1918.	
			SICK — Remained Off OR 2 31 / Admitted Off OR 2 31 / To 98 F.A. Off OR — 21 / Remaining Off OR 2 10	Sick Off OR — 1
			WOUNDED — 2 62 / — 2 62 / — 2 30 / — 2 51	
			Routine — Evacuation of Sick and Wounded Evacuation of Sick and Wounded auxilliary from Forward Area	
			Capt. J.B. Mackay R.A.M.C. reported for temporary duty.	
			Sick and Wounded passed through 7 Amb. during 24 Hrs ending noon 24th Oct 1918.	
	24 Oct		SICK — Remained Off 1 OR 40 / Admitted Off 1 OR 7 / To 98 F.A. Off OR 411 / Died Off OR 6 / Remaining Off OR 6	
			WOUNDED — 10 / 1 47 / 1 50 / — 1 / — 6	
			Lt Col. L.D. Snow A.S.O. R.A.M.C. admitted to hospital, 98 F.A. Sick. Major M. Whittlewood R.A.M.C. assumed temporary command of 97 Amb.	G.J.

Army Form C. 2118.

WAR DIARY
or
INTELLIGENCE SUMMARY.
(Erase heading not required.)

97(P) Field Ambulance

Place	Date	Hour	Summary of Events and Information	Remarks and references to Appendices
CYGNEN	1915		Sick and Wounded passed through 7 Amb. during 24 hrs ending hour 28 Oct 1915.	
				Remaining
			Received / Admitted / To 95 F.A. / OK	Off / OR
	25/10	0504	SICK / WOUNDED — OFF: — OR: 6 / OFF: 2 OR: 43 / OFF: 2 OR: 49 / OFF: — OR: —	— / 1
			— / 2 / 10 / 9 / —	
			6 / 3 / 53 / 3 / 58 / —	
			Routine — Evacuation of Sick and Wounded etc	SDC
			Sick and Wounded passed through 7 Amb. during 24 hrs ending hour 26 Oct 1915.	
			Received / Admitted to 95 F.A. / OK / Remaining	
			OFF / OR — OFF / OR — OFF / OR	
	26/10	1201	SICK / WOUNDED — NIL	
			— / 1 / — / 1 / —	
			Routine — Evacuation of Sick and Wounded etc to 95 F.A	SDC
			Sick and Wounded passed through 7 Amb during 24 hrs ending hour 27 Oct 1915.	
	27/10	0704	— NIL —	
			Routine — Evacuation of Sick and Wounded to ADS	SDC

Army Form C. 2118.

WAR DIARY
or
INTELLIGENCE SUMMARY.
(Erase heading not required.)

97 (CD) Field Ambulance.

Instructions regarding War Diaries and Intelligence Summaries are contained in F. S. Regs., Part II. and the Staff Manual respectively. Title pages will be prepared in manuscript.

Place	Date	Hour	Summary of Events and Information	Remarks and references to Appendices
ROLLEGHEM T.2.a.2.6 Sheet 29	25 Oct		SICK and WOUNDED passed through F. Amb during 24 hr ending noon 25th Oct 1918. NIL	
			Surgeon Lieut. H.O. BLANDFORD. R.N. reported for duty and was taken on the strength of 97 Fd Amb.	SDS
			SICK and WOUNDED passed through F. Amb during 24 hr ending noon 29th Oct 1918.	
			Remained / Admitted / To 98FA / Remaining OFF OR / OFF OR / OFF OR / OFF OR SICK — / 1 36 / 1 / 35 WOUNDED — / 2 35 / 2 / 35	
			Capt. OP PECKITT RAMC reported for duty from Hospital on discharge. Lieut. E.B. BRIGROSE RAMC granted leave to UK from 29.10.18 to 12.11.18	SDS
			Sick and Wounded passed through F. Amb during 24 hrs ending noon 30 Oct 1918.	
30 Oct			Remained / Admitted / To S.C.C. / Remaining OFF OR / OFF OR / OFF OR / OFF OR SICK — 35 / — 76 / — 40 / — 71 WOUNDED — 35 / — 76 / — 40 / — 71	
			Capt J.B. MACKAY RAMC proceeded to 96 Field Amb for duty	SDS

Army Form C. 2118.

WAR DIARY
or
INTELLIGENCE SUMMARY.
(Erase heading not required.)

97 (C.P.) Field Ambulance

Instructions regarding War Diaries and Intelligence Summaries are contained in F. S. Regs., Part II. and the Staff Manual respectively. Title pages will be prepared in manuscript.

Place	Date	Hour	Summary of Events and Information	Remarks and references to Appendices
ROLLEGHEM	31/10		Sick and Wounded passed through L Amb during 24 hrs ending noon 31 Oct. 1918	
			<table> Remaining / Admitted / To 97 FA / Totals / Remaining OFF OR / OFF OR / OFF OR / OFF OR / OFF OR SICK: 71 / 10 / 10 / 76 / 52 WOUNDED: / / 12 / 12 / </table>	
			Routine - Hospital - Collection and Evacuation of Sick.	Sudden S. 41 O.C. 97 F.A.

WAR DIARY
or
INTELLIGENCE SUMMARY.

Army Form C. 2118.

97th (6.?) Field Ambulance. November 1918.

Volume XXXVII

Place	Date 1918	Hour	Summary of Events and Information	Remarks and references to Appendices
ROLLEGHEM T.2.a.2.6 (Ref. 9.9)	1 Nov		Sick and Wounded passed through & Evac. during 24 hrs ending Noon 1st Nov 1918	

Sick and Wounded — week ending Noon 1st Nov 1918:

	Remaining		Admitted		Transfs from 98 BA		To 66 CCS		To 98th BA		Remaining	
	OFF	OR	OFF	OR	OFF	OR	OFF	OR	OFF	OR	OFF	OR
SICK		52		8		28		7		19		62
WOUNDED		52		8		28		7		19		62

Routine Hospital work, collection of sick 15
Lt Col L.D. PHIL. D.S.O. R.A.M.C. reported from Hospital

Ist Nov G.S. Wand?
D.D.M.S.

| 2 Nov | | | Sick and Wounded passed through & Evac. during 24 hrs ending Noon 2nd Nov 1918 | |

	Remaining		Admitted		Transfs from 98		To 66 CCS		To 98th BA		To Duty		Remaining	
	OFF	OR	OFF	OR	OFF	OR	OFF	OR	OFF	OR	OFF	OR	OFF	OR
SICK		62		6				12		17		1			51
WOUNDED		62		6				12		17		1			51

Routine Hospital work

| 3 Nov | | | Sick and Wounded passed through & Evac. during 24 hrs ending Noon 3 Nov 1918 | |

	Remaining		Admitted				To 66 CCS		To 98 BA				Remaining	
	OFF	OR	OFF	OR			OFF	OR	OFF	OR			OFF	OR
SICK		51		10				5		1				55
WOUNDED		51		10				6		1				55

Routine Hospital work

Army Form C. 2118.

WAR DIARY
of
INTELLIGENCE SUMMARY.

97th (C.P.) Field Ambulance

(Erase heading not required.)

Instructions regarding War Diaries and Intelligence Summaries are contained in F. S. Regs. Part II. and the Staff Manual respectively. Title pages will be prepared in manuscript.

Place	Date 1918	Hour	Summary of Events and Information	Remarks and references to Appendices
POLLEGHEM	4 Nov	4 hrs	Sick and WOUNDED passed through F. Amb. during 24 hrs ending Noon 4th Nov 1918. **Remaining** OFF/OR 55 — / **Admitted** OFF/OR —/4 / **Trsfrd to 96 FA** OFF/OR 3/1 / **To C.C.S.** OFF/OR 1/— / **To Duty** OFF/OR —/11 / **Remaining** OFF/OR 50/1 SICK 55 / — / 4 / 3 / 1 / — / 11 / 50 WOUNDED — / 1 / 4 / 1 / — / 1 / — / 1 / 51 Routine Hospital work.	208
HOOGMOLEN O.23.d.5.9 Sheet 29.	5 Nov		Sick and WOUNDED passed through F. Amb. during 24 hrs ending Noon 5th Nov 1918. **Remaining** / **Admitted** / **Trsfrd from 96 FA** / **To C.C.S.** / **To 96th FA** / **To Duty** / **Remaining** SICK 50 / 5 / — / 29 / — / 13 / 13 / — WOUNDED 1 / 5 / — / 29 / — / 14 / 13 / — Unit moved by road to HOOGMOLEN. Surg Lieut. H.O. BLANFORD, R.N. and 1 Tent Sub Section (a temporary A.D.S. with Reserve Medical Unit Capt. C.R. REBBITT R.A.M.C. and Capt. G. M° KENZIE R.A.M.C.) moved with Bearers to take over line.	209
	6 Nov		Sick and WOUNDED passed through to Station during 24 hrs ending Noon 6 Nov 1918. **Admitted** / **Trsfrd from 96 FA** / **To 96th FA** / **Died** / **Remaining** SICK 1 / — / 4 / 4 / — / 1 / — / — / 1 / — WOUNDED 1 / — / 4 / 4 / — / 1 / — / — / 1 / — Routine — Main Dressing Station Major M.W. LITTLEWOOD R.A.M.C. admitted to Hospital. sick.	210

Army Form C. 2118.

WAR DIARY
of
INTELLIGENCE SUMMARY.   91st (C.P.) Field Ambulance

(Erase heading not required.)

Instructions regarding War Diaries and Intelligence Summaries are contained in F. S. Regs., Part II. and the Staff Manual respectively. Title pages will be prepared in manuscript.

Place	Date	Hour	Summary of Events and Information	Remarks and references to Appendices
HOOGMOLEN	1/11/18		SICK and WOUNDED passed through D.Amb. during 24 hrs ending Noon Nov 1st 1918	
			Admitted / To 96 D.A. / Remaining	
			OFF / OR / OFF / OR	
			SICK 1 / 2 / — / 2	Nil
			WOUNDED 1 / 1 / 1 / 2	
			Routine — Main Dressing Station and A.D.S.	S.D.S.
	2/11		SICK and WOUNDED passed through D.Amb. during 24 hrs ending Noon Nov 2nd 1918	
			Admitted / To 96th D.A. / Remaining	
			OFF / OR / OFF / OR	
			SICK — / 2 / — / 2	Nil
			WOUNDED 1 / 1 / 1 / 1	
			Routine Capt. C.F. BRADLEY R.C. R.P. reported from 6 F.A. to take place	S.D.S.
			SICK and WOUNDED passed through D.Amb. during 24 hrs ending Noon 3/11/18	
			SICK	Nil
			WOUNDED	
AUTRYVE V.a.5.4 Clerl' 20	3/11	9 a.m.	Unit moved by road to AUTRYVE and established M.D.S. Major W.S. DONKS R.A.M.C. reported from leave	S.D.S.

Army Form C. 2118.

WAR DIARY
or
INTELLIGENCE SUMMARY.

97th (C.T.) Field Ambulance.

(Erase heading not required.)

Instructions regarding War Diaries and Intelligence Summaries are contained in F.S. Regs., Part II. and the Staff Manual respectively. Title pages will be prepared in manuscript.

Place	Date	Hour	Summary of Events and Information	Remarks and references to Appendices
WATERLOO E.5.b.9.3 Sheet 37.	10/11/18	10 hrs	SICK and WOUNDED passed through F. Amb. during 24 hrs ending 10am 10th Nov 1918	
			SICK — Nil	
			WOUNDED — Nil	
			Unit moved by road and established M.A.S. and A.D.S.	SF
FLOBECQ T.27.a.8.5 Sheet 30	11/11/18		SICK and WOUNDED passed through to Field during 24 hrs ending Noon 11th Nov 1918	
			SICK — Nil	
			WOUNDED — Nil	
			Unit moved by road to FLOBECQ	
			Capt. G.H. KEARNEY R.A.M.C. for temporary duty at 36 Div. Reception Camp S.O.S.	
			SICK passed through 36 Div Amb. during 48 hrs ending Noon 12th Nov 1918	
	12 Nov			Admitted / Remaining
				OFF O.R. / OFF O.R.
			SICK	10 / 10
				10 / 10
			Major M.W. LITTLEWOOD R.A.M.C. reported from Hospital	SOS

Army Form C. 2118.

WAR DIARY
or
INTELLIGENCE SUMMARY.
(Erase heading not required.)

97th (CP) Field Ambulance

Place	Date	Hour	Summary of Events and Information	Remarks and references to Appendices
FIOBECQ	13/11/18		Sick paraded through Dte Andics during 24hrs ending Noon 13th Nov 1918	
			Remaining / Admitted / Remaining OFF / OR / OFF / OR / OFF / OR SICK — / 10 — / 5 — / 15	
			Routine Hospital Work	
			Sick paraded through Dte Andel during 24hrs ending Noon 14th Nov 1918	
			Remaining / Admitted / Remaining OFF / OR / OFF / OR / OFF / OR SICK — / 15 — / 9 — / 24	
			Unit moved by road to RENAIX Lieut E. B. RINGROSE R.A.M.C reported from leave.	
RENAIX X.16.d.central Sheet 59.	15/11/18		Sick paraded through Dte Andts during 24hrs ending Noon 15th Nov 1918	
			Remaining / Admitted / Remaining OFF / OR / OFF / OR / OFF / OR SICK — / 24 — / 17 — / 41	
			Routine Collection of Sick &c	

Army Form C. 2118.

WAR DIARY
or
INTELLIGENCE SUMMARY.   97th (CP) Field Ambulance

(Erase heading not required.)

Instructions regarding War Diaries and Intelligence Summaries are contained in F. S. Regs., Part II. and the Staff Manual respectively. Title pages will be prepared in manuscript.

Place	Date	Hour	Summary of Events and Information	Remarks and references to Appendices
HEESTERT P25 c.4.5 Sheet 9a.	16/11	16.00	Sick disposed through DA etc etc during 24 hrs ending noon 16th Nov 1918	
			Remaining / Admitted / To C.C.S. / To Reg.Mt / To Duty / Remaining OFF OR / OFF OR / OFF OR / OFF OR / OFF OR / OFF OR	
			SICK 1 41 / 1 15 / 1 / 9 / 6 / 40	
			SICK 1 41 / 1 15 / 1 / 9 / 6 / 40	
			Unit moved by road to HEESTERT	SOS
HELBEKE M20 c.8.4 Sheet 9a.	17/11	17.00	Sick passed through DA etc etc during 24 hrs ending noon 17th Nov 1918	
			Remaining / To Reg.Mt 86 F.A. / / / / Remaining OFF OR / OFF OR / / / / OFF OR	
			SICK 40 / 38 / / / / 2	
			SICK 40 / 38 / / / / 2	
			Unit moved by road to HELBEKE and then Bivrouac Rail Station	SOS
	18/11	18.00	Sick passed through DA etc etc during 24 hrs ending Noon 18th Nov 1918	
			Remaining / Admitted / Transfers to 96th / / / Remaining OFF OR / OFF OR / OFF OR / / / OFF OR	
			SICK 2 / 12 / 13 / / / 27	
			2 / 12 / 13 / / / 27	
			Surg.Lt. H.O. BLANFORD R.N. reported from Reserve Medical Unit	SOS

Army Form C. 2118.

WAR DIARY
of
INTELLIGENCE SUMMARY.
(Erase heading not required)

97th (CP) Field Ambulance

Instructions regarding War Diaries and Intelligence Summaries are contained in F.S. Regs., Part II. and the Staff Manual respectively. Title pages will be prepared in manuscript.

Place	Date	Hour	Summary of Events and Information							Remarks and references to Appendices
AELBEKE	19/5		SICK parade during 24 hrs. & D.R.S. during 24 hrs ending Noon Novem. 19th 1918							
				Remaining		Admitted		To C.C.S.	Remaining	
				OFF	OR	OFF	OR	OFF OR	OFF OR	
	19/11		SICK		27		34	2	59	
					27		34	2	59	
			Major M.W. LITTLEWOOD. R.A.M.C granted leave to U.K. from 19.11.18 to 3.12.18 Sd.							
			SICK parade during 24 hrs and D.R.S. during 24 hrs ending Noon 20th Nov 1918							
				Remaining		Admitted		To C.C.S. To 96 BTN	Remaining	
				OFF	OR	OFF	OR	OFF OR OFF OR	OFF OR	
	20/11		SICK		59	2	25	2 32 2	50	
					59	2	25	2 32 2	50	
			Capt. C.R. REEKITT. R.A.M.C for temporary duty with 2/14 Bn. London Regt Sd.							
			SICK parade during 24 hr Amb. & D. R.S. during 24 hrs ending Noon 21st Nov 1918							
				Remaining		Admitted		Transfrm 96BTN To C.C.S To Duty	Remaining	
				OFF	OR	OFF	OR	OFF OR OFF OR OFF OR	OFF OR	
	21/11		SICK		50	1	28	1 22 2	55	
					50	1	28	1 22 2	55	
			Routine Hospital work							

Army Form C. 2118.

WAR DIARY
or
INTELLIGENCE SUMMARY.   97th (CP) Field Ambulance

(Erase heading not required.)

Instructions regarding War Diaries and Intelligence Summaries are contained in F. S. Regs., Part II. and the Staff Manual respectively. Title pages will be prepared in manuscript.

Place	Date 1918	Hour	Summary of Events and Information	Remarks and references to Appendices
NEIBEKE			Sick passed through 2d Amb. + D.R.S. during 24 hrs ending noon 22nd Nov 1918	
			<table><tr><td colspan="2">Remained</td><td colspan="2">Admitted</td><td colspan="2">Offrs from 96th FA</td><td colspan="2">Thrs from 96th FA</td><td colspan="2">To 66 C.S</td><td colspan="2">To Duty</td><td colspan="2">Remaining</td></tr><tr><td>OFF</td><td>OR</td><td>OFF</td><td>OR</td><td>OFF</td><td>OR</td><td>OFF</td><td>OR</td><td>OFF</td><td>OR</td><td>OFF</td><td>OR</td><td>OFF</td><td>OR</td></tr><tr><td></td><td>55</td><td>1</td><td>35</td><td></td><td>4</td><td>1</td><td>-</td><td></td><td>2</td><td></td><td>10</td><td></td><td>12</td><td></td><td>73</td></tr><tr><td></td><td>55</td><td>1</td><td>35</td><td></td><td>4</td><td>1</td><td></td><td></td><td>2</td><td></td><td>10</td><td></td><td>12</td><td></td><td>73</td></tr></table>	
			Routine - Hospital work	Sd
			Sick passed through 2d Amb. + D.R.S. during 24 hrs ending noon 23rd Nov 1918	
	22 Nov		<table><tr><td colspan="2">Remained</td><td colspan="2">Admitted</td><td colspan="2">Trspfm 96thFA</td><td colspan="2">Trspfm 98thFA</td><td colspan="2">To 66 C.S</td><td colspan="2">To Duty</td><td colspan="2">Remaining</td></tr><tr><td>OFF</td><td>OR</td><td>OFF</td><td>OR</td><td>OFF</td><td>OR</td><td>OFF</td><td>OR</td><td>OFF</td><td>OR</td><td>OFF</td><td>OR</td><td>OFF</td><td>OR</td></tr><tr><td></td><td>73</td><td>2</td><td>26</td><td></td><td>5</td><td></td><td>4</td><td></td><td>2</td><td></td><td>12</td><td></td><td>3</td><td></td><td>93</td></tr><tr><td></td><td>73</td><td>2</td><td>26</td><td></td><td>5</td><td></td><td>4</td><td></td><td>2</td><td></td><td>12</td><td></td><td>3</td><td></td><td>93</td></tr></table>	
			Routine - Hospital work	Sd
			Sick passed through 2d Amb. + D.R.S. during 24 hrs ending noon 24th Nov 1918	
	24 Nov		<table><tr><td colspan="2">Remained</td><td colspan="2">Admitted</td><td colspan="2">Trsfr fm 96thFA</td><td colspan="2">Trsfr fm 98thFA</td><td colspan="2">To 66 C.S</td><td colspan="2">To Duty</td><td colspan="2">Remaining</td></tr><tr><td>OFF</td><td>OR</td><td>OFF</td><td>OR</td><td>OFF</td><td>OR</td><td>OFF</td><td>OR</td><td>OFF</td><td>OR</td><td>OFF</td><td>OR</td><td>OFF</td><td>OR</td></tr><tr><td></td><td>93</td><td></td><td>11</td><td></td><td>3</td><td></td><td>5</td><td></td><td></td><td></td><td>8</td><td></td><td>9</td><td></td><td>95</td></tr><tr><td></td><td>93</td><td></td><td>11</td><td></td><td>3</td><td></td><td>5</td><td></td><td></td><td></td><td>8</td><td></td><td>9</td><td></td><td>95</td></tr></table>	
			Capt J. E. BRADLEY, R.C., U.S.A for temporary duty with 2/23 Bn London Regt	Sd

Army Form C. 2118.

WAR DIARY
or
INTELLIGENCE SUMMARY.
(Erase heading not required.)

97th (B.P.) Field Ambulance

Instructions regarding War Diaries and Intelligence Summaries are contained in F.S. Regs., Part II. and the Staff Manual respectively. Title pages will be prepared in manuscript.

Place	Date 1918	Hour	Summary of Events and Information	Remarks and references to Appendices
RELBEKE	25/11		Sick passed through the Amb. & R.C.S. during 24 hrs ending Noon 25th Nov 1918.	
			<table><tr><th rowspan="2">Remaining</th><th colspan="2">Admitted thr from 96FA</th><th colspan="2">To CCS</th><th colspan="2">To Duty</th><th colspan="2">Remaining</th></tr><tr><th>OFF</th><th>OR</th><th>OFF</th><th>OR</th><th>OFF</th><th>OR</th><th>OFF</th><th>OR</th></tr><tr><td>SICK</td><td>95</td><td>2</td><td>21</td><td>10</td><td>2</td><td>11</td><td></td><td>20</td><td></td><td>89</td></tr><tr><td></td><td>95</td><td>2</td><td>21</td><td></td><td>2</td><td>11</td><td></td><td>20</td><td></td><td>89</td></tr>	
			Routine - Hospital Work.	Sgd.
	26/11		Sick passed through the Amb. & R.C.S. during 24 hrs ending Noon 26th Nov 1918.	
			<table><tr><th>Remaining OFF OR</th><th>Admitted OFF OR</th><th>Transfers from 96FA BY FA OFF OR</th><th>To CCS OFF OR</th><th>To Duty OFF OR</th><th>Remaining OFF OR</th></tr><tr><td>SICK 89</td><td>1 40</td><td>8</td><td>2 2</td><td>1</td><td>10</td><td>120</td></tr><tr><td>89</td><td>1 40</td><td>8</td><td>2 2</td><td>1</td><td>10</td><td>120</td></tr>	Sgd.
			Routine - Hospital Work	
	27/11		Sick passed through District & R.C.S during 24 hrs ending Noon 27th Nov 1918.	
			<table><tr><th>Remaining OFF OR</th><th>Admitted OFF OR</th><th>Transfers from 96FA OFF OR</th><th>To CCS OFF OR</th><th>To Duty OFF OR</th><th>Remaining OFF OR</th></tr><tr><td>SICK 120</td><td>53</td><td>7</td><td>133</td><td>30</td><td>17</td></tr><tr><td>120</td><td>53</td><td>7</td><td>133</td><td>30</td><td>17</td></tr>	Sgd.
			Routine - Hospital Work	

Army Form C. 2118.

WAR DIARY
or
INTELLIGENCE SUMMARY.

97th (CD) Field Ambulance

(Erase heading not required.)

Instructions regarding War Diaries and Intelligence Summaries are contained in F. S. Regs., Part II. and the Staff Manual respectively. Title pages will be prepared in manuscript.

Place	Date 1918	Hour	Summary of Events and Information	Remarks and references to Appendices
LA VIGNE E.1.A.4.4 Sheet 36	28/10		SICK passed through Field Ambce for 24 hrs Ending Noon 28th Nov 1918 <table><tr><td colspan=2>Remaining</td><td colspan=2>Admitted</td><td colspan=2>To C.C.S.</td><td colspan=2>To Duty</td><td colspan=2>Remaining</td></tr><tr><td>OFF</td><td>OR</td><td>OFF</td><td>OR</td><td>OFF</td><td>OR</td><td>OFF</td><td>OR</td><td>OFF</td><td>OR</td></tr><tr><td>SICK</td><td>17</td><td>3</td><td>53</td><td>3</td><td>65</td><td></td><td>5</td><td></td><td></td></tr><tr><td></td><td>17</td><td>3</td><td>53</td><td>3</td><td>65</td><td></td><td>5</td><td></td><td></td></tr></table> Unit moved by road to LA VIGNE area. Capt. G.F. BRIDGLEY M.C. U.S.A. reported from 2/23 Bn London Regt SICK passed through Field Ambce for 24hrs Ending Noon 29th Nov 1918 NIL	Nil
LA HUTTE FARM D.26.a.5.5 Sheet 36	29/11		SICK Unit moved by road to LA HUTTE FARM	S.D.1
LAVENTIE M.4.d.1.9 Sheet 36	30/11		SICK passed through Field Ambce for 24hrs Ending Noon 30th Nov 1918 <table><tr><td colspan=2>Admitted</td><td colspan=2>To C.C.S.</td><td colspan=2>Remaining</td></tr><tr><td>OFF</td><td>OR</td><td>OFF</td><td>OR</td><td>OFF</td><td>OR</td></tr><tr><td>SICK</td><td>3</td><td>31</td><td>3</td><td>31</td><td></td><td></td></tr><tr><td></td><td>3</td><td>31</td><td>3</td><td>31</td><td></td><td></td></tr></table> Unit moved by road to LAVENTIE.	Nil S.D.1

Army Form C. 2118

Volume XXXVIII
97th (C2) Field Ambulance
December 1918.

No. 82 38

WAR DIARY
or
INTELLIGENCE SUMMARY
(Erase heading not required.)

Instructions regarding War Diaries and Intelligence Summaries are contained in F. S. Regs., Part II. and the Staff Manual respectively. Title Pages will be prepared in manuscript.

Place	Date 1918	Hour	Summary of Events and Information				Remarks and references to Appendices
ST VENANT P.10.c.1.9 Q.a.l.36a	1 Dec		Sick passed through the Amb. & D.B.S. during 24 hrs ending Noon. 1st Dec. 1918.				
				Admitted		Remaining	
				To G.C.S.	O.R.	O.R.	
			SICK		9	2	St Venant O.C. 97 F.A.
					9	21	
			Unit moved by road from LAVENTIE to ST. VENANT.				
			Sick passed through the Amb. & D.R.S. during 24 hrs ending Noon 2nd Dec. 1918.				
				Remained	Admitted	To Amber	To G.C.S.	Remaining
				O.R.	O.R.	OFF	O.R.	OFF	O.R.	O.R.
EBBLINGHEM T.15.c.0.8 G.a.k.27	2 Dec		SICK	2	25	2	21	6
				2	25	2	21	6
			Unit moved by road to EBBLINGHEM.				
			Sick passed through the Amb. & D.R.S. during 24 hrs ending Noon 3rd Dec. 1918.				
				Remained	Admitted		Remaining
				O.R.	O.R.		O.R.
	3 Dec		SICK	6	8		14	S.S
				6	8		14
			Routine - Prepare oiled for Divisional Rest Station.				

Army Form C. 2118

WAR DIARY
or
INTELLIGENCE SUMMARY

97th (C.D.) Field Ambulance

(Erase heading not required.)

Place	Date 1918	Hour	Summary of Events and Information	Remarks and references to Appendices
EBBLINGHEM	4 Dec		SICK parade through Bearers + B.R.S. during 24hr. ending Noon 4th Dec 1918	
			Remained / Transfers from B.S.P. / Admitted / To B.C.S. / To Duty / Remaining	
			O.R.: 14 / OFF: 1, O.R: 11 / OFF: -, O.R: 14 / OFF: 1, O.R: 1 / OFF: -, O.R: 1 / O.R: 37	S.P.S
			SICK 14 / 11 / 14 / 1 / 1 / 37	
			Routine — Hospital TBRS	
	5 Dec		SICK parade through Bearers + B.R.S. during 24hrs ending Noon 5th Dec 1918	
			Remained / Admitted / Transfers / To B.C.S. / To Duty / Remaining	
			O.R: 37 / OFF: 1, O.R: 31 / OFF: 2, O.R: 12 / OFF: 3, O.R: 8 / OFF: -, O.R: 6 / O.R: 66	S.P.S
			SICK 37 / 31 / 12 / 3 / 8 / 6 / 66	
			Surgeon Lieut. H.O. BLANFORD R.N. proceeded to 34th Stationary Hospital for temporary duty	
			Capt. C.E. BRADLEY R.A.M.C.R. granted leave to U.K. 5.6.19 to 19.12.18	
			Capt. G.H. KEARNEY R.A.M.C.	
	6 Dec		SICK parade through Bearers + B.R.S. during 24hrs ending Noon 6th Dec 1918	
			Remained / Admitted / Transfers / To B.C.S. / To Duty / Remaining	
			O.R: 66 / OFF: 1, O.R: 19 / OFF: 1, O.R: 6 / OFF: 1, O.R: 7 / OFF: -, O.R: 1 / O.R: 83	S.P.S
			SICK 66 / 19 / 6 / 7 / 1 / 83	
			Capt G.H. KEARNEY R.A.M.C. proceeded to 34th Stationary Hospital for temporary duty	
			Capt. C.K. REDDITT R.A.M.C. reported from 2/4 Bn London Regt.	

WAR DIARY
or
INTELLIGENCE SUMMARY

Army Form C. 2118

97th (E) Field Ambulance

(Erase heading not required.)

Place	Date 1918	Hour	Summary of Events and Information										Remarks and references to Appendices
EBBLINGHEM			SICK Passed Through 30 Amber + D.R.S during 24 hrs Ending Noon 7th Dec 1918										
				Remained		Admitted		Transfers		To G.G.S		To Duty	
				OFF	OR	OFF	OR	OFF	OR	OFF	OR	OFF	OR	Remaining OFF OR
	7 Dec		SICK	—	83	—	22	—	6	1	9	—	19	— 83
														— 83
			Routine - Hospital + A.R.S											S.D.S
			SICK Passed Through 30 Amber + D.R.S during 24 hrs Ending Noon 8th Dec 1918										
				Remained		Admitted		Transfers		To G.G.S		To Duty		Remaining
				OFF	OR	OFF	OR	OFF	OR	OFF	OR	OFF	OR	OFF OR
	8 Dec		SICK	—	83	3	20	—	12	3	1	—	5	— 109
			Pt N				4							— 109
			Routine - Hospital + A.R.S											S.D.S
			SICK Passed Through 30 Amber + D.R.S during 24 hrs Ending Noon 9th Dec 1918										
				Remained		Admitted		Transfers		To G.G.S		To Duty		Remaining
				OFF	OR	OFF	OR	OFF	OR	OFF	OR	OFF	OR	OFF OR
	9 Dec		SICK	—	109	—	11	—	11	—	9	—	17	— 105
				—	109	—	11	—	11	—	9			— 105
			Routine - Hospital + A.R.S											S.D.S

Army Form C. 2118.

WAR DIARY
or
INTELLIGENCE SUMMARY. 97th (E.D) Field Ambulance

(Erase heading not required.)

Instructions regarding War Diaries and Intelligence Summaries are contained in F. S. Regs., Part II. and the Staff Manual respectively. Title pages will be prepared in manuscript.

Place	Date 1918	Hour	Summary of Events and Information									Remarks and references to Appendices
EBBLINGHEM	10 Dec		Sick parade through St Ambroise + R.C.S. during 24 hrs ending 10 hr Dec 1918									
				Remained		Admitted		Transfers		To Duty		Remaining
				OFF	OR	OFF	OR	OFF	OR	OFF	OR	OFF	OR
			SICK		105	2	26		7		10		14	2	114
					105	2	26		7		10		14	2	114
			P. of W		5						5					A.S.S
			Routine – Hospital + A.R.S.												
	11 Dec		Sick passed through St Ambroise + D.R.S during 24hrs ending Noon 11th Dec 1918									
				Remained		Admitted		Transfers		To Duty		Remaining
				OFF	OR	OFF	OR	OFF	OR	OFF	OR	OFF	OR
			SICK	2	114		17		14		5		20	2	117
				2	114		17		11		5		20	2	117
			Capt. E. BRADLEY M.C. U.S.A. reported from leave												5
	12 Dec		Sick passed through St Ambroise + D.R.S during 24 hrs ending 12 hr Dec 1918									
				Remained		Admitted		Transfers		To Duty		Remaining
				OFF	OR	OFF	OR	OFF	OR	OFF	OR	OFF	OR
			SICK	2	117		17		3		10		17	2	110
				2	117		17		3		10		17	2	110
			Routine – Hospital + A.R.S												A.S.S

Army Form C. 2118.

WAR DIARY
or
INTELLIGENCE SUMMARY. 97th (C.P.) Field Ambulance
(Erase heading not required.)

Instructions regarding War Diaries and Intelligence Summaries are contained in F. S. Regs., Part II. and the Staff Manual respectively. Title pages will be prepared in manuscript.

Place	Date 1915	Hour	Summary of Events and Information								Remarks and references to Appendices
EBLINGHEM			Sick Losses through 2d Ambce + FDRS during 24 hrs ending Noon 13th Dec 1915								
				Remained	Admitted	Transfers		To G.C.S.		To Duty	
				OR	OR	OFF	OR	OFF	OR	OR	
	13 Dec		SICK	110	24		3		4	8	
				110	24		3		4	8	
			P of W		2				2		
			Lt/G. H. KEARNEY R.A.M.C. and Surg. Lt. W.D. BLANFORD R.N. reported from No 44 Stationary Hospital								125 Remaining 125
			Sick passed through 2d Ambce + FDRS during 24 hrs ending Noon 14th Dec 1915.								
				Remained	Admitted	Transfers		To G.C.S.		To Duty	Remaining
				OR	OFF	OR	OFF	OR	OFF	OR	OR
	14 Dec		SICK	125	1	22		15	1	7	14	141
				125	1	22		15	1	7	14	141
			P of W			1				1		
			Routine — Hospital F.A.R.S.								501
			Sick passed through 2d Ambce + FDRS during 24 hrs ending Noon 15th Dec 1915								
				Remained	Admitted	Transfers		To G.C.S.		To Duty	Remaining
				OR	OR	OFF	OR	OFF	OR	OR	
	15 Dec		SICK	141	27		13		7	25	149
				141	27		13		7	25	149
			Routine — Hospital F.A.R.S.								

Army Form C. 2118.

WAR DIARY
or
INTELLIGENCE SUMMARY.   97th (69) Field Ambulance

(Erase heading not required.)

Instructions regarding War Diaries and Intelligence Summaries are contained in F. S. Regs., Part II. and the Staff Manual respectively. Title pages will be prepared in manuscript.

Place	Date	Hour	Summary of Events and Information	Remarks and references to Appendices
EBBLINGHEM	1918			
	16 Dec		SICK Passed through 56 Ambce + D.R.S. during 24 hrs ending Noon 16th Dec 1918.	
			Remained Admitted Transfers To 66&8 To Duty Remaining	
			O.R. O.R. O.R. O.R. O.R.	
			SICK 149 13 9 10 145	875
			Routine – Hospital + D.R.S.	
	17 Dec		SICK Passed through 56 Ambce + D.R.S. during 24 hrs ending Noon 17th Dec 1918.	
			Remained Admitted Transfers To 66s To Duty Remaining	
			O.R. O.R. O.R. O.R. O.R.	
			SICK 145 17 3 15 149	895
			P of W 3 3	
			Routine – Hospital + D.R.S.	
	18 Dec		SICK Passed through 56 Ambce + D.R.S. during 24 hrs ending Noon 18th Dec 1918.	
			Remained Admitted Transfers To 66s To Duty Remaining	
			O.R. O.R. O.R. O.R. O.R.	
			SICK 149 8 2 13 19 155	895
			Major M. Littlewood R.A.M.C. reported from leave	

Army Form C. 2118.

WAR DIARY
or
INTELLIGENCE SUMMARY.

97th (CD) Field Ambulance

(Erase heading not required.)

Place	Date	Hour	Summary of Events and Information	Remarks and references to Appendices
EBBLINGHEM	19/12/18		SICK passed through the Amb. & D.R.S during 24hrs ending Noon 19th Dec 1918	
			Retained / Admitted / Transfers To C.C.S. / To Duty / Remaining	
			O/R / O/R / O/R / O/R / O/R	
			SICK 125 / 9 / 9 / 3 / 24 / 116	
			Routine - Hospital F.D.R.S.	
			SICK passed through the Amb. & D.R.S during 24hrs ending Noon 20th Dec 1918	
			Retained / Admitted / Transfers To C.C.S. / To Duty / Remaining	
			OFF / O/R / OFF / O/R / OFF / O/R / OFF / O/R / OFF / O/R	
			SICK 116 / 1 / 25 / 1 / 7 / 1 / 22 / / 113	
			P of W / / 3 / / 1 / / 3 / / /	
			Routine - Hospital F.D.R.S	
	20/12		SICK passed through the Amb. & D.R.S during 24hrs ending Noon 21st Dec 1918	
			Retained / Admitted / To C.C.S / To Duty / Remaining	
			O/R / O/R / O/R / O/R / O/R	
			SICK 113 / 15 / 5 / 12 / 111	
			P of W / 2 / 2 / / /	
	21/12		Routine - Hospital F.D.R.S.	

Army Form C. 2118.

WAR DIARY
or
INTELLIGENCE SUMMARY.
(Erase heading not required.)

97th (C@) Field Ambulance

Instructions regarding War Diaries and Intelligence Summaries are contained in F. S. Regs., Part II. and the Staff Manual respectively. Title pages will be prepared in manuscript.

Place	Date 1918	Hour	Summary of Events and Information	Remarks and references to Appendices
EBLINGHEM			Sick passed through Eb Ambce + DRS during 24hrs ending Noon 22nd Dec 1918.	
			Remained / Admitted / Transfer / To 6 GS / To Duty / Died / Remaining OR OR OR OR OR OR	
	19 Dec		SICK 111 13 2 6 11 1 108	SoC
			Routine - Hospital YARS	
			Sick passed through Eb Amblce + DRS during 24hrs ending Noon 23rd Dec 1918.	
			Remained / Admitted / Transfer / To 6 GS / To Duty / Remaining OR OR OR OR OR OR	
	23 Dec		SICK 108 14 3 7 15 103	SoC
			Routine - Hospital YARS	
			Sick passed through Eb Ambce + DRS during 24hrs ending Noon 24th Dec 1918.	
			Remained / Admitted / Transfer / To 6 GS / To Duty / Remaining OR Off OR Off OR OR OR	
	24 Dec		SICK 103 1 25 1 8 10 40	SoC
			Major W.E. Dennis RAMC proceeded to England for Demobilisation.	

Army Form C. 2118.

WAR DIARY
or
INTELLIGENCE SUMMARY.   97th (C.D.) Field Ambulance

(Erase heading not required.)

Place	Date 1918	Hour	Summary of Events and Information	Remarks and references to Appendices
EBBLINGHEM	25 Dec		Sick passed through B.R.S. Ambces & D.R.S. during 24 hrs ending Noon 25th Dec 1918	
			Remained / Admitted / Transfer / To Duty	
			O.R. / O.R. / OFF O.R. / OFF O.R. / OFF O.R.	
			SICK 110 / 10 / 1 5 / 1 8 / Remaining O.R. 107	
			Routine Hospital & A.P.C.	
	26 Dec		Sick passed through Bd. Amba & D.R.S during 24 hrs ending Noon 26th Dec 1918	
			Remained / Admitted / To DRS / To Duty	
			O.R. / OFF O.R. / OFF O.R. / O.R.	
			SICK 107 / 2 13 / 2 5 / 1 Remaining O.R. 116	
			Routine Hospital & A.P.C.	
	27 Dec		Sick passed through Bd. Ambce & D.R.S during 24 hrs ending Noon 27th Dec 1918	
			Remained / Admitted / Transfer / To Duty	
			O.R. / O.R. / O.R. / O.R.	
			SICK 116 / 18 / 1 3 / 21 Remaining O.R. 111	
			Surgeon Lieut H.O. BLANFORD R.N. proceeded to 98 L/R Field Ambulance for temporary duty	

Army Form C. 2118.

WAR DIARY
or
INTELLIGENCE SUMMARY. 97th (8.D) Field Ambulance

(Erase heading not required).

Instructions regarding War Diaries and Intelligence Summaries are contained in F. S. Regs., Part II. and the Staff Manual respectively. Title pages will be prepared in manuscript.

Place	Date 1915	Hour	Summary of Events and Information	Remarks and references to Appendices
EBBLINGHEM	28 Dec		Sick parade. Known strength + ORS during 24hrs ending 10am 28th Dec 1915	
				Received OR	Admitted OR	To O&S OR	To Duty OR	Remaining OR
			SICK	111	24	10	20	105
			Capt CR Reckitt RAMC proceeded on leave to U.K. from 28th Dec to 11th Jan 1919	
			Sick parade. Known strength of Officers + ORS during 24hrs ending Noon 29th Dec 1915	
				Remaining OFF OR	Admitted OFF OR	Transfers OFF OR	To O&S OFF OR	To Duty OFF OR	Remaining OFF OR
			SICK	105	1 26	3	1 8	8	118
	29 Dec		Routine - Hospital + ARS	
			Sick parade. Known strength of Officers + ORS during 24hrs ending Noon 30th Dec 1915	
				Remaining OFF OR	Admitted OFF OR	Transfers OFF OR	To O&S OFF OR	To Duty OFF OR	Remaining OFF OR
			SICK	118	2 15	3	2 9	9	118
	30 Dec		Routine - Hospital + ARS	

Army Form C. 2118.

WAR DIARY
or
INTELLIGENCE SUMMARY.
(Erase heading not required.)

97th (C.P.) Field Ambulance

Instructions regarding War Diaries and Intelligence Summaries are contained in F. S. Regs., Part II. and the Staff Manual respectively. Title pages will be prepared in manuscript.

Place	Date 1918	Hour	Summary of Events and Information	Remarks and references to Appendices
EBBLINGHEM	31 Dec		Sick parade. Running total admitted & Ros during 24 hrs ending Noon 31st Dec 1918	
			Remained on R. / admitted on R. / To C.C.S. To Duty on R. / Remaining on R.	
			Sick No. 118 / 96 / 3 / 14 / 127	
			Routing - Hospital & D.R.S.	Scotland 2nd F.A / 0 - 31 F.A

30ᵗʰ DIV
Box 2100

14/3490

To 91.7 a

COMMITTEE FOR THE
MEDICAL HISTORY OF THE WAR
10 MAR 1919
Date

Army Form C. 2118.

WAR DIARY
or
INTELLIGENCE SUMMARY.

97th (2/9) Field Ambulance

(Erase heading not required.)

Instructions regarding War Diaries and Intelligence Summaries are contained in F. S. Regs., Part II. and the Staff Manual respectively. Title pages will be prepared in manuscript.

Place	Date	Hour	Summary of Events and Information									Remarks and references to Appendices
EBBLINGHEM	1.1.19		Sick passed through Field Ambulance + D.R.S during 24 hrs ending Noon 1st Jan 1919									
				Remained		Admitted		Transfers	To G.C.S		To Duty	Remaining
				OFF	OR	OFF	OR	OFF	OR	OFF	OR	OFF	OR
			SICK		127		23		5		17		15		123	Nil
"	2.1.19		Sick passed through Field Ambulance + D.R.S during 24 hrs ending Noon 2nd Jan 1919									
				Remaining		Admitted		Transfers	To G.C.S		To Duty	Remaining
				OFF	OR	OFF	OR	OFF	OR	OFF	OR	OFF	OR
			SICK		123	1	12		3	1	36		18		84	Nil
"	3.1.19		Sick passed through Field Ambulance + D.R.S during 24 hrs ending Noon 3rd Jan 1919									
				Remaining		Admitted		Transfers	To G.C.S		To Duty	Remaining
				OFF	OR	OFF	OR	OFF	OR	OFF	OR	OFF	OR
			SICK		84	1	18		29	1			11		62	

Army Form C. 2118.

WAR DIARY
or
INTELLIGENCE SUMMARY.   97th (6th) Field Ambulance

(Erase heading not required.)

Instructions regarding War Diaries and Intelligence Summaries are contained in F. S. Regs., Part II. and the Staff Manual respectively. Title pages will be prepared in manuscript.

Place	Date	Hour	Summary of Events and Information					Remarks and references to Appendices
EBBLINGHEM	4/1/19		Sick forward through Field Ambulances + D.R.S. during 24 hrs ending Noon 4th Jan 1919					
				Remained	Admitted	To C.C.S.	To Duty	Remaining
				O.R.	O.R.	O.R.	O.R.	O.R.
			SICK	62	21	28	11	44
								Nil
"	5/1/19		Sick passed through Field Ambulance + D.R.S. during 24 hrs ending Noon 5th Jan 1919					
				Remained	Admitted	To C.C.S.	To Duty	Remaining
				O.R.	O.R.	O.R.	O.R.	O.R.
			SICK	44	10	29	11	14
								Nil
"	6/1/19		Sick passed through Field Ambulance + D.R.S. during 24 hrs ending Noon 6th Jan 1919					
				Remained	Admitted	Totals	To Duty	Remaining
				O.R.	O.R.	O.R.	O.R.	O.R.
			SICK	14	12	15	9	2
			CAPT G H KEARNEY RAMC is taken off the strength & posted to 2/23 London Regt.					

Army Form C. 2118.

WAR DIARY
or
INTELLIGENCE SUMMARY.   91st (CD) Field Ambulance

(Erase heading not required.)

Place	Date	Hour	Summary of Events and Information				Remarks and references to Appendices
ARNEKE	7.1.19		Sick passed through Field Ambulance & D.R.S. during 24 hrs ending Noon 7th Jan 1919				
					Remaining O.Rs		
			SICK		2		
			Left Hollinghem by road to ARNEKE				Nil
SOEX	8.1.19		Sick passed through St Andre during 24 hrs ending Noon 8th Jan 1919				
					Remaining O.Rs		
			SICK		2		
			Arrived ARNEKE 2pm 7th Left ARNEKE by road for SOEX				Nil
DUNKIRK	9.1.19		Sick passed through D.A. Ambce during 24 hrs ending Noon 9th Jan 1919				
				To Duty O.R	Remaining O.R		
			SICK	2	1		
			Left SOEX by road for DUNKIRK arrived DUNKIRK.				

Army Form C. 2118.

WAR DIARY
or
INTELLIGENCE SUMMARY.   97th (CP) Field Ambulance

(Erase heading not required.)

Place	Date	Hour	Summary of Events and Information	Remarks and references to Appendices
DUNKIRK	10/1/19		DUNKIRK. Unit camped on sand dunes near ST POL. DUNKIRK, under canvas.	Nil
"	12.1.19		Erection of Nissen Huts for O.R.	Nil
"	14.1.19		Routine evacuation of sick from 30th Divisional Unit at PETROIT & MALO.	Nil
"	16.1.19		The majority of personnel are now housed in Huts.	Nil
"	18.1.19		No 1. Detraining Station is now run by two shifts of the Ambulance personnel.	Nil
"	23.1.19		Demobilization commenced, undergoing a detachment of two men proceeding from Place d'Armes and Lieut, DUNKIRK.	Nil

R. Cullingford Major
O.C. 97th

Army Form C. 2118.

WAR DIARY
OF
INTELLIGENCE SUMMARY. 97th (C.P) Field Ambulance

Instructions regarding War Diaries and Intelligence Summaries are contained in F. S. Regs., Part II. and the Staff Manual respectively. Title pages will be prepared in manuscript.

(Erase heading not required.)

Place	Date	Hour	Summary of Events and Information	Remarks and references to Appendices
DUNKIRK	24.1.19		Lt.Col SMITH DSO. RAMC proceeded on 14 day's leave to the United Kingdom. Major M.W. LITTLEWOOD RAMC takes over temporary command. Capt. EVANS, FRANKLIN, & CRANN are attached for rations & accommodation.	Nil
"	26.1.19		Capt. C.E. BRADLEY MC USA is now the only M.O. on the strength, in addition to Lt.Col SMITH & Major LITTLEWOOD.	Nil
"	28.1.19		Inspection of demobilizing men now takes place at a Central Inspection Room. 7 men are now examined at the Dressing Station.	Nil
"	30.1.19		Allotment for demobilization is now increased to 16 per week.	Nil
"	31.1.19		Supplementary rations on arrangements created to meet the day's intakes of demobilizing men.	Nil

M.W. Littlewood
Major RAMC
O.C. 97 F.A.

140/3601

Feb. 1919

94 F.A.

COMMITTEE FOR THE
2 SEP 1919
MEDICAL HISTORY OF THE WAR

27/8

Army Form C. 2118.

WAR DIARY
of
INTELLIGENCE SUMMARY. 97th (2D) Field Ambulance
(Erase heading not required.)

Place	Date	Hour	Summary of Events and Information	Remarks and references to Appendices
DUNKIRK	1/9/19	Routine	Running Delivour No II	S.S.Sland
	9/9/19	Routine	Running Delivous No II.	do.
	10/9/19	Routine	Running Delivous No II. Lt. Col. L.D. Shaw D.S.O. Returned from leave.	do.
	11/9/19	Routine	Running Delivous No II.	do.
	12/9/19	Routine	Capt. C.E. Bradley M.C. USA proceeded on leave U.K.	do.
	13/9/19	Routine	Capt. C.E. Bradley M.C. USA reported from leave U.K.	do.
	22/9/19	Routine	Running Delivous No II.	do.
	23/9/19	Routine	Running Delivous No II.	do.

S.D.Shaw
Lt. Col. R.A.M.C.
O.C. 97th Field Amb.

140/3601

94R 7 A.

2 SEP 1919
MEDICAL HISTORY OF THE WAR

Army Form C. 2118

WAR DIARY
or
INTELLIGENCE SUMMARY 97th Field Ambulance
(Erase heading not required.)

Instructions regarding War Diaries and Intelligence Summaries are contained in F. S. Regs., Part II. and the Staff Manual respectively. Title Pages will be prepared in manuscript.

14/B

Place	Date	Hour	Summary of Events and Information	Remarks and references to Appendices
DURHAM	1/3/19		ROUTINE. Receiving Relicees No II.	J5241
	6/3/19		ROUTINE. Receiving Relicees No II. Major M.Y. Litchwood. R.A.M.C. demobilised to U.K.	97 Chavasse Major Ram at 97 F.A. Amb Mr
	9/3/19		ROUTINE. Receivent Relicees No II. Major I.B. Chavasse. M.C. Reported for Duty.	Mr
	10/3/19		ROUTINE. Receiving Relicees No II. Capt. G.E. Bensley. N.C.U.S.A. demobilised to U.S.A.	Mr
	13/3/19		ROUTINE. Receiving Relicees No II. Lt. Col. L.D. Shaw. D.S.O. R.A.M.C. Returned to U.K. on expiration of contract. Major I.B. Chavasse. M.C. R.M.C. took over command of Unit 97 F.A.	Mr
	14/3/19		ROUTINE. Receiving Relicees No II.	Mr
	24/3/19		ROUTINE. Receiving Relicees No II.	Mr
	31/3/19		ROUTINE. Receiving Relicees No II.	Mr

J.B. Chavasse
Major R.A.M.C.
o.c. 97 Field Ambulance

Army Form C. 2118.

WAR DIARY
or
INTELLIGENCE SUMMARY.

97th Field Ambulance

(Erase heading not required.)

Place	Date	Hour	Summary of Events and Information	Remarks and references to Appendices
St Pol-sur-Mer	1/4/19	ROUTINE	Lending Personnel to Delouser No II	WR 4
	6/4/19	ROUTINE	Lending Personnel to Delouser No II	
	10/4/19	ROUTINE	Lending Personnel to Delouser No II	
	17/4/19	ROUTINE	Lending Personnel to Delouser No II	
	24/4/19	ROUTINE	Lending Personnel to Delouser No II	
	30/4/19	ROUTINE	Lending Personnel to Delouser No II	

PBMorgan
Major RAMC
OC 97th Field Ambce

16/3/85-
Cased

13 AUG 1919

94th F.A.

Nov 1919

Army Form C. 2118

WAR DIARY
or
INTELLIGENCE SUMMARY
(Erase heading not required.)

MAY - 1919.

67 Yr August
NL 67 43

Place	Date	Hour	Summary of Events and Information	Remarks and references to Appendices
DUNKERQUE S.P.H.	May 1.	1.	Took over temporary Command of Unit fm Major H.F.B. CHAVASSE who left unit & took over duties of M.O. to H.Q. Troops BOULOGNE.	Cross
			Jno. Elliot Major R.A.M.C.	
	2.		Routine work in Camp & to 2 detainees M.	
	3.		N.Y.S. of infantieren etc.	
	4.		ditto	
	5.		Inspection of camp & equipment by Lt Col. BEGBIE A.D.M.S. Dunkerque P.B.	
May 10th			Took over command fm Major T.S. Elliot because Cinq[que] capitaine	
June 2nd			Routine work with any during my tour of duty	
June 3rd			Handed over command to Capt. O'NEILL G.B. Purnell N.S.M.C.(T) proceeding on duty U.K. BOULS. Calais.	
			Cinq[que] Capitaine	

140/3585-
encl

13 AUG 1919

94. F.O.

June/1919

Army Form C. 2118

WAR DIARY
or
INTELLIGENCE SUMMARY
(Erase heading not required.)

97th Field Ambulance

June – 1919.

Place	Date 1919	Hour	Summary of Events and Information	Remarks and references to Appendices
DUNKERQUE. ST POL.	June 3rd		Took over command from Capt W. Jones Bennet. This day. Geo. Murrell (Capt Q.W. Bennet).	Ceases
	21st		The Medical & Surgical Stores and Equipment were returned this day to No 14 Base Depot Medical Stores Calais.	
	23rd		The Ordnance equipment was despatched to D.O.O. (Demobilization Depot.) Meyville this day.	

Geo. J. Murrell
Capt. Q.W. Bennet
O.C. 97th Field Ambulance

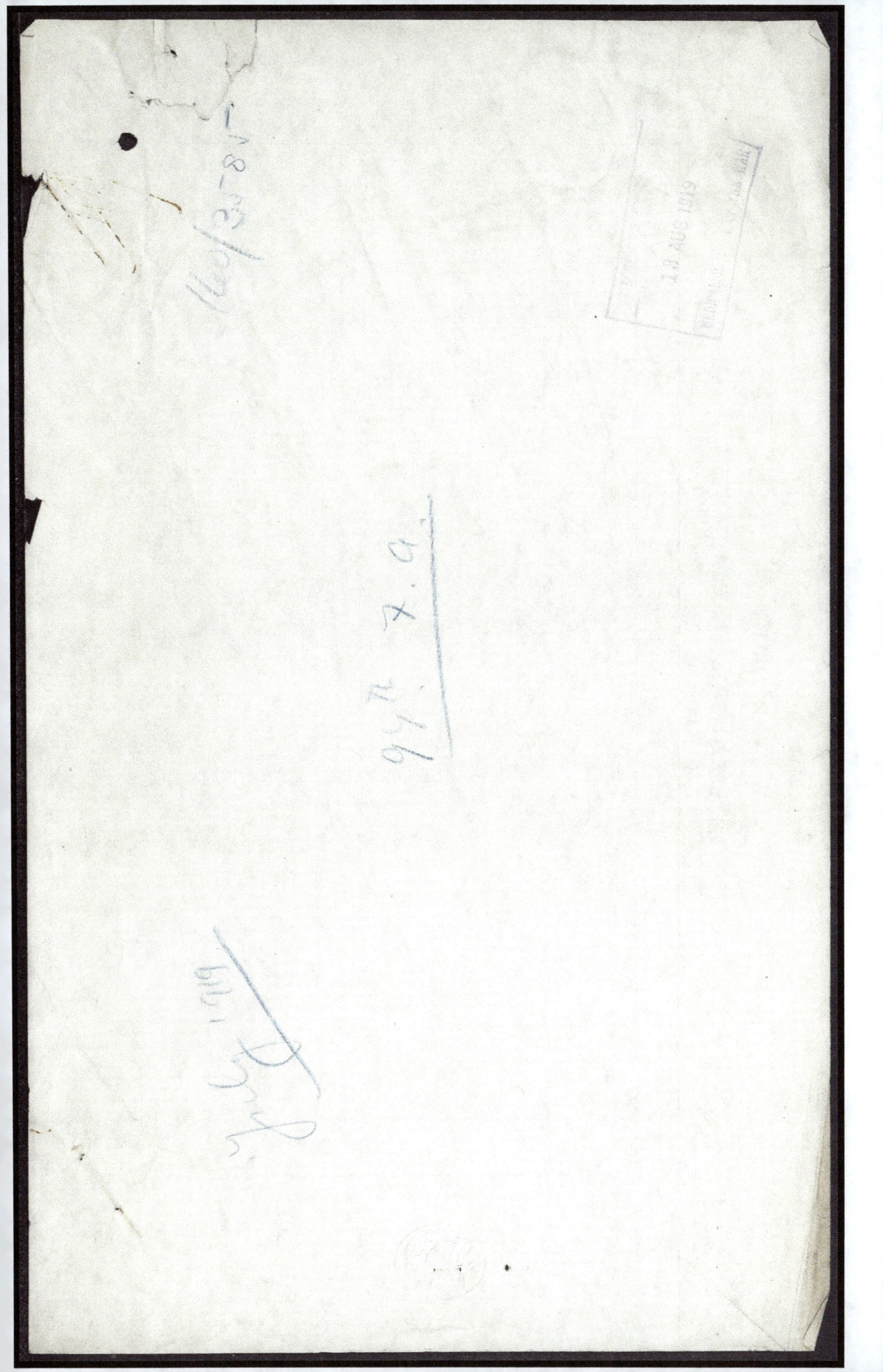

Original

Army Form C. 2118

WAR DIARY
or
INTELLIGENCE SUMMARY

(Erase heading not required.)

97th Field Ambulance

July 1919.

Instructions regarding War Diaries and Intelligence Summaries are contained in F. S. Regs., Part II. and the Staff Manual respectively. Title Pages will be prepared in manuscript.

Place	Date	Hour	Summary of Events and Information	Remarks and references to Appendices
Dunkerque St Pol 3/Mbr.	July 2.		1 Officer and 11 Other Ranks transferred to No 4 General Hospital on disbandment of the Unit.	V81 57

Geo. Hurst Capt. RAMC
O.C. 97 Field Ambulance.

www.ingramcontent.com/pod-product-compliance
Lightning Source LLC
Chambersburg PA
CBHW081428300426
44108CB00016BA/2323